LITERACY PLACE®

TABLE OF CONTENTS

CHAPTER BY CHAPTER

THEME
We are always adding
to our life story.

UNIT 1

TABLE OF CONTENTS

WHAT AN IDEA!

THEME
People solve problems by inventing new things.

UNIT 2

TABLE OF CONTENTS

DISCOVERY TEAMS

THEME

When we work as a team, we learn new things about our world.

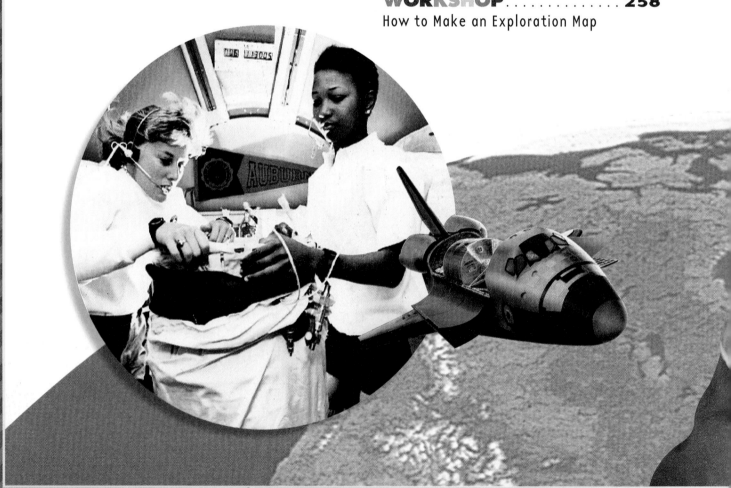

UNIT 3

TABLE OF CONTENTS

The Funny Side

THEME

Sometimes humor is the best way to communicate.

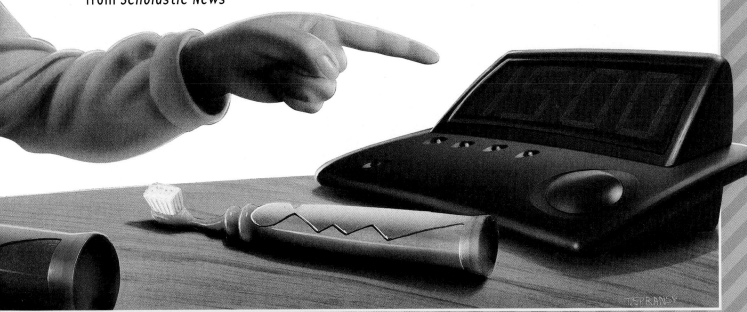

UNIT 4

NATURE GUIDES

THEME

Gathering and using information help us understand and describe the natural world.

UNIT 5

TABLE OF CONTENTS

IT TAKES A LEADER

THEME

In every community there are people who inspire others to take action.

JACKIE ROBINSON

UNIT 6

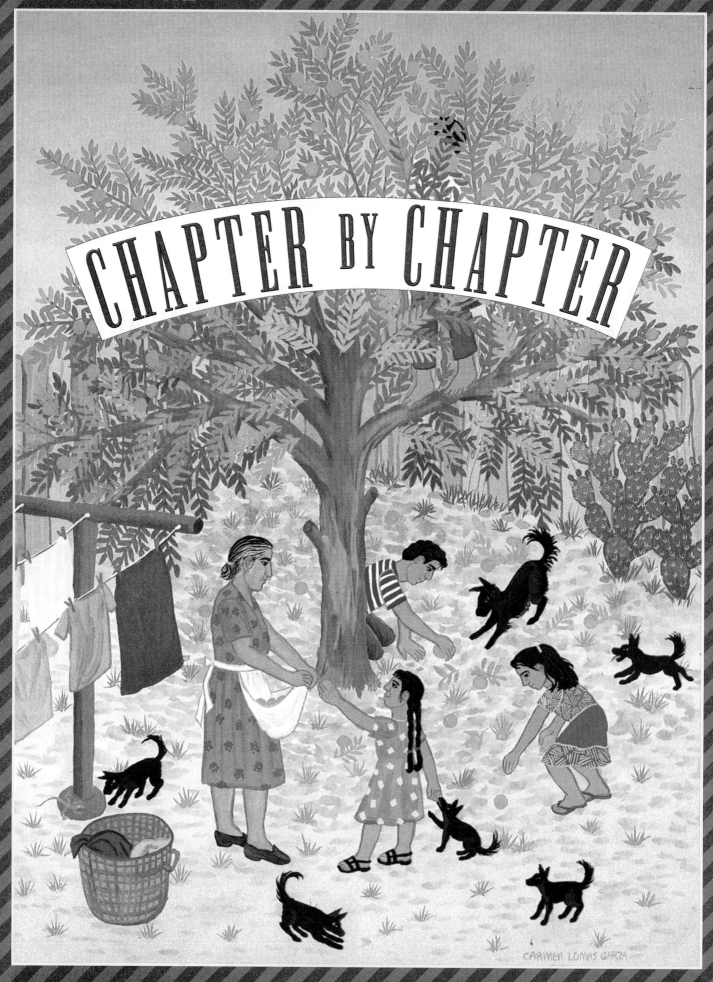

CHAPTER BY CHAPTER

CARMEN LOMAS GARZA

CHAPTER BY CHAPTER

THEME
We are always adding
to our life story.

www.scholastic.com
Visit the kids' area of
www.scholastic.com for the
latest news about your favorite
Scholastic books. You'll find sneak
previews of new books, interviews
with authors and illustrators, and
lots of other great stuff!

UNIT 1

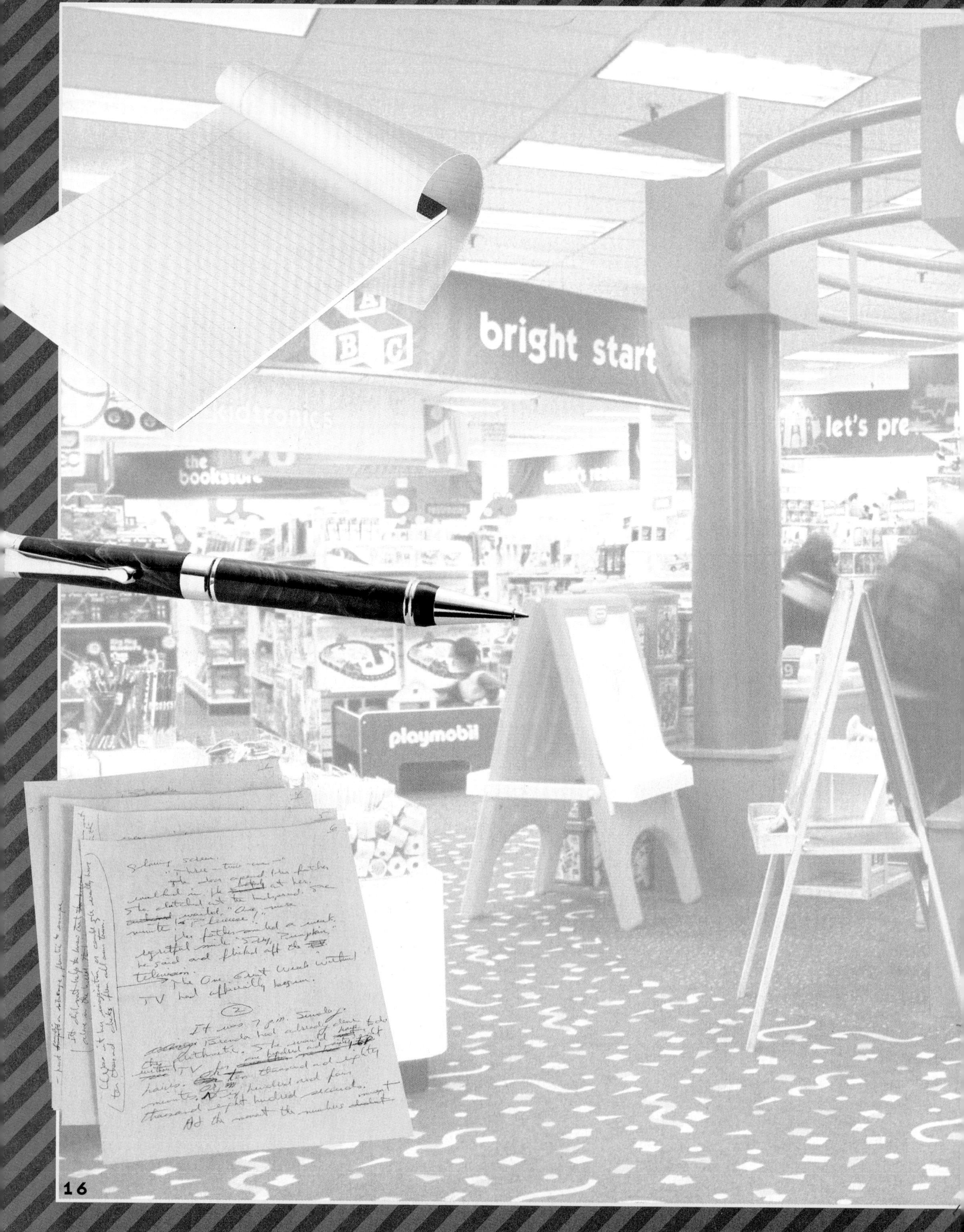
bright start
let's pre
the bookstore
playmobil

Welcome to
LITERACY PLACE

Bookstore

We are always adding to our life story.

Young Arthur

by
Robert D. San Souci

illustrated by
Jamichael Henterly

AWARD WINNER

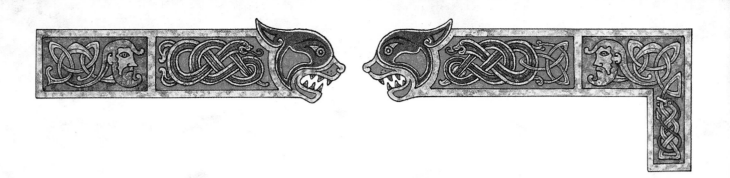

King Uther heard the baby's wail and leaped to his feet. There was a sharp rap at the chamber door, and a servant entered grinning happily. "You have a son," he told the king. Uther's joy knew no bounds. When he was ushered into Queen Igerna's bedchamber, Uther looked lovingly at mother and son. "The boy's name shall be Arthur," he declared, "and he shall be a great king. For Merlin has foretold that he will one day rule the greatest kingdom under heaven."

But Uther's happiness did not last. His beloved queen died soon after Arthur's birth, and sadness sapped the king's spirit. He lost interest in ruling, and Merlin was unable to rouse him from his melancholy. "Unrest grows throughout the land," Merlin warned. "Your old foes are rising in rebellion. Give the babe into my keeping, for you have enemies even at court."

Anxious for his son's safety, Uther agreed. So Merlin, disguised as a beggar, took the infant Arthur to Sir Ector and his lady, who lived some distance from the court and all its dangers. He told them nothing about the child, save that his name was Arthur. The couple had recently lost their infant son and welcomed Arthur as their own.

Soon rebellion divided the kingdom. Uther, reclaiming his old spirit, rallied his knights and barons. With Merlin always beside him, he drove back his enemies.

But as Uther celebrated his victory in the town of Verulum, traitors poisoned the town's wells. The king and his loyal followers were stricken. Merlin alone escaped. Though he tried his healing arts on Uther, he was forced to confess, "Sire, there is no remedy."

"Then," said the dying monarch, "I declare that my son shall be king of all this realm after me. God's blessing and mine be upon him." With these words, Uther died.

When the rebels entered Verulum, only Merlin was alive.

"Tell us where Uther's son is hidden," they demanded, "so that we can slay him and end Uther's line."

But Merlin vanished before their eyes.

21

Young Arthur was raised as a son in Sir Ector's house. He learned to read and write alongside his foster brother, Kay, who was four years older. By the time he was fifteen, Arthur was a tall, handsome, quick-witted lad. Though he had great strength, he also had a gentle manner.

Kay, who had recently been knighted, decided to train Arthur in the knightly arts himself. But Kay was vain and jealous of the favor Arthur found with their father, so he was a harsh taskmaster. Arthur came away from his lessons in swordsmanship with many bruises and cuts. When he complained, Kay replied, "A knight must be thick-skinned and ready to bear even grievous wounds without flinching." Yet if Arthur so much as pricked his brother, Kay would bellow loudly for the physician.

Eventually Kay appointed Arthur his apprentice. This was an honor the younger boy would happily have forgone. However, seeing that Sir Ector wished it so, Arthur sighed and agreed. But he felt in his heart that he already was a knight, though no lord had dubbed him such.

Both Arthur and Kay knew it was vital to learn the arts of war. Their kingdom was still at the mercy of upstart lords who ruled by fire and sword.

The story of Uther's lost son, the true heir to the throne, would have been forgotten but for Merlin. One Christmas Eve, the long-absent magician reappeared and summoned the bishops, lords, and common folk to London's square. There he drove a broadsword halfway into a huge stone. Written on the blade in blazing gold letters were the words: "Whoso pulleth out the sword from this stone is born the rightful King of England."

In the days that followed, knights and barons, cowherds and bakers, an endless parade of would-be kings eagerly pulled at the sword. But none could loosen it, let alone draw it forth.

When they accused Merlin of trickery, he said, "The rightful king has not yet come. God will make him known at the proper time."

Now it happened that a great tournament was held in London. Among those who came were Sir Ector, Sir Kay, and young Arthur, who served Kay. So eager was the boy to see the jousts that he forgot to pack Kay's sword. There was great upset when the mistake was discovered.

"Woe to you, boy," snarled Kay, "if your error costs me the victory I would otherwise win today!"

Even Sir Ector scolded Arthur and ordered, "Go back directly and fetch the missing sword."

Angry at his carelessness and impatient to see the contests, Arthur started homeward. Then he suddenly reined in his horse.

In the deserted city square was a massive stone with a sword plunged into its center. "Surely that sword is as good as the one left at home," he said. "I will borrow it. When Kay is finished, I will return it to this curious monument."

So saying, he dismounted, scrambled up the stone, took the sword handle, and tugged. The sword did not move. Impatient to return to the tournament, he pulled again. This time, the sword slid easily out of the stone. In his haste, he did not notice the words upon the blade. Shoving the weapon into his belt, he remounted and raced to where Sir Kay waited his turn upon the field.

The moment he saw the golden words upon the blade, Kay began to tremble with excitement. When Arthur asked what was amiss, Kay shouted, "Go! Get away! You have caused enough trouble."

But Arthur was curious. So he followed as Kay ran to Sir Ector. "Look, Father!" cried Kay. "Here is the sword of the stone. Therefore, it is I who must be king of all this land!"

When Sir Ector and the others saw the sword and read the golden inscription, they began to shout, "The sword from the stone! The king's sword!"

Hearing only this much, Arthur thought that he had stolen a king's weapon. As people hurried excitedly toward Kay, Arthur spurred his horse away, certain he had committed a great crime.

Looking back, he saw Kay and Sir Ector ride off, surrounded by the greatest lords of the realm. Were they taking Kay to trial? he wondered. Had he brought ruin upon Sir Ector's household?

"A true knight would not run away," he said to himself, "and I am a true knight in my heart." Fearful, but determined to do what was right, the boy wheeled his horse around.

The great square was now filled with people. Just how terrible a crime had he committed?

Upon the stone stood Kay, holding the sword. The crowd shouted each time he held the blade aloft. Then silence fell over the throng: Merlin had appeared at the edge of the square. People stood aside to let the magician approach the stone.

"Are you the one who pulled the sword from the stone?" Merlin asked.

"I am holding it, am I not?" Kay replied.

"The rightful king could pull it free a hundred times," said Merlin. "Slip the sword into the groove and pull it out again."

With a shrug, Kay reinserted the sword. But when he tried to jerk it free, it would not budge.

Suddenly all eyes turned toward Arthur, who was pushing his way through the crowd, bellowing at the top of his lungs. "It wasn't Kay's fault! I brought him the sword!"

Merlin peered closely at Arthur. Then he smiled and said, "Climb up and draw the sword from the stone."

Uncertainly Arthur clambered up beside Kay. Grasping the pommel, he easily pulled the sword out.

Then Merlin cried, "This is Arthur, son of Uther Pendragon, Britain's destined king."

An astonished Sir Ector knelt to pay the boy homage, followed by Kay and many others. But all around, there was growing confusion and dispute. Some cried, "It is the will of heaven! Long live the king!" while others cried, "It is Merlin's plot to put a beardless boy, a puppet, on the throne, and so rule the land."

The cries of "Long live King Arthur!" soon carried the day. But many powerful knights and barons rode away angry, vowing never to accept Arthur as their king.

Arthur was crowned in London. But it was the custom for Britain's high king to be crowned a second time as King of Wales. So Arthur, Merlin, and his court rode to the old walled city of Caerleon.

On the day of his coronation feast, enemy lords laid siege to the city. They breached the gates and battled their way into the great hall.

Just when all seemed lost, Arthur rose up like a blazing fire against his enemies. In the struggle, his sword was shattered. Brandishing his broken weapon, he led a counterattack that drove the rebels from the hall and from the city.

Though the city was secure, the king's forces were outnumbered by the enemy beyond the walls. More rebels joined the siege of Caerleon hourly.

In the great hall, Arthur stared unhappily at his broken sword. "If I had a proper king's sword, I would rout those rebels once and for all," he boasted.

"You have courage and a strong right arm," said Merlin. "In a short time, you have shown you have the makings of a just and wise ruler. These things are more important than a sword, no matter how finely made. The people trust you."

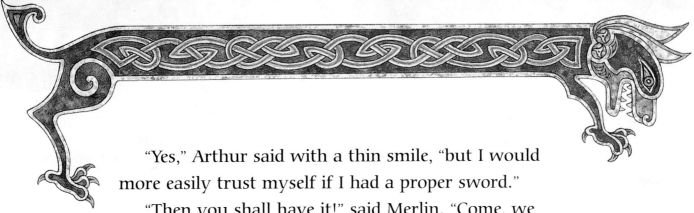

"Yes," Arthur said with a thin smile, "but I would more easily trust myself if I had a proper sword."

"Then you shall have it!" said Merlin. "Come, we have a great distance to travel in a short time."

"How can we go anywhere?" Arthur protested. "We are surrounded by enemies."

"Take my hand," said Merlin. "Don't be afraid. If you speak or cry out, you will undo everything."

Without hesitation, Arthur clasped Merlin's hand. It seemed to him that they were wrapped in pale smoke. Then they flew like ghosts along corridors, unseen by the guards. They passed through the huge doors of the hall, though they were closed. Down the deserted streets they raced.

Arthur felt excited, afraid, dizzy. Many times he choked back a cry. But he kept silent, his fingers twined with Merlin's.

They reached the city walls, and poured like rising smoke up the battlements; they poured down the outer walls like rainwater. They sped past the tents and watchfires of the enemy camp, then across the meadows and through the trees beyond.

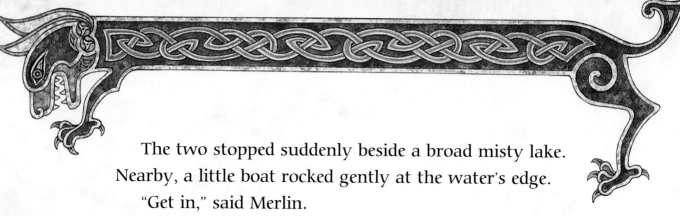

The two stopped suddenly beside a broad misty lake. Nearby, a little boat rocked gently at the water's edge.

"Get in," said Merlin.

Arthur did so, and the magician followed.

"There are no oars," said Arthur.

"They are not needed," Merlin replied. Indeed, the boat was already drifting toward the center of the lake, where the reflected moon shimmered like a pool of liquid silver. When they reached the brightness, a woman's arm thrust up, holding a great sword.

"This is the sword you seek—one truly worthy of a king. It is called Excalibur," said Merlin. "Take it."

Arthur took hold of the handle by wrapping his fingers around the woman's pale fingers. At his touch, the ghostly arm vanished, and the sword remained in his grasp.

Then the boat carried them swiftly back to shore. There they were wrapped again in Merlin's smoky magic, and returned unseen to the great hall.

When he found himself seated once more before the great fire, Arthur wondered if he had had a waking dream. But Excalibur lay across his knees.

At dawn, Arthur, brandishing Excalibur, led his army against the enemy just emerging from their tents. They had assumed that Arthur would keep his weaker force behind the walls. While the rebels hastened to form battle lines, Merlin magically scattered their watchfires. The flame and smoke from burning tents added to their confusion.

But it was Arthur who carried the day. The marvelous sword he carried flashed in the light of the rising sun as it rose and fell, rose and fell. Excalibur seemed to have a life of its own as it flickered right or left to wound or slay an enemy.

The battle was fierce, and where the fighting was the most desperate, there was King Arthur, raging like a young lion. When the three most powerful rebel lords set upon him, Excalibur burned as bright as the sun itself, blinding Arthur's enemies. Then he fell upon them and drove them off. And when the knights saw their lords in flight, they broke and ran.

Then the common folk of Caerleon rushed out, armed with clubs and staves. They harried the stragglers until none of the enemy remained upon the field.

King Arthur had won his first battle. Though his soldiers urged him to pursue and punish his foes, he said, "We need fear those lords no longer. They are beaten and have nothing left them but their honor. I will not slay them to take that away."

Merlin nodded, saying, "Such mercy may well turn those enemies to friends in time."

"Friends or enemies, I will meet them as true king of the realm," Arthur replied, sheathing Excalibur.

"Now," said Merlin, "your real work begins. You must raise the castle my dreams name Camelot, and gather around you the greatest knights from near and far. Then you will establish a reign of such nobility, justice, and wisdom that all ages will celebrate Arthur the King, whose fame will grow with every passing generation."

from THE **Knight's** HANDBOOK

by CHRISTOPHER GRAVETT

ARMOR AND WEAPONS

Great lords and kings needed knights to help them defend their lands, and wage war on their rivals. In battle, knights charged with their lances lowered, knocking the opposing knights from their horses.

COATS OF MAIL

Only knights could usually afford to keep several horses and wear full armor. The earliest knights wore coats of "mail" that weighed about 15 kg (33 lb). Mail was made from thousands of iron rings, each one linked to four others, and closed by a tiny rivet. By adding or removing rings, the coat could be tailored like a suit. From the twelfth century, knights wore long mail sleeves that went over the hands like mittens, and mail leggings. The coat of mail had to be flexible so that the knight could move easily. To make it more comfortable, a padded garment was often worn underneath. This also cushioned heavy blows from weapons. Over their armor, knights began to wear a cloth "surcoat" or tunic, sometimes decorated with their coat-of-arms.

THE HELMET

At first, the only armor made from solid steel plates was the helmet. This was usually conical, with a noseguard to protect the face from blows. By about 1200, some knights were using helmets fitted with a face mask. These developed into the "helm," which covered the whole head, and had eyeslits and breathing holes. In the fourteenth and early fifteenth centuries, knights wore a type of helmet called a "basinet." Because of the visor's strange shape, this helmet was known as a "hound's hood!"

Under their surcoats, these French knights are wearing a mixture of mail and plate armor.

READY FOR THE FIGHT!

What the well-dressed knight and his horse
wear when going to battle

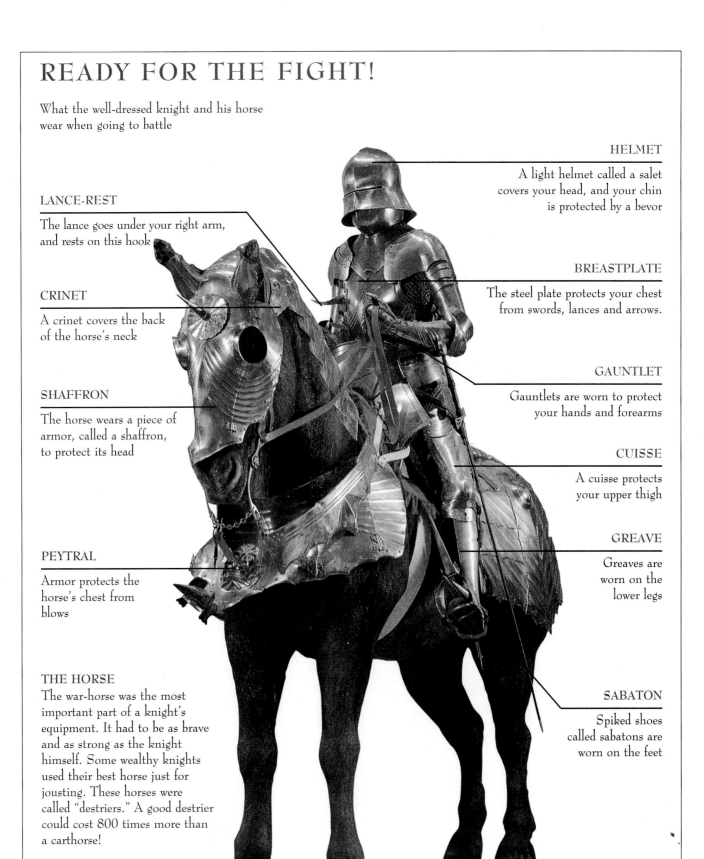

HELMET

A light helmet called a salet
covers your head, and your chin
is protected by a bevor

LANCE-REST

The lance goes under your right arm,
and rests on this hook

CRINET

A crinet covers the back
of the horse's neck

BREASTPLATE

The steel plate protects your chest
from swords, lances and arrows.

GAUNTLET

Gauntlets are worn to protect
your hands and forearms

SHAFFRON

The horse wears a piece of
armor, called a shaffron,
to protect its head

CUISSE

A cuisse protects
your upper thigh

GREAVE

Greaves are
worn on the
lower legs

PEYTRAL

Armor protects the
horse's chest from
blows

THE HORSE

The war-horse was the most
important part of a knight's
equipment. It had to be as brave
and as strong as the knight
himself. Some wealthy knights
used their best horse just for
jousting. These horses were
called "destriers." A good destrier
could cost 800 times more than
a carthorse!

SABATON

Spiked shoes
called sabatons are
worn on the feet

SUITS OF STEEL

Mail was strong, but it could be pierced by sharp weapons, so to protect themselves further, fourteenth-century knights began to wear a "coat of plates" over their mail. This was a sleeveless cloth garment lined with steel plates. Sometimes a solid breastplate would be attached to protect the chest, and the arms and legs were also covered in plate. Later, the plates were worn uncovered, and held together by rivets, leather straps, buckles, and laces. By 1400, wealthy knights were clad from head to toe in shining metal.

HIGH FASHION

Armorers (the people who made the armor) gave the steel plates a fashionable shape, and some were beautifully decorated. A knight's suit was specially made for him, but it would still have cost less than his best war-horse.

CARTWHEELS

The suit of armor weighed less than the pack a modern soldier carries on his back, and knights in full armor could easily mount their horses. Some knights even boasted that they could turn cartwheels, or leap into the saddle!

An iron-clad knight says good-bye to his family. A piece of armor called a shaffron protects the horse's head.

HERALDRY

In the twelfth century, knights began to wear special patterns so that they could be recognized at contests and in battle. The code that controlled who could have which shapes and colors is called "heraldry."

COATS-OF-ARMS

A knight often wore his family's design on his cloth tunic or "surcoat," and this is what gave us the term "coat-of-arms." The knight's horse was dressed in a long covering called a "trapper," which was decorated with the knight's design. The coat-of-arms would also be painted on the knight's shield, and on a flag called a "banner." The knight's wife and family could use the coat-of-arms on their clothes and possessions, too.

Knights recognized each other in battle by their coats-of-arms

HERALDIC COLORS

Knights chose all sorts of designs for their coats-of-arms: some knights liked to have animals like lions and dolphins on their shields, others preferred geometric shapes. There were rules to prevent families from having the same arms, and to make designs easier to see. The animals had to be drawn in a certain way, and there were rules about how colors were used. Silver and gold were called "metals," and these could be placed on top of or under red, blue, black, or green. The well-dressed knight sometimes attached a colorful crest to the top of his helmet. The crest could be made from leather or wood. This made it easier for heralds and friends to identify the knight in a tournament or battle.

A BRAVE MESSENGER

"Heralds" kept records of coats-of-arms, and tried to enforce the rules. Kings and great lords had their own heralds, who wore their masters' arms on a loose coat called a "tabard." Heralds had the dangerous job of acting as messengers between courts, delivering challenges to tournaments, or even to war. Their other important duties included shouting out the names of contestants at tournaments, and identifying the dead on the battlefield by their coats-of-arms.

FOOD

Knights were fighting men, so they had to be fit and strong. Like all nobles, they ate lots of meat and fish, but very few vegetables. Wild boar, peacock, and even whale might be served at a feast!

THE LORD'S TABLE

Cows, sheep, pigs, chickens, pheasants, and partridges were kept on the manor to provide meat for the household. The ducks, geese, swans, and other waterfowl that lived on rivers and ponds within the estate would also end up on the lord's table.

THE HALL

The whole household ate together in the hall. Instead of plates, everyone except the nobles was given a thick slab of coarse bread, called a trencher, to place their meat on. When the bread had become soggy with gravy, it was thrown to the dogs, or given to the poor.

The lord and his family ate from silver platters, and sat at a raised table at one end of the hall. The less important you were, the farther away you would sit from the lord and the saltcellar that marked the division between the nobles and the common

people. As a knight, you would sit "above the salt."

PASS THE SALT

In medieval times, the best way to stop meat from rotting was to preserve it in salt. To make the meat taste better, cooks added garlic, onions, mustard, and garden herbs to their dishes. In the lord's household, the cook would also have exotic spices like black pepper, cloves, ginger, and nutmeg that came from distant lands and were very expensive.

With their meat, nobles had fine white bread made from wheat flour. Peasants had to make do with coarse, dark bread, and vegetables, which, apart from cabbages and onions, were thought unfit to be served at a knight's table. As a treat, peasants might have an egg or a little bacon.

Cooks prepare a sumptuous feast at a noble household

KNIGHTLY PASTIMES

When knights were not fighting, training, or competing in a tournament, they liked to dance and play games.

ACROBATS AND MINSTRELS

At dinner, the lord and his household would be entertained by acrobats, jugglers, fire-eaters, and comedians. Minstrels told funny stories, recited poetry, and sang songs accompanied

by fiddles, harps, bagpipes, hurdy-gurdies, and other instruments. Minstrels traveled from court to court, so they would often bring exciting news and gossip from other parts of the country. Sometimes, as a surprise, the lord entered the hall in disguise, performed a mime and disappeared again.

Musicians playing a hurdy-gurdy and bagpipes.

DANCING AND GAMES

Dancing was a good opportunity for knights to court the ladies! In the ring dance, everyone held hands and danced in a large circle. In another dance, couples danced together then changed partners. There were also games to play, like "hoodman blind," in which a blindfolded person had to catch and identify the others. Knights enjoyed games of strategy like checkers (draughts), backgammon, and chess. Chess was introduced to Europe from the Middle East, probably by knights returning from the crusades. Noble ladies liked to play board games, too.

THINK ABOUT READING

Answer the questions in the story map.

SETTING

1. Where and when does the legend take place?

CHARACTERS

2. Who are the main characters?

3. How are Arthur and Kay different?

GOAL

4. What prediction is made when Arthur is born?

EVENTS

5. What happens to Arthur after King Uther dies?

6. Why does Arthur pull the sword from the stone the first time?

7. How does Arthur prove that he is the rightful King of England?

ENDING

8. After King Arthur wins his first battle, what does Merlin tell him to do?

WRITE A LEAD FOR A NEWSPAPER ARTICLE

It's front-page news! Picture the crowd's excitement when Arthur pulls the sword from the stone the second time. Imagine that you are a newspaper reporter at the scene. Write a lead, or first paragraph, for a newspaper article about the event. Be sure that your lead gives the most important facts, including *who, what, where, when, why,* and *how.*

LITERATURE CIRCLE

The legend of *Young Arthur* and *The Knight's Handbook* give a picture of life in the Middle Ages. Think of other stories that you have read, movies you have seen, or TV shows you have watched about knights during this time. They may be about King Arthur, knights of his Round Table, or other characters. Talk about how these stories are like *Young Arthur.* Tell how they are different. Record your ideas on a Venn diagram.

AUTHOR
ROBERT D. SAN SOUCI

Award-winning author Robert D. San Souci always carries a notepad for jotting down book ideas. Ideas come to him when he reads and researches in the library or wanders around listening to people talk. He says, "I love to listen for the flow and rhythm of the language that different people use." San Souci also reads newspapers for inspiration. "I look for bizarre little tidbits . . . . I keep a file of these clippings called my 'Weird File,' and periodically I go through it for ideas."

MORE BOOKS BY
ROBERT D. SAN SOUCI

- *Young Guinevere*
- *Young Lancelot*
- *Cut From the Same Cloth: American Women of Myth, Legend and Tall Tale*

CHEROKEE SUMMER

by Diane Hoyt-Goldsmith
photographs by Lawrence Migdale

PHOTO
BIOGRAPHY

From CHEROKEE

AWARD
WINNER

S U M M E R

by Diane Hoyt-Goldsmith

photographs by Lawrence Migdale

My name is Bridget. I live in a small town called Okay, Oklahoma in the northeastern part of the state. In summer, the countryside is a patchwork of green pastures and golden fields. Farmers raise cotton, grain, soybeans, and corn while ranchers fatten cattle and hogs. There are dense forests of oak and hickory that shade the valleys, and rolling fields of hay that ripen in the summer heat.

Before Oklahoma became a state in 1907, the place where I live was part of Indian Territory. I am a Cherokee Indian and a member of the Cherokee Nation. My people have a long history and a great heritage. Our strong traditions have given us an identity to be proud of.

AREA OF DETAIL

CHEROKEE COUNTY →
Illinois River
Tahlequah
Okay · *Lake Tenkiller*
Muskogee

Tulsa ·

★ Oklahoma City

OKLAHOMA

Summer Fun

Summer is a special time for my family. The weather is hot and humid so we go outdoors as much as possible. One of our favorite pastimes is hunting for crawdads. My father and his twin brother used to catch them when they were little boys. Now my dad is an expert.

First we drive out to Grandfather's house and fix up some gigs—poles with a fork on the end for catching crawdads. Grandfather helps us make them out of a piece of wire and river cane. He cuts the wire from a clothes hanger and with a pliers, shapes it into a fork with two prongs. Then we tie it to the cane with a piece of string.

We go hunting at Spring Creek. It flows behind the house where my father grew up. My great-grandmother, Mary Belle Russell, raised him and she still lives there.

The best place to look for crawdads is under the rocks near the banks of the creek. If we creep along quietly, we might find one lying out in clear view. Then, a quick jab with the gig and we have caught one. Sometimes we can turn a rock over slowly and find one hiding underneath.

My father is fast and catches three or four crawdads before I can even get to the water. Then he stands back and watches my brother, sister, and me. It doesn't take us long to catch enough to fill a coffee can. I usually catch the most.

Soon it's time to cook the crawdads. We build a twig fire on the shore with some dry leaves, tiny pieces of wood, and bits of wild grapevine.

After we get the fire going, we fill the can that holds the crawdads with water from the creek. We heat the can on stones over the fire. Soon the water starts to boil. When the crawdads turn a bright red, they are cooked and ready to eat. Nothing is more delicious than a fresh crawdad cooked over a twig fire on a hot summer day.

Bridget's grandfather splits a piece of river cane and puts the double-prong fork into the end to make a gig for catching crawdads.

Bridget's mother has gone hunting for crawdads every summer since she was a child. Breaking the sticks into small pieces, she helps her husband start a fire on the shore to cook the crawdads.

The Cherokee Language

My mother's parents can both speak our native language. Although my grandmother reads and writes in Cherokee, many of the younger people have stopped learning and using the language altogether.

Grandmother teaches the Cherokee language in an adult class during the school year. She has taught me a few words in Cherokee, and I like having a Cherokee name. Grandmother says that there are things she can say in Cherokee that are hard to translate into English. Our language is part of our history and our identity as a tribe. That is why we don't want to lose it.

The Cherokee language is spoken by combining eighty-five different sounds. The written language has a separate character for each sound, so Cherokee is written by using this syllabary, rather than by using an alphabet.

The Cherokees have had a written language since 1821. The syllabary was the invention of a man named Sequoyah. The English alphabet took four thousand years to develop, but Sequoyah invented our syllabary in just nine years.

kah-MAH-mah
BUTTERFLY

yo-nah
BEAR

ee-NAH-dah
SNAKE

When Sequoyah created our written language, he could neither read nor write in English. He watched the Europeans write and receive letters, and decided to come up with the same system for his own people.

Sequoyah was very artistic and the characters he drew for the Cherokee syllabary were done with a calligrapher's grace and beauty. Later on, as people began to use the syllabary to print books and newspapers, many original characters were changed to look more like English letter forms. However, in Cherokee the letters stand for different sounds. For example, a "D" in Cherokee stands for the sound "ah" and an "R" stands for "eh."

The Nation's TSA-LA-GI (*TSA-lah-gee*) Library is located in the old prison building. The people who work there try new ways of teaching children to become literate in the Cherokee language. For example, the Nation has a program in which Cherokee is taught in the schools. There is even a new computer program for students learning our language. When you type the sound of a Cherokee word on the computer, a mechanical voice pronounces it. Then the proper letter comes up on the screen. It is fun to use.

Another way to teach the language is by telling stories. The library puts on puppet shows in the schools, and the actors use Cherokee stories, characters, and words.

For our people, legends have been a good way for the elders to teach children about Cherokee life and the proper way to behave. Sometimes the stories explain something about the natural world. The stories almost always have a moral, and they are entertaining too.

Possum Learns a Lesson

A CHEROKEE LEGEND
retold by Sequoyah Guess

Long, long ago in the days when animals could talk, Possum had a big, bushy tail. It was even more beautiful than Fox's, and Possum was proud of it. He loved to show it off to his friends. Every day he combed it a hundred times to keep it looking shiny.

The rest of the animals grew tired of Possum's showing off. They got together and discussed what they could do to teach him a lesson. Then they came up with a plan.

Rabbit went over and talked to Possum.

"We're going to have a dance tonight," he said, "and it's in honor of your tail."

"Great! Great!" Possum replied. "But you know I'll need a special chair to sit on so I can show it off."

"Of course," Rabbit answered. "We'll get a nice chair for you. But in the meantime, I'll help you get ready. You won't have to do a thing. Just sit back and relax."

Possum was really thrilled to have so much attention paid to his tail. He lay back while Rabbit carefully washed and combed it. Possum was so relaxed and happy that he soon fell asleep.

While Possum snored peacefully, Rabbit whistled for his friend Cricket. It was time to put the rest of the plan into action. Cricket came and shaved off all the hairs on Possum's tail. Then he helped Rabbit wrap some cloth around it.

When Possum woke up, Rabbit told him, "I've got this cloth over your tail to keep it nice for tonight." Possum didn't give it

a thought. He was full of excitement and couldn't wait for the dance to begin.

When night came, all the birds and the animals gathered for the dance. Chanting their ancient songs, they moved around the fire in a perfect circle, singing and dancing.

Rabbit said to Possum, "You should go out there and dance. We are all waiting to see your most wonderful tail." As he spoke, he started to unwrap Possum's tail.

Possum was in such a hurry to dance that he didn't look back. He did not notice that anything was wrong. He danced and sang, circling the fire with a huge grin on his face.

"Look at my tail," he sang. "I've got a beautiful tail. There's no tail like mine."

The animals started to giggle. They said "Oooooh!" and "Aaaaah!" Then they started to laugh out loud.

At first, Possum thought they were admiring his tail. He kept on singing. Each time he passed the animals, he sang "Look at my beautiful tail!" But the more the animals laughed, the more Possum wondered, What's wrong? Why are they making fun of me?

Then he turned and looked behind him. His beautiful tail was pink and bare! Instead of being big and bushy, it was skinny and ugly.

Possum was so embarrassed that he fell backward, his big smile frozen on his lips.

Possum never got his bushy tail back. And to this day, all opossums have a hairless tail. If you startle an opossum when you are walking in the woods, he'll play dead and grin just like Possum did. Possum learned it is not smart to brag about anything too much. ■

A Summer Stomp Dance

For the Cherokees, dancing around a fire is not something that only happens in legends and stories. Special stomp dances are still held every weekend all year round by the traditional people in the tribe. Our people keep the spirit of ancient teachings alive by singing the songs that we have learned from past generations. Because these have never been written down, the elders teach the words and melodies to their children. Attending a stomp dance has become a very special part of my summer.

Before the dances begin, the Cherokees often prepare a special feast called a "Hog Fry." Everything is cooked outdoors over an open fire. It takes all afternoon to make an evening meal for the crowd.

The Cherokees are known for their hospitality. It is a tradition that anyone who comes to a stomp dance will be fed. The meal is a time for sharing. It creates an atmosphere of friendship for the dances that follow.

Stomp dances have been performed for centuries. They are still danced by the tribes of the Southeast—the

Small pieces of pork are added to hot lard in a cast-iron kettle to cook. The stove was made out of a fifty-gallon oil drum. A hole for adding wood has been cut into the sides near the bottom.

Cherokees, Creeks, Seminoles, and Shawnees. The dancers believe that the rhythmic songs and movements of the dance help put them back in balance with the world. Dancing gives them peace of mind.

Men, women, and children are free to participate in the dances. Children begin to dance when they are very young, following the movements of their parents and grandparents.

At a stomp dance, dancers from many tribes gather to visit, feast, and worship. The dances begin after dinner and usually last all night long.

Some of the girls wear a modern version of shackles, made with tin cans rather than turtle shells. The cans make a nice sound when filled with tiny pebbles.

On long summer afternoons, when I have the chance to be alone, I like to draw pictures and let my mind wander. I dream about what I will do when I grow up and how I will live. Perhaps I'll be an artist or a dancer. I might be a doctor or a teacher. I might even be the chief of my tribe.

For now, I feel lucky to have a loving family and to live in a beautiful place. I am proud of my Cherokee heritage, and I will work hard to keep it strong. Soon it will be time to go back to school. The weather will turn cold and the leaves will fall. But I will have the memories of this Cherokee summer—a special time in my life.

The summer hay crop near Tahlequah is harvested and collected into bales for drying. The giant hay rolls are a good place to be alone to think and dream.

from FAMILY PICTURES

♦ *Cuadros de familia* ♦

by CARMEN LOMAS GARZA

The pictures in this book are all painted from my memories of growing up in Kingsville, Texas, near the border with Mexico. From the time I was a young girl I always dreamed of becoming an artist. I practiced drawing every day; I studied art in school; and I finally did become an artist. My family has inspired and encouraged me for all these years. This is my book of family pictures.

Los cuadros de este libro los pinté de los recuerdos de mi niñez en Kingsville, Texas, cerca de la frontera con México. Desde que era pequeña, siempre soñé con ser artista. Dibujaba cada día; estudié arte en la escuela; y por fin, me hice artista. Mi familia me ha inspirado y alentado todos estos años. Este es mi libro de cuadros de familia.

Oranges

We were always going to my grandparents' house, so whatever they were involved in we would get involved in. In this picture my grandmother is hanging up the laundry. We told her that the oranges needed picking so she said, "Well, go ahead and pick some." Before she knew it, she had too many oranges to hold in her hands, so she made a basket out of her apron. That's my brother up in the tree, picking oranges. The rest of us are picking up the ones that he dropped on the ground.

Naranjas

Siempre íbamos a la casa de mis abuelos, así que cualquier cosa que estuvieran haciendo ellos, nosotros la hacíamos también. En este cuadro, mi abuela está colgando la ropa a secar. Nosotros le dijimos que las naranjas estaban listas para cosechar, y ella nos respondió:–Vayan pues, recójanlas. En un dos por tres, tenía demasiadas naranjas para sostenerlas en las manos, así que convirtió su delantal en canasta. Ése es mi hermano, en el árbol, recogiendo naranjas. El resto de nosotros estamos recogiendo las que él deja caer al suelo.

Watermelon

It's a hot summer evening. The whole family's on the front porch. My grandfather had brought us some watermelons that afternoon. We put them in the refrigerator and let them chill down. After supper we went out to the front porch. My father cut the watermelon and gave each one of us a slice.

It was fun to sit out there. The light was so bright on the porch that you couldn't see beyond the edge of the lit area. It was like being in our own little world.

Sandía

Es una noche calurosa de verano. Toda la familia está en el corredor. Mi abuelo nos había traído unas sandías esa tarde. Las pusimos en el refrigerador para enfriarlas. Después de la cena, salimos al corredor. Mi padre cortó la sandía y nos dio un pedazo a cada uno.

Era divertido estar sentados allá afuera. La luz del corredor era tan fuerte que no se podía ver más allá del área que estaba iluminada. Era como estar en nuestro propio pequeño mundo.

61

Think About Reading

Write your answers.

1. Why are members of the Cherokee nation so interested in learning the Cherokee language?

2. How can you tell that Bridget's family is important to her?

3. If you could spend a summer with Bridget's family, which activity do you think you would enjoy most? Why?

4. How do the photographs and captions in the selection help you learn about Bridget's life?

5. In what ways are *Cherokee Summer* and *Family Pictures* alike?

Write a Caption

The paintings in *Family Pictures* are a little like photographs. They show Carmen Lomas Garza's family doing things together. Choose one of the pictures and write a caption for it. In your caption, be sure to tell where the family members are and describe what they are doing. Include how the family members feel about the activity.

Literature Circle

Cherokee Summer and *Family Pictures* are both about families. Talk about the kinds of information presented in each selection. How are the two families alike? Which selection gives a clearer picture of the family's life? What other things would you like to learn about each family?

AUTHOR AND PHOTOGRAPHER
Diane Hoyt-Goldsmith and Lawrence Migdale

When Diane Hoyt-Goldsmith grew up in Oregon, she always loved to read and draw. A beautiful piece of Native American art inspired her to research her first book, *Totem Pole*. Lawrence Migdale always takes the colorful photographs that illustrate Diane's books. As a team, this author and photographer have created over fifteen books about children from different cultures in the Americas.

MORE BOOKS BY
Hoyt-Goldsmith and Migdale

- *Celebrating Chinese New Year*
- *Apache Rodeo*
- *Buffalo Days*
- *Hoang Anh: A Vietnamese-American Boy*

How to
Make a Book Jacket

Have you ever picked up a book because you liked the way the cover looked? You can learn a lot about a book from its cover illustration and the information found on the book jacket.

What is a book jacket? A book jacket is made up of several parts. The front cover shows the title of the book, the name of the author, and artwork related to the book. The inside front flap has a paragraph about the book, while the back cover may have quotes from reviewers or a photo of the author.

The title is on the cover.

The author's name is below the title.

When I Was Nine
by James Stevenson

My own children are grown up now; that's how old I am. But sometimes I look back and I remember . . .

In that pre-World War II time, the radios were bigger, the cars larger, and the days seemed to be longer. But some things were exactly as they are now: arithmetic, older brothers, and the ecstasy of jumping into an icy mountain stream. This evocation of a summer in the 1930s is the perfect answer for every grandchild (and child) who has ever said, "Tell me about when you were little."

The inside flap gives a summary of the book.

Pictures give clues to what the book is about.

1 Brainstorm

What words and pictures tell a story about you? Get out your notebook and jot down things you like to do, places you like to go, people you know, talents you have, and all the words you can think of that tell about you.

TOOLS

- pencil and ruler
- construction paper
- colored markers
- picture of you
- glue

My best friend

2 Investigate

When you've finished your list, put check marks next to your best ideas. Decide on a title for your book. Then look at some book jackets to see what pictures, titles, and designs they use. Write down some ideas for your own jacket design. Think about what colors you want to use and what pictures should go on your cover.

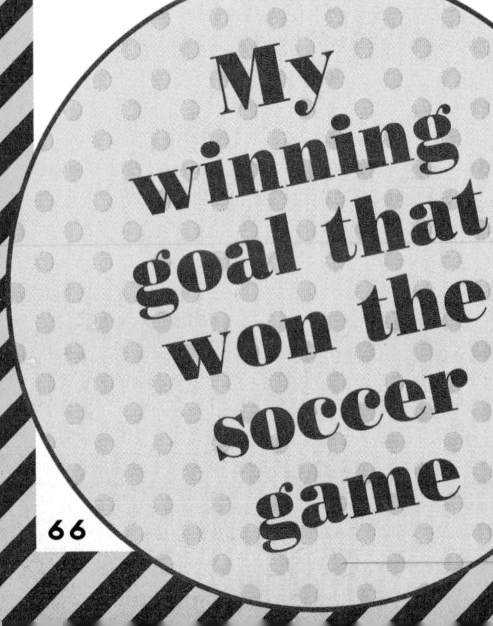

My family's trip to Chicago

My winning goal that won the soccer game

3 Write Flap Copy

After deciding on a cover design, the next step is to write a brief paragraph that describes what your book is about. This paragraph is like a short book report. It goes inside the front flap of your book cover and is called flap copy. The more interesting the flap copy, the more likely that people will read your book. Be sure to use lots of details when you write your paragraph.

Tips
- Having trouble drawing? Try using some family photos—but ask first! Or use some pictures from magazines and make a collage.
- Don't be afraid to use lots of bright colors. Remember, a book jacket has to catch your eye!

The first time I rode a bicycle

The time that the dog ate my birthday cake

4 Make Your Book Jacket

- Fold a piece of construction paper in half to make the jacket. Then fold down the inside flaps.
- Draw the design you want on the cover, and then add the title and your name.
- Put your flap copy on the inside of the front flap.
- If you want, decorate the back cover with a picture of yourself or some "quotes" from made-up book reviews.

If You Are Using a Computer . . .

Create your book cover on the computer. You can choose a border that you like and clip art that tells about you. After you've decided on what to call your book, type the title and your name with a special font.

THINK
How do you think famous people choose what to put in their autobiographies?

Jerry Spinelli
Author ▶

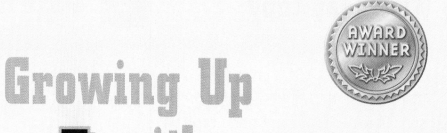

Growing Up with Jerry Spinelli

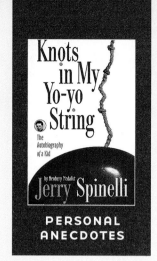

JERRY SPINELLI

What's it like to grow up? Author Jerry Spinelli has his own opinions. Here he describes some of the growing pains and challenges he experienced as a fourth grader and as a Little League ball player.

Fourth Grade Heartache

I was in fourth grade when Judy Brooks broke up with me. Judy was my neighbor. She lived up the street at 718 George Street in Norristown, Pennsylvania, where I grew up. As a matter of fact, George Street is Oriole Street in a few of my books, and Norristown is the town of Two Mills in *Maniac Magee*, *Dump Days*, and *The Bathwater Gang*.

Judy and I were an item for about four years. Then in the fourth grade she informed me that she hated all boys— and that included me. Well, I told her that if that was the case, then I hated all girls. For the next year or two I was into a pretty severe girl-hating stage. By the way, in *Fourth Grade Rats* the girl in the book that the boy really likes is named Judy Billings. She just happens to have the same first name and same initials as Judy Brooks!

This is me in fourth grade, the year Judy Brooks broke up with me. Can you imagine any girl dumping such a cute little face?

Neighbors

On summer evenings my father and I would go out after dinner and toss a baseball because I wanted to be a Major League shortstop. The Seeton's house was perpendicular to ours—their dining room windows faced our backyard. One evening, my father and I were throwing the ball, and my aim wasn't too accurate. I threw the ball over my father's head right through the Seeton's dining room window. I was a real coward at times like that, so it was up to my father to tell the Seetons what had happened, and offer to pay for it.

After a week or so, the window was fixed. But then a couple of days later my father and I were playing catch again and I did the same thing! It's just unbelievable—same window, same baseball—and my father took care of it again. And the most amazing thing about the whole episode was that none of the Seetons ever said anything about it. Mr. Seeton may have been fuming behind the walls of his own house, but he never said anything to me. I just got off scott free—all I had to deal with was my own conscience.

Overnight Fright

I had two best friends in the fourth grade—Roger Adelman and Johnny Seeton, and I have a little story about each of those friends. My Roger Adelman story makes me cringe, even today, to think of what a baby I was. You see, I was never one to go to camp for weeks at a time or even overnight. I went to YMCA day camp, but I never stayed overnight. To me that seemed too adult. But Roger Adelman went away to Boy Scout camp for a week or two at a time.

Even though I wasn't the type to do this, somehow I ended up with a pup tent. I put it up in my yard and the next thing I knew, I was inviting Roger Adelman to come down and sleep over. So he came down and my mother, as mothers will do, had all kinds of comforts—blankets and snacks and some kind of lantern light. So we had our snacks and chatted and played cards, and then turned out the light and lay down in the pup tent. Roger went to sleep immediately like a veteran Boy Scout. But I was wide awake, nervous and spooked for about an hour or so. Finally, I shook Roger's shoulder to tell him that I had to go back in the house. My last memory is of me picking up my blanket and heading in the back door of my house while Roger trudged off the three or four blocks to his house.

You are looking at the 1953 50-yard dash champion of Norristown, Pennsylvania, grade schools. Wisely, I retired from track after that.

71

Adventure at the Creek

Another day I was down at the creek with Johnny Seeton. I had been standing in the water, which was only about a foot deep. When I came up out of the creek I saw that there were leeches—what we used to call bloodsuckers—all over my shins. Well, I knew what to do in case of a rattlesnake bite from reading books and watching movies. You'd just get out your old trusty knife, make an X-shaped cut at the bite mark, and suck out the poison. So I figured, well, I guess you do something similar for leeches. I must have thought they were poisonous. So I brushed the leeches off my legs—

I did not have the nerve to start making cuts—and I told Johnny to start sucking. The last thing I remember was a kid with horror in his eyes turning and running and racing up the steep bank, and that was the last of Johnny that I saw that afternoon. And I went with wet shins and bare feet to my house wondering if I was going to die in a few days because my friend wouldn't suck out the poison.

A Happy Ending

I want to end by saying that in spite of some unpleasant memories, fourth grade wasn't all bad. In fact, one of the best things I remember from that time is my teacher, Miss Coleman. As the years go by, I tend to appreciate her more and more. That's why I dedicated my book *Fourth Grade Rats* to her.

Here I am having lunch at a school I visited. As you can see, I'll do anything for a free lunch.

I had <u>two</u> best friends in the fourth grade. Here's a poem I wrote about the situation.

Stuck

In fourth grade
for some reason we had
this test
and one of the questions was:
<u>Who is your best friend?</u>
I was really stuck
because I could not decide
between Roger Adelman
who was in my class
and Johnny Seeton
who was my neighbor.
Surely the one I didn't choose
would be offended.
The answer space
was still a blank
when the teacher called
for papers.
Quickly,
I wrote in both names.
I never found out
how well I did.

—Jerry Spinelli

Shortstop

From ages eleven to sixteen, if someone asked me what I wanted to be when I grew up, I gave one of two answers: "A baseball player" or "A shortstop."

Major league baseball—that was the life for me. And I wanted to live it only as a shortstop. When I trotted onto a diamond, I instinctively headed for the dusty plain between second and third. I never wanted to play any other position. When we got up sandlot games, no one else occupied shortstop. They knew it was mine.

I was eleven when I first played Little League baseball. To give as many kids as possible a chance to participate, the Little League declared that some of us would share uniforms with others. And so the season was exactly half over when I pedaled my bike up to Albert Pascavage's house to pick up his uniform: green socks, green caps, gray woolen shirt, and pants with green trim. I packed my precious cargo into my bike basket and drove it carefully home. I was a member of the Green Sox.

During one game in that half season I played second base—apparently no one told the manager I was going to be a major league shortstop. Our opponent was the Red Sox. The batter hit a ground ball right at me. I crouched, feet spread, glove ready, as I had been taught in the *Times Herald* baseball school. I could hear the ball crunching along the sandy ground. It hit my glove—but not the pocket. Instead it glanced off the fat leather thumb and rolled on behind me.

Here I am at age 12 in 1953—a shortstop for the Green Sox.

My first error!

I was heartbroken. I stomped my foot. I pounded my fist into the stupid glove.

When the inning was over and I slunk to the Green Sox bench, the manager was waiting for me. I thought he was going to console me. I thought he would say, "Tough luck, Jerry. Nice try," and then tousle my hair.

That's not what happened.

At age 4, in 1945, I am a budding ballplayer.

What he really did was glare angrily at me, and what he really said was, "Don't you ever do that again." He pointed out that while I was standing there pounding my glove, two Red Sox runs had scored. "Next time you miss the ball, you turn around and chase it down. You don't just stand there feeling sorry for yourself. Understand?"

I nodded. And I never forgot.

Like most of the kids in my class, I got better at sports simply by growing older. I went from being one of the worst players in Little League as an eleven-year-old, to making the all-star team as a twelve-year-old. The following year I was the only seventh grader to start on the Stewart Junior High School team—at shortstop, of course. It mattered little that I was not very good at hitting a curve ball, since most pitchers threw only fastballs.

During the summer of junior high school I played in a baseball league called Connie Mack Knee-Hi, for thirteen- to fifteen-year-olds. Before each game, one team would line up along the first-base line, the other team along third base. The umpire stood on the pitcher's mound, took off his cap, and read aloud the Sportsmanship Pledge, pausing after each line so the rest of us could repeat it in chorus. We pledged ourselves to be loyal to, among other things, "clean living and clean speech." In the final line we promised to be "a generous victor and a gracious loser."

In the Knee-Hi summer of 1955, I had little chance to be a gracious loser. My team, Norristown Brick Company, swept through the local league undefeated, winning our games by an average score of 12–1. One score was 24–0. One team simply refused to show up. Our pitchers threw four no-hitters, three by Lee Holmes. Opposing batters could no more hit Bill Bryzgornia's fastball than spell his name. We were a powerhouse.

We beat Conshohocken two out of three to gain the state playoffs. Three wins there put us into the title game. On a bright Saturday afternoon at War Memorial Field in Doylestown, Norristown Brick Company defeated Ellwood City 4–2, to become Connie Mack Knee-Hi champions of Pennsylvania.

Two buddies (Anthony Greco and Bob Hopple) and me (left), heading off to a dance at Grace Lutheran Church, 1955. I'm wearing my Knee-Hi State Champions jacket.

In the awards ceremony after the game, we were given jackets saying STATE CHAMPIONS. Ellwood City players got trophies. A jacket would eventually wear out and be thrown away, leaving me with nothing to show for our great triumph. But a trophy was immune to frayed cuffs and moth holes. A trophy would be forever. I watched as each Ellwood City player walked up for his trophy and half-wished I had been on the losing side.

A week later, during a banquet at the Valley Forge Hotel in downtown Norristown, to my relief, we were each given a magnificent trophy.

Chucking dust on a four-base diamond was only part of the baseball life. There was the long list of major league batting averages to pore over each Sunday in *The Philadelphia Inquirer*. There was the baseball encyclopedia, my first history book, to study. Long before I knew the difference between Yorktown and Gettysburg, I knew Ty Cobb's lifetime batting average (.367) and Cy Young's total career pitching victories (511).

There were cards to flip. We bought bubblegum just to get the baseball cards, and then we dueled. Slip one corner of the card between forefinger and middle finger and flip outward, Frisbee-like, toward a wall. The kid whose card lands closest to the wall picks up the other kid's cards. The stacks of cards I won this way would be worth a fortune today, if I had kept them.

There were baseballs to tape. Seldom in our sandlot games did we have a ball with a real stitched horsehide cover still on it. Most often the balls were covered in black utility tape. A white ball was a real treat. It meant that someone had sneaked into the medicine chest at home and used up half a roll of first-aid tape.

There were hours to spend bouncing tennis balls off neighbors' brick walls, any wall but that of the mysterious barber across the street. For hours each week I scooped up the rebounding grounders, practicing to be a great shortstop. Considering the thumping I gave those houses, it's a wonder I was never chased off. Maybe the people behind the walls understood that in my mind I was not really standing on George Street but in the brown dust of Connie Mack Stadium, out at shortstop, fielding hot shots off the bat of Willie Mays.

And there was the glove. My glove bore the signature of Marty Marion, slick-fielding shortstop of the St. Louis Cardinals.

Each year at the end of summer vacation, I rubbed my glove with olive oil from the kitchen cabinet. Then I pressed a baseball deep into the pocket of the glove, curled the leather fingers about the ball, and squeezed the whole thing into a shoebox. Standing on a chair, I set the box high on a closet shelf. Baseball season was officially over.

For the next six months we would hibernate, shortstop and glove, dreaming of the Chiclets-white bases at Connie Mack Stadium, feeling in the palm the hard, round punch of a grounder well caught.

MENTOR

Jerry Spinelli

Author

JOHN · NEWBERY · MEDAL

FOR THE
MOST DISTINGUISHED
CONTRIBUTION
TO
AMERICAN LITERATURE
FOR CHILDREN

JERRY SPINELLI
1991

Authors are full of the "write" stuff.

As an author of children's books, Jerry Spinelli is so successful that writing is his full-time job. But he never thought much about writing when he was growing up. "My dream was to play baseball. I was going to be a shortstop in the major leagues."

PROFILE

Name: Jerry Spinelli

Occupation: author

Pets: a rat named Daisy and Chi-Chi the chinchilla

Favorite thing to read: Bugs Bunny comics

Book that won the Newbery Medal: *Maniac Magee*

Special skills: flipping baseball cards

QUESTIONS
for Jerry Spinelli

Discover how Jerry Spinelli became a writer.

Q What made you decide to become a writer instead of a baseball player?

A When I was sixteen my high school football team won a big game. I was so excited—I wrote a poem about it. A local newspaper published the poem. That's when I decided to become a writer.

Q And how did you become a writer?

A Well, first I became a grown-up. And I thought, *Now on to the important stuff!* So I tried writing grown-up novels about important stuff. But nobody wanted to publish them.

Q What made you decide to try children's books?

A I married my wife Eileen, a writer who already had five kids. One night, one of our little angels snuck into the refrigerator and swiped a piece of fried chicken I was saving for lunch. When I discovered the chicken was gone, I wrote about it. That piece of writing became my first published novel, *Space Station Seventh Grade*. At the time I had no idea I was going to write a children's book.

Q Do you have a regular writing schedule?

A I usually write in the morning from 10:00 to noon. Then after dinner, I write some more from 9:00 to midnight. I like working at night.

Q Are your childhood memories important to your writing?

A When I was growing up, I didn't think my childhood was special. It was full of kid stuff: bike riding, flipping baseball cards, and catching poison ivy. It wasn't until I started writing about it that I realized what an adventure it had been!

Q What do you like best about your job?

A The best part is being able to make a living from what I do. I was able to quit my job as an editor of a magazine. I love writing, and the fact that I get paid for it is an added bonus.

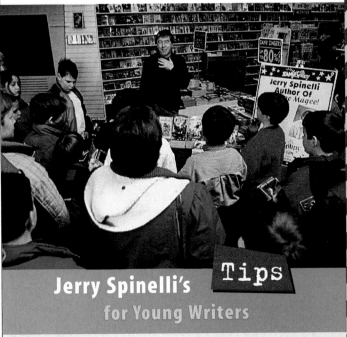

Jerry Spinelli's Tips
for Young Writers

1 Subject Matter: See how successful authors write for themselves as well as for their audience.

2 Trust Your Ideas: Remember to listen to your ideas.

3 Keep Writing: Whether playing the piano, baseball, or writing, the more you do something, the more you will improve. Have fun with it!

HARTRANFT SCHOOL
JUNE 1953

Think About Reading

Write your answers.

1. What are four main events that Jerry experienced during fourth grade?

2. Why do you think Jerry grew to appreciate his fourth grade teacher?

3. What experiences have you had that are similar to one of Jerry's stories? What did you do?

4. In "Shortstop," what does eleven-year-old Jerry learn when he fails to catch the ground ball?

5. What was important to Jerry between the ages of eleven and sixteen? What is important to him as an adult?

Write a Fan Letter

Write a fan letter to author Jerry Spinelli. Tell him what you like best about his writing and explain why. You may also wish to share with him something funny or important that has happened to you in fourth grade. Be sure to include the date, a greeting, and a closing in your letter.

Literature Circle

Talk about the advice that Jerry Spinelli gives to young writers. What pointers does he give for writing? Which do you think are most important? How does he use his own advice in his writing? Why do you think that this advice makes him a good writer? What advice would you give to him?

AUTHOR

Jerry Spinelli

As a child, Jerry Spinelli had many careers—salamander finder, flat-stone creek skipper, railroad-car counter, and tin-can stomper, to name just a few. Although each "job" was short-lived, the experiences help Jerry add real-life details to his writing. He says, "Write what you care about. That's when you are going to do your best writing."

MORE BOOKS BY

Jerry Spinelli

- *Maniac Magee*
- *Dump Days*
- *Report to the Principal's Office*

AFRICAN TALE

86

Mufaro's Beautiful Daughters

AN AFRICAN TALE
BY JOHN STEPTOE

A LONG TIME AGO, in a certain place in Africa, a small village lay across a river and half a day's journey from a city where a great king lived. A man named Mufaro lived in this village with his two daughters, who were called Manyara and Nyasha. Everyone agreed that Manyara and Nyasha were very beautiful.

Manyara was almost always in a bad temper. She teased her sister whenever their father's back was turned, and she had been heard to say, "Someday, Nyasha, I will be a queen, and you will be a servant in my household."

"If that should come to pass," Nyasha responded, "I will be pleased to serve you. But why do you say such things? You are clever and strong and beautiful. Why are you so unhappy?"

"Because everyone talks about how kind *you* are, and they praise everything you do," Manyara replied. "I'm certain that Father loves you best. But when I am queen, everyone will know that your silly kindness is only weakness."

Nyasha was sad that Manyara felt this way, but she ignored her sister's words and went about her chores. Nyasha kept a small plot of land, on which she grew millet, sunflowers, yams, and vegetables. She always sang as she worked, and some said it was her singing that made her crops more bountiful than anyone else's.

One day, Nyasha noticed a small garden snake resting beneath a yam vine. "Good day, little Nyoka," she called to him. "You are welcome here. You will keep away any creatures who might spoil my vegetables." She bent forward, gave the little snake a loving pat on the head, and then returned to her work.

From that day on, Nyoka was always at Nyasha's side when she tended her garden. It was said that she sang all the more sweetly when he was there.

Mufaro knew nothing of how Manyara treated Nyasha. Nyasha was too considerate of her father's feelings to complain, and Manyara was always careful to behave herself when Mufaro was around.

Early one morning, a messenger from the city arrived. The Great King wanted a wife. "The Most Worthy and Beautiful Daughters in the Land are invited to appear before the King, and he will choose one to become Queen!" the messenger proclaimed.

Mufaro called Manyara and Nyasha to him. "It would be a great honor to have one of you chosen," he said. "Prepare yourselves to journey to the city. I will call together all our friends to make a wedding party. We will leave tomorrow as the sun rises."

"But, my father," Manyara said sweetly, "it would be painful for either of us to leave you, even to be wife to the king. I know Nyasha would grieve to death if she were parted from you. I am strong. Send me to the city, and let poor Nyasha be happy here with you."

Mufaro beamed with pride. "The king has asked for the most worthy and the most beautiful. No, Manyara, I cannot send you alone. Only a king can choose between two such worthy daughters. Both of you must go!"

That night, when everyone was asleep, Manyara stole quietly out of the village. She had never been in the forest at night before, and she was frightened, but her greed to be the first to appear before the king drove her on. In her hurry, she almost stumbled over a small boy who suddenly appeared, standing in the path.

"Please," said the boy. "I am hungry. Will you give me something to eat?"

"I have brought only enough for myself," Manyara replied.

"But please!" said the boy. "I am so *very* hungry."

"Out of my way, boy! Tomorrow I will become your queen. How dare you stand in my path?"

After traveling for what seemed to be a great distance, Manyara came to a small clearing. There, silhouetted against the moonlight, was an old woman seated on a large stone.

The old woman spoke. "I will give you some advice, Manyara. Soon after you pass the place where two paths cross, you will see a grove of trees. They will laugh at you. You must not laugh in return. Later, you will meet a man with his head under his arm. You must be polite to him."

"How do you know my name? How dare you advise your future queen? Stand aside, you ugly woman!" Manyara scolded, and then rushed on her way without looking back.

Just as the old woman had foretold, Manyara came to a grove of trees, and they did indeed seem to be laughing at her.

"I must be calm," Manyara thought. "I will *not* be frightened." She looked up at the trees and laughed out loud. "I laugh at you, trees!" she shouted, and she hurried on.

It was not yet dawn when Manyara heard the sound of rushing water. "The river must be up ahead," she thought. "The great city is just on the other side."

But there, on the side, she saw a man with his head tucked under his arm. Manyara ran past him without speaking. "A queen acknowledges those who please her," she said to herself. "I will be queen. I will be queen," she chanted, as she hurried on toward the city.

Nyasha woke up at the first light of dawn. As she put on her finest garments, she thought how her life might be changed forever beyond this day. "I'd much prefer to live here," she admitted to herself. "I'd hate to leave this village and never see my father or sing to little Nyoka again."

Her thoughts were interrupted by loud shouts and a commotion from the wedding party assembled outside. Manyara was missing! Everyone bustled about, searching and calling for her. When they found her footprints on the path that led to the city, they decided to go on as planned.

As the wedding party moved through the forest, brightly plumed birds darted about in the cool green shadows beneath the trees. Though anxious about her sister, Nyasha was soon filled with excitement about all there was to see.

They were deep in the forest when she saw the small boy standing by the side of the path.

"You must be hungry," she said, and handed him a yam she had brought for her lunch. The boy smiled and disappeared as quietly as he had come.

Later, as they were approaching the place where the two paths crossed, the old woman appeared and silently pointed the way to the city. Nyasha thanked her and gave her a small pouch filled with sunflower seeds.

The sun was high in the sky when the party came to the grove of towering trees. Their uppermost branches seemed to bow down to Nyasha as she passed beneath them.

As last, someone announced that they were near their destination.

Nyasha ran ahead and topped the rise before the others could catch up with her. She stood transfixed at her first sight of the city. "Oh, my father," she called. "A great spirit must stand guard here! Just look at what lies before us. I never in all my life dreamed there could be anything so beautiful!"

Arm in arm, Nyasha and her father descended the hill, crossed the river, and approached the city gate. Just as they entered through the great doors, the air was rent by piercing cries, and Manyara ran wildly out of a chamber at the center of the enclosure. When she saw Nyasha, she fell upon her, sobbing.

"Do not go to the king, my sister. Oh, please, Father, do not let her go!" she cried hysterically. "There's a great monster there, a snake with five heads! He said that he knew all my faults and that I displeased him. He would have swallowed me alive if I had not run. Oh, my sister, please do not go inside that place."

It frightened Nyasha to see her sister so upset. But, leaving her father to comfort Manyara, she bravely made her way to the chamber and opened the door.

On the seat of the great chief's stool lay the little garden snake. Nyasha laughed with relief and joy.

"My little friend!" she exclaimed. "It's such a pleasure to see you, but why are you here?"

"I am the king," Nyoka replied.

And there, before Nyasha's eyes, the garden snake changed shape.

"I am the king. I am also the hungry boy with whom you shared a yam in the forest and the old woman to whom you made a gift of sunflower seeds. But you know me best as Nyoka. Because I have been all of these, I know you to be the Most Worthy and Most Beautiful Daughter in the Land. It would make me very happy if you would be my wife."

And so it was that, a long time ago, Nyasha agreed to be married. The king's mother and sisters took Nyasha to their house, and the wedding preparations began. The best weavers in the land laid out their finest cloth for her wedding garments. Villagers from all around were invited to the celebration, and a great feast was held. Nyasha prepared the bread for the wedding feast from millet that had been brought from her village.

Mufaro proclaimed to all who would hear him that he was the happiest father in all the land, for he was blessed with two beautiful and worthy daughters—Nyasha, the queen; and Manyara, a servant in the queen's household.

AWARD WINNER

from *My Song Is Beautiful*

YOU AND I

by Mary Ann Hoberman

Only one I in the whole wide world
And millions and millions of you,
But every you is an I to itself
And I am a you to you, too!

But if I am a you and you are an I
And the opposite is also true,
It makes us both the same somehow
Yet splits us each in two.

It's more and more mysterious,
The more I think it through:
Every you everywhere in the world is an I;
Every I in the world is a you!

Students from Brooklyn, New York P.S. 16 created this self-portrait quilt from painted fabric that they stitched together.

Think About Reading

Answer the questions in the story map.

SETTING
1. Where and when does the story take place?

CHARACTERS
2. Who are the main characters in the story?

GOAL
3. Why is the message that arrives from the king important to Mufaro?

EVENTS

4. What three people does Manyara meet on her way to the city? How does she treat them?

5. How does Nyasha treat the people she meets on her way to the city?

6. What does Nyasha do when she meets the garden snake in the city?

SOLUTION
7. What does Nyasha learn about Nyoka, the snake?

8. What happens to Mufaro's two daughters in the end?

Write an Interview

What is it like to be queen of the land? Write an interview with Nyasha. Ask three questions and write the answers she might give. Make sure your questions begin with words such as *who*, *what*, *where*, *why*, *when*, and *how*. Avoid using questions that can be answered *yes* or *no*.

Literature Circle

The author of the poem "You and I" says that all people are "the same somehow." Do you agree that all people have something in common? Talk about Mufaro's two daughters. How are they different? In what ways are they alike? With which young woman would you rather spend time? Why? Record your ideas about the two daughters on a chart.

AUTHOR AND ILLUSTRATOR
John Steptoe

As a child, John Steptoe began drawing pictures and telling stories to go with them. It's no surprise that he published his first picture book when he was only nineteen. Steptoe dedicated *Mufaro's Beautiful Daughters* to the children of South Africa. In this story, Steptoe found a new way to express his pride in his African heritage. In his Caldecott Award acceptance speech he said, "This award gives me hope that children... will be encouraged to love themselves enough to accomplish the dreams that I know are in their hearts."

MORE BOOKS BY
John Steptoe

- *The Story of Jumping Mouse: A Native American Legend*
- *Birthday*
- *Stevie*

How to

Write a Personal Narrative

Pick a chapter from your life and write about it!

Ever think about writing a book starring you as the main character? Many authors do just that when they write a personal narrative. In a personal narrative, authors share their memories and experiences with others. Each story is told using the first-person point of view, as though the author is speaking directly to the reader.

Choose a Story to Tell

Decide on a topic for your personal narrative. Think of important events in your life that you'd like to share with others. Maybe it's something that's really amusing or exciting or heart-warming. After you've decided what to write about, ask yourself these questions. What is my story about? When did it happen?

Where did it take place? Who else was there? Think about these questions when you're writing your outline.

Tips
- Ask your family for details about the event you chose for your story.
- What age were you when the story took place?
- What did you look like?
- Write your story as though you are talking to a friend.

TOOLS

- notebook and pencil

- memories about events in your life

- people who can help you remember dates and details

2 Make an Outline

Now that you have your story idea, it's time to organize your material. Like any story, your personal narrative should have a beginning, a middle, and an end. Think about the story you want to tell, and divide your paper into three sections. Then write a few sentences in each section that tell what happened in that part of your story. This outline will help you organize your personal narrative.

How Am I Doing?

Before you start writing, take a few minutes to ask yourself these questions.

• Do I have a clear idea of what I want to write about?

• Have I decided on the mood of my story? Is it funny, sad, or something else?

• Is the outline of my story clear and organized?

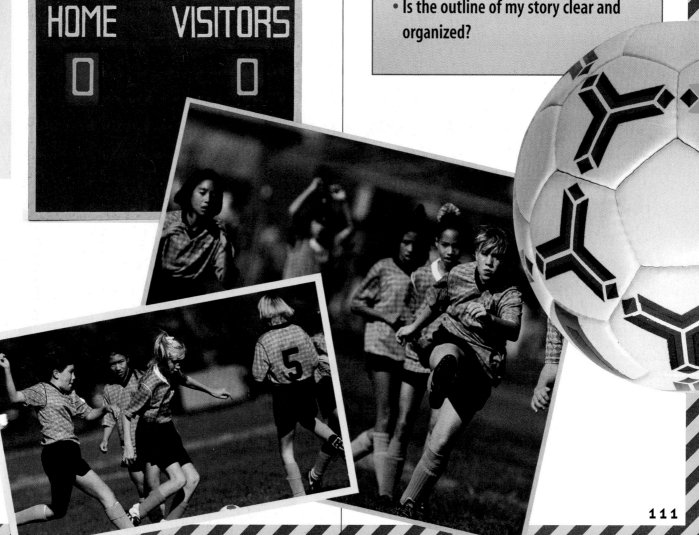

Write Your Personal Narrative

Once you've finished your outline, it's time to write your story. Use the ideas in your outline, and then add lots of details. Search your memory to find sensory details that will make your personal narrative come alive. What sounds, tastes, and smells do you remember? What colors remind you of the event you are writing about? Be sure to write your story using the first-person point of view.

4 Present Your Story

Here are some ways to present your story. Whatever form you choose, illustrate your narrative with drawings or photos.

- Make a book by stapling several sheets of paper together. If you made a book jacket, you can use that as the cover!

- Create a poster by arranging your writing with pictures and photos on a piece of posterboard.

- Write to a friend and tell your story in letter form.

- Turn your narrative into a script for a play.

- If you want to, you can share your personal narrative with the rest of the class.

If You Are Using a Computer . . .

Try drafting your personal narrative in the Report format on the computer. Choose clip art to illustrate your work. To make your narrative ready to present, you can print it out and use the book cover from the Workshop, or you can make a new title page. If you like, you also can use the Record and Playback Tools as you work on your story.

CONGRATULATIONS

You've read about other people's lives and thought about your own. Every experience is a new chapter.

Jerry Spinelli
Author ▶

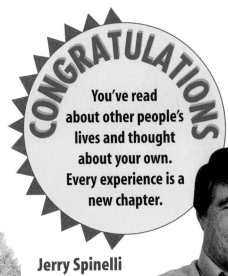

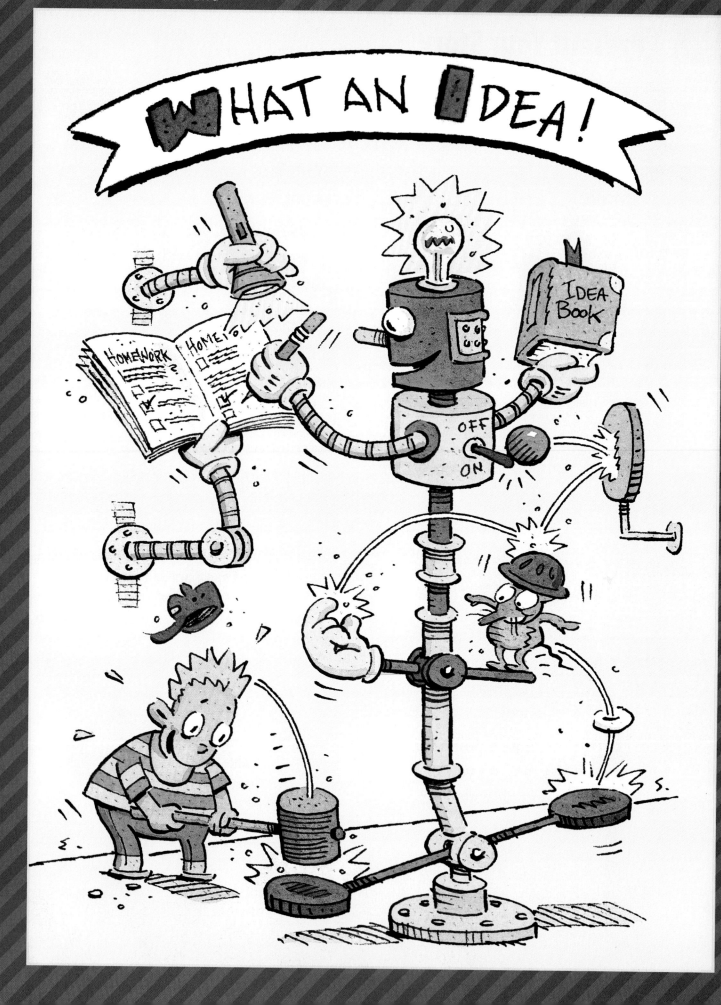

WHAT AN IDEA!

THEME

People solve problems by inventing new things.

www.scholastic.com

Visit the kids' area of **www.scholastic.com** for the latest news about your favorite Scholastic books. You'll find sneak previews of new books, interviews with authors and illustrators, and lots of other great stuff!

UNIT 2

milk jug

seat cushion trim waste

polystyrene cups

recycled cotton canvas
or recycled polypropylene

trim waste from diaper
manufacturing

soda bottles

wetsuit trim waste

recycled
EVA foam

tire rubber and
recycled rubber

coffee filters
and file folders

magazines and cardboard

Welcome to

LITERACY PLACE

Inventor's Office

People solve problems by inventing new things.

A PIECE of STRING

IS A WONDERFUL THING

by **JUDY HINDLEY**   illustrated by **MARGARET CHAMBERLAIN**

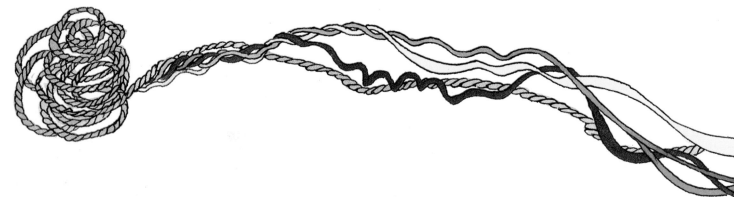

*W*hat a wonderful
thing string is!
Just think of the things
you can do with string!

Let us sing a song
about string—
what a wonderful thing it is!
When you think of the things
that you do with string,
you have to admit
it's a marvelous bit
to have in your kit:

My friend's uncle said, "You should never go anywhere without change for a phone call, a pencil stub, and a piece of string."

for a fishing line, a boat, a kite,
somewhere to hang your socks to dry;
for tying up packages, fastening gates,
leading you safe through a treacherous cave;
for a spinning top, a skipping rope,
a bracelet, a necklace, a drawstring purse . . .
there's just about no end of things
a person can do with a piece of string!
And then you wonder,
from time to time,
how did a thing like
string begin?

← slipknot

A slipknot can hitch
a boat, a horse,
a swing...

three small knots   three big knots   three small knots

= · · · — — — · · ·
= Morse code for S.O.S.

In New Guinea, people make fishing nets out of spiderwebs. They leave a wooden frame with a colony of spiders, who spin their webs around it. In the British Museum, I saw a spiderweb hat that was made this way.

Back in the days
when mammoths roamed,
and they didn't have chains
and they didn't have ropes
for hauling around or
lifting things up—

(well, they didn't have any connecting things:
buttons or braces or buckles or laces,
or latches or catches or bolts or belts,
or tabs or clasps or hooks and eyes . . .
Velcro patches! ribbons! ties!
zips or grips or snaps or clips)—
well how did anyone
THINK IT UP?

Did they chat as they sat
near the fire at night,
eating their prehistoric fish,
and say, "What we need
to get it right
is a thing like hair,
but long and strong,
a thing to tie on a piece of bone:
what a wonderful fishing line
that would make!"?

After which, I suppose,
they went out to the lake
and tickled the fish
with their cold, bare hands—
for they didn't have nets
if they didn't have string.
How they all must have wished
that they had such a thing!

For a long time the only spears were pointed sticks.
Much later, a chip of stone would be tied to
the stick with a sinew.

So how on earth
do you think they discovered it?
Do you think somebody
just tripped over it?
Was it an accident?
Was it a guess?
Did it emerge
from a hideous mess?
Did it begin with
a sinuous twig,
a whippety willow,
a snaky vine?

Did it happen that somebody,
one dark night,
winding his weary way home alone,
got tripped by the foot on a loop of vine
and fell kersplat! and broke a bone;
and then, as he lay in the dark, so sad,
and yelled for help (and it didn't come)
he got thoroughly bored with doing that
and invented—a woolly-rhinoceros trap?

In order to hunt successfully, people had to start working as a team.
But there's always a slowpoke...

Oh, it might have occurred
in a number of ways
as the populace pondered
the fate they faced—
as they huddled in caves
in the worst of the weather,
wishing for things like
tents
and clothes,
as they hugged furry skins
to their shivering bodies
and scraps of hide
to their cold, bare toes

And they had no suspenders
or snaps or connectors
or buttons or toggles
or zippers or pins—
so HOW did they hold up
their trousers, then?
They must have said,
"Oh! A piece of string
would be SUCH a fine thing
to have around the cave!"

Teams of hunters drove their prey over cliffs...
or possibly into holes hidden by vines.

They needed a noose for an antelope foot.
They needed a thing to string a bow.
They needed nets, and traps, and snares
for catching their venison unaware
and leading the first wild horses home.

A single fiber of wool is as strong as a thread of gold.

SPINNING A THIN THING FROM A FAT THING
Yarn is spun from sheep's fleece, cotton tufts, or even birds' down.
Try spinning with cotton. Pull and stretch it very gently,
very steadily, twisting it really tight as it draws out.

Well, they must've gone on to try and try
as hundreds of thousands of years went by,
twisting and braiding and trying out knots
with strips of hide and rhinoceros guts,
spiders' webs and liana vines,
reeds and weeds and ribs of palm,
slippery sinews, muscles, and thongs,
elephant grasses three feet long,
and wriggly fish-bone skeletons.

And they spun out the fibers
of vegetable fluff,
and they felted the hairs of a goat,
and they knitted and twisted
and braided and twined

and invented . . .

TURNING A THIN THING INTO A FLAT THING

The next trick is weaving and knitting to make fabric.
Tiny short hairs laid down higgledy-piggledy, then
wetted and pressed together, can be turned into felt.

the three-ply rope!
What a wonderful thing!
A very fine thing!
The KING of string
is rope!

You can lift up pots
from an echoing well with it,
fling it to make a bridge;
you can haul along hulking hunks
of stone for building a pyramid
(and they did).

The Egyptians made rope from bulrushes, camel hair, and flax.

The oldest rope ever discovered came from a tomb in Egypt. It was made from flax 5000 years ago.

Sometimes rope was even made from women's hair.

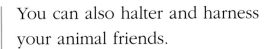

You can also halter and harness
your animal friends.

And then again, when life gets tough
and it's time to be moving along,
you can use it to lash your luggage fast
to a camel, a goat, a raft, a boat—
oh! a stringable thing
is the only thing
to have when you're afloat!

Making Rope

One man twists two strands clockwise and walks forward.

A second man makes sure the strands of rope are laid tightly together.

A third man closes the strands by twisting this tool counterclockwise and walks backward as the rope is formed.

But they still
went on and on,
sticking and spinning
and looping and gluing
and tying and trying out
more and more types,
quicker and quicker
crazier, slicker

early cart

The pontoon bridge was an early bright idea. It began with a row of boats all roped together.

Roman crane

early gravity railway

Isambard Kingdom Brunel went up in a hot-air balloon to lay the first rope of the famous Clifton Suspension Bridge in Bristol, England.

early flying machine

Hot metal can be stretched into rails and cables, ropes, and delicate wires.

for pulleys and ladders
and hoses and bridges
and fences and winches
and wires and pipes.

Where on earth
have we come to now?
What would a town
ever do without string
and things that go stringing along?
Candlewicks, rackets, and violins,
telephones, plumbing, and railroad lines,
things that fasten and fuse and fix
and click and stick and link.

Can you even begin
to count the ways
that things connect
with other things?
It could just about
scramble your brain!

And to think it began
(though we'll never know when)
with somebody choking
on elephant gristle,
or trying to chew
through the stem
of a thistle,
or just stumbling into
the thing!

Oh, what we've done
with a piece of string
is a marvelous thing,
an amazing thing—
some would say
a crazy thing!
And one of these days
I might just go away
and begin it
all over
again . . .

Amazing

B.C.

3500s B.C.

The wheel is invented by the Sumerians in what is now Iraq.

A.D.

A.D. 100s

Paper is invented in China by Ts'ai Lun. Knowledge of papermaking eventually spreads to Europe by way of the Islamic world.

A.D. 200s

The Maya are the first to use the number zero.

Mayan 0

A.D. 1280s

Eyeglasses are developed in Italy.

A.D. 1450s

The printing press is invented in Germany.

Inventions & Discoveries

1593

Galileo Galilei devises the first thermometer.

1656

The first successful pendulum clock is invented by Christiaan Huygens. This clock improves the accuracy of timekeeping.

1783

The Montgolfier brothers are the first to construct and ride in a hot-air balloon in France.

1809

Mary Dixon Kies becomes the first woman to receive a U.S. patent for her invention of a weaving process.

1871

Margaret Knight invents a machine that makes paper bags. She later patents 21 more inventions.

1   2   3   4

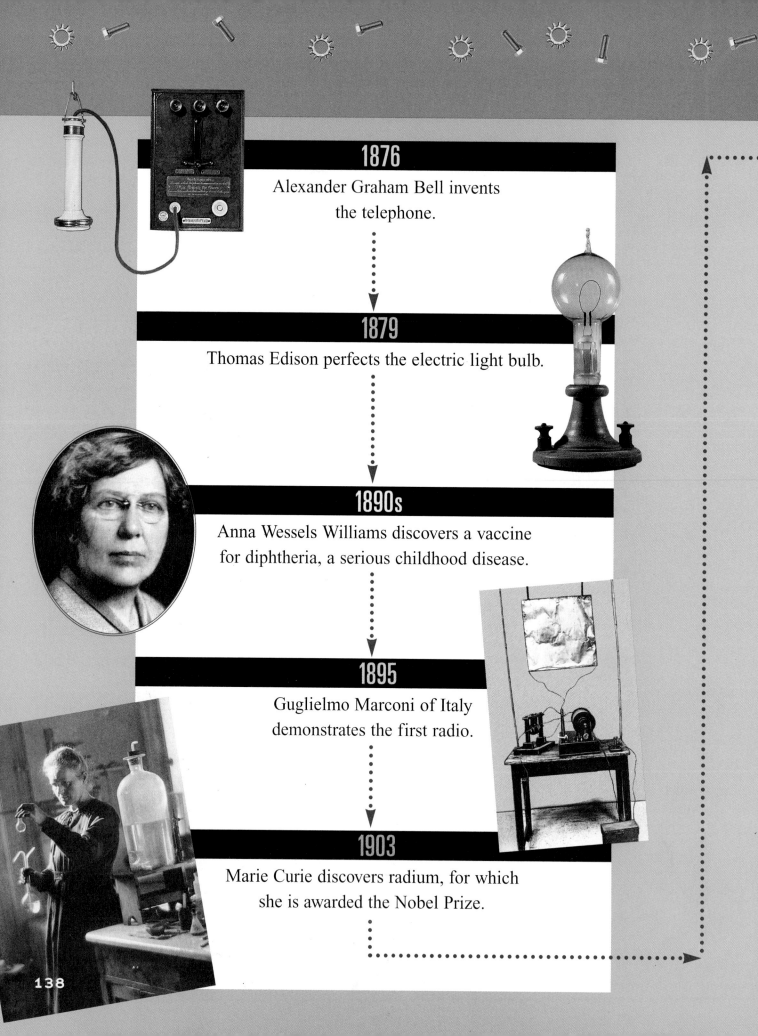

1876

Alexander Graham Bell invents the telephone.

1879

Thomas Edison perfects the electric light bulb.

1890s

Anna Wessels Williams discovers a vaccine for diphtheria, a serious childhood disease.

1895

Guglielmo Marconi of Italy demonstrates the first radio.

1903

Marie Curie discovers radium, for which she is awarded the Nobel Prize.

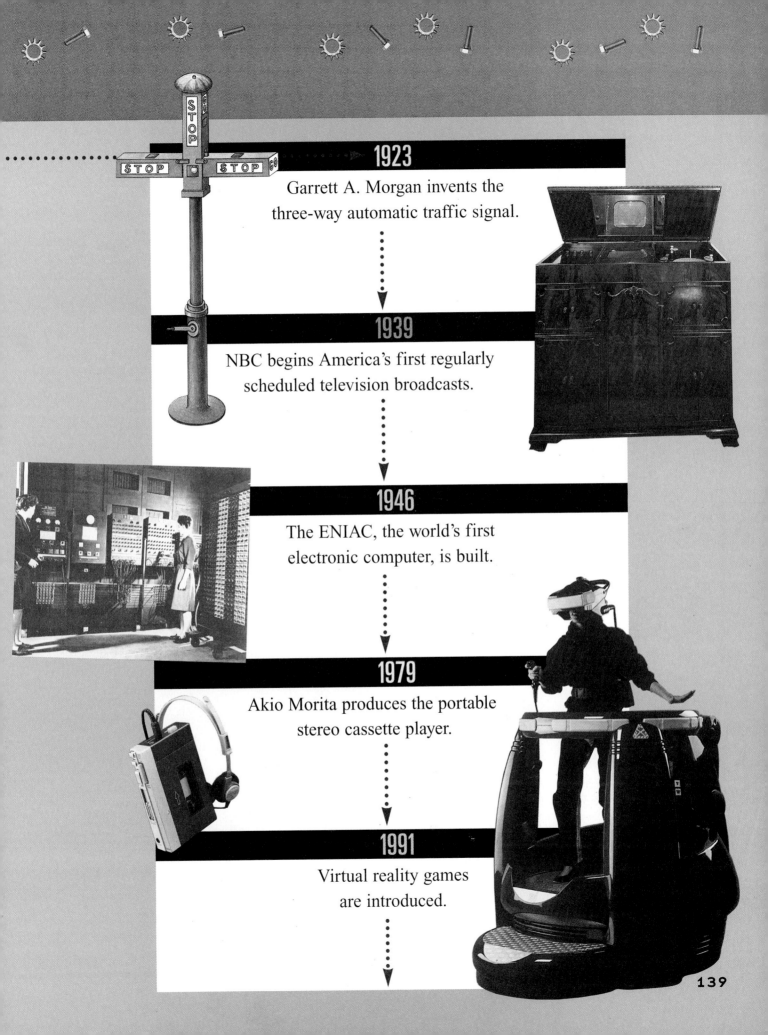

1923
Garrett A. Morgan invents the three-way automatic traffic signal.

1939
NBC begins America's first regularly scheduled television broadcasts.

1946
The ENIAC, the world's first electronic computer, is built.

1979
Akio Morita produces the portable stereo cassette player.

1991
Virtual reality games are introduced.

THINK ABOUT READING

Write your answers.

1. What are three ways people used string long ago? What are three ways they use string today?

2. What does the author mean by "a piece of string"?

3. Which three uses of string are most important in your life? Explain the reasons for your choices.

4. *A Piece of String Is a Wonderful Thing* is nonfiction. How does the author make the factual information about string entertaining?

5. Which discovery or invention on the time line do you think is as important as string? Explain your answer.

Write a Poster

Choose one of the uses of string or one of the inventions or discoveries on the time line. Write a poster that advertises the invention and persuades people that it is an important discovery. Make up a catchy slogan for the poster. Use colorful adjectives and precise verbs in your writing.

Literature Circle

Look around your classroom for examples of ways that string is used. Don't forget to look at your clothing, too. Talk about how each use of "string" solves a problem. You may wish to record your findings on a chart. Then, have a conversation about your ideas for new inventions with string.

AUTHOR
Judy Hindley

Judy Hindley enjoys writing humorous poetry and creating information-packed nonfiction books like *A Piece of String Is a Wonderful Thing*. She has written over 30 children's books on a variety of topics from knights to science. Although Ms. Hindley grew up in California, she now lives in England and writes full time.

MORE BOOKS BY
Judy Hindley

- *The Wheeling and Whirling-Around Book*
- *Time Traveller Book of Knights and Castles*
- *A Song of Colors*

Invention Book

The Invention of

Sneakers

How rubber-soled shoes with canvas uppers became known as "sneaks" or "sneakers" is not exactly known. The reason may be the obvious one—rubber and canvas shoes are very quiet. But the phenomenal popularity of the sneaker has more to do with its comfort and style than with the ability to sneak around quietly.

The story of the rubber-soled sneaker begins with the development of rubber. For many centuries, the natives of Central and South America commonly used the gum that oozed from the bark of certain trees to cover and protect the bottoms of their feet. Their technique was to apply the gum directly in thin layers, curing each layer with gentle heat from a fire. The result was a coating that covered the bottom of the wearer's foot and protected it from rough land.

SNEAKERS

A British traveler, in the late 1700s, became fascinated with these strange-looking foot coverings, but he was even more intrigued with the possibility of using the gum to make other products. He collected several samples of the gum and the products the natives made from it and returned to England, where he showed the new substance to his chemist friend Joseph Priestley. Priestley's first discovery was that the gum had the unique ability to cleanly erase pencil marks by briskly rubbing the paper with it—so he enthusiastically named the substance "rubber."

For the next fifty years, several products made of rubber were manufactured— mostly water-proof containers and coverings to protect all kinds of things from the rain. And by 1820 someone finally designed a rubber cover that the wearer could stretch over his leather shoes to protect them in wet or muddy weather. These rubber "overshoes" quickly found their way to America, and the new novelty product became an instant success—but not for long.

This drawing shows how the Mayans made shoes by covering their feet with melted rubber.

SNEAKERS

In an attempt to make money on the popular imported fad, many New England shoe manufacturers hastily set up factories, making rubber overshoes in various styles that incorporated hand-painted designs and other decorations. But within just a few years the attraction had diminished, as wearers soon discovered that pure rubber became obnoxiously smelly and sticky in hot weather, and brittle enough to crack into small pieces during cold weather. By 1823 no one wanted anything to do with rubber overshoes.

About that time, Charles Goodyear, a young out-of-work hardware salesman, decided to take on the challenge of eliminating rubber's shortcomings. Goodyear's interest became a hobby and then a serious undertaking. Soon he was dedicating all his time and money to making rubber a more stable product. Goodyear believed that the solution involved adding certain chemicals to the pure rubber gum and finding the right way to cure the mixture.

Experiment after experiment failed, and Charles Goodyear went broke. He borrowed money from friends and businessmen, but he still couldn't find the right formula. Eventually Goodyear was arrested and put into debtor's prison for failing to pay back his creditors.

SNEAKERS

While the shoe industry still tried to bring back the fad by introducing various new styles of rubber overshoes, the sticky, smelly, and often brittle substance found little acceptance as footwear. In 1834 an inventor named Wait Webster patented a process for attaching rubber to the soles of shoes and boots with uppers made of leather, but the combination did nothing to eliminate the original problems with rubber.

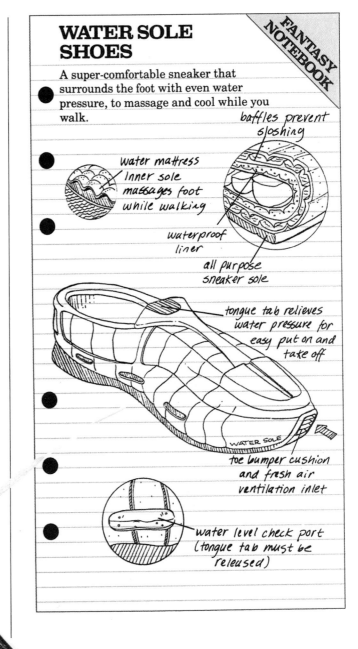

WATER SOLE SHOES

FANTASY NOTEBOOK

A super-comfortable sneaker that surrounds the foot with even water pressure, to massage and cool while you walk.

baffles prevent sloshing

water mattress inner sole massages foot while walking

waterproof liner

all purpose sneaker sole

tongue tab relieves water pressure for easy put on and take off

WATER SOLE

toe bumper cushion and fresh air ventilation inlet

water level check port (tongue tab must be released)

An artist's rendition of Charles Goodyear at work, just as he discovered the process of vulcanization.

By 1838 Charles Goodyear was at his experiments again; this time another rubber enthusiast, Nathaniel Hayward, joined him. They discovered that if they mixed sulfur with the gum rubber and then left it in the sun to bake slowly, the mixture would form a rubbery but not sticky outer skin. Goodyear was sure he was on the track to the solution, but Hayward wasn't so convinced. So Goodyear paid Hayward for his contribution and optimistically went on experimenting alone.

One year later, Charles Goodyear got lucky. He was mixing up a batch of gum rubber, sulfur, and white lead when a glob of the mixture fell off his stirring utensil and onto the hot stovetop. When the mass cooled and Goodyear went to remove it, he discovered that the rubber had cured perfectly—consistently rubbery throughout and not sticky at all! He then discovered that his new "metallic" rubber (he called it "metallic" because of the lead in the mixture) was more elastic and considerably less brittle. Goodyear named the process for making metallic rubber vulcanization, after the Roman god of fire, Vulcan.

SNEAKERS

Now that a better rubber had been invented, a better rubber shoe could be made. Charles Goodyear licensed his vulcanization process to several shoe companies and also to manufacturers of all types of rubber products. Some companies made rubber-soled shoes, rubber shoe covers, or even all-rubber shoes, and one shoe manufacturer, Thomas Crane Wales, made a waterproof boot of rubberized cloth with a rubber sole, called "Wales patent Arctic gaitors." But the first real sneaker with laced canvas uppers and vulcanized rubber soles came in 1868 from the Candee Manufacturing Company of New Haven, Connecticut. These canvas-and-rubber "croquet sandals" were made to appeal strictly to the wealthy, and they were sold through the exclusive Peck and Snyder Sporting Goods Catalog.

Fortunately, the Candee Company's marketing scheme didn't work as planned, and people who never thought of playing croquet began wearing the light and comfortable canvas-and-rubber shoes. By 1873 the shoes were commonly called sneaks or sneakers. And by the beginning of the twentieth century, everyday people often wore 60¢ canvas-and-rubber sneakers, while the rich wore more expensive models with silk, satin, and white duck uppers, trimmed in bows for women and elk skin for men.

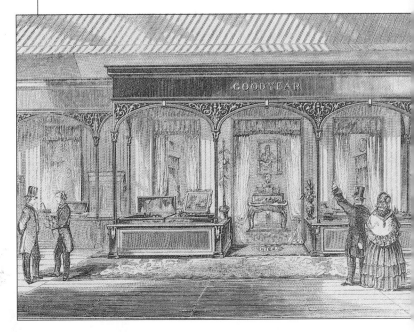

A print of Charles Goodyear's exhibition of rubber products at the famous Crystal Palace in Sydenham, England, from 1893.

SNEAKERS

While the sneaker became increasingly popular as a comfortable, stylish casual shoe, it also was being used as a sporting shoe. Special types of sneakers were being made for all kinds of popular sports and games. In 1909 the basketball sneaker was introduced, and a year later the Spalding Company invented a rubber sneaker sole with molded suction cups for better traction. In 1915 the U.S. Navy ordered non-slip sneakers to be used aboard ships.

A picture of the early Spalding tennis shoes in action.

In 1917 Henry McKinney, the public relations director for the National India Rubber Company (owned by the U.S. Rubber Company), decided it was time to call the canvas-and-rubber shoe

An early advertisement for Spalding tennis shoes.

something different from the ever-popular sneaker. After reviewing more than 300 suggestions, he selected the name "Peds" (from the Latin word meaning "foot"). However, McKinney soon discovered that another company used "Peds," and he quickly switched to the now-famous brand name "Keds." The idea worked, and for a while the Keds name was just as familiar as sneakers.

Many other companies tried to create new sneaker fads, and some succeeded. Over the past seventy-odd years, "new, improved" models have appeared with features such as arch cushions, colored uppers, colored rubber soles, side venting outlets, waffle soles, and most recently, curved-sole "running" shoes. Today the sneaker is by far America's most popular and comfortable shoe style, accounting for over one-quarter of all shoes sold—and very few are worn for croquet.

Fantasy Inventions

The sneaker has come a long way since the early twentieth century and there is no reason you can't invent another variation on this old favorite.

Slug Glue Dispenser. A healthy live slug is placed inside the glue dispenser carrying case. When glue is needed, a portion of the case bottom is removed and the slug is allowed to walk across the area to be glued.

Shoe Shine Vending Machine. Provides a quick shoe shine for people on the move. Shine selection options include rainy day waterproofing, military spit shine, different color shade, and a computerized shoe condition report.

New Sneaker Smell Renewer. A spray that gets rid of old sneaker smell and replaces it with the smell of a new pair of shoes.

Headlight Shoes. Shoe toe headlights and red heel taillights provide safety for nighttime joggers and walkers.

MENTOR

Julie Lewis

Inventor

Inventor + Problem = Solution!

Julie Lewis is an inventor who cares about the environment. Her most successful invention tackles a problem that is becoming bigger every day—too much garbage. Can garbage be turned into something useful? After some experimenting, Lewis came up with a solution: shoes!

PROFILE

Name: Julie Lewis

Occupation: inventor and founder of Deja Shoe Inc.

Special skills: ability to see a problem and solve it

Favorite invention: the telephone

A problem that needs an inventive solution: air pollution

Previous jobs: bread factory worker, nutrition teacher, waitress

Favorite book in fourth grade: *Harriet the Spy* by Louise Fitzhugh

QUESTIONS
for Julie Lewis

Learn how Julie Lewis found a practical solution to an environmental problem.

Q What gave you the idea to invent shoes out of trash?

A My college roommate was in nursing school. One cold day, she hung her polyester nursing-school pants on the radiator. They melted. That's when I realized that some fabrics were made of plastics. Later, when I thought of using recycled materials to make cloth, I remembered her pants melting.

Q How did that help you come up with your invention?

A It made me think of what gets recycled: aluminum, plastics, and even tire rubber. I had some sandals made from old tires, which gave me the idea of combining different types of recycled "garbage" to make shoes.

Q How did you turn garbage into shoes?

A It took me a few years to develop a cloth made from recycled plastics. Then I made some model shoes with it. My two kids thought it was funny. They'd say, "Oh, there's Mom trying to invent again."

Q What was the next step?

A I didn't know anything about making shoes, but I wasn't afraid to ask. First I talked to Bill Bowerman, a shoe designer and co-founder of Nike Shoes. I explained my idea, and showed him what I'd done. He made me a model of the first Deja shoe.

Q Did you start a company with just one shoe?

A That model shoe was all I needed. I applied for a grant from an Oregon agency in charge of recycling. I presented a business plan and an explanation of how to turn recycled materials into shoes. They awarded me $110,000 to start my company.

Q Do you feel that you've solved the problem of waste in the environment?

A Not at all. I'm proud of our success in recycling, but there's so much more to do!

Julie Lewis's Tips
for Young Inventors

1 Don't be discouraged if someone says your idea is dumb.

2 Look for alternative solutions. If a solution doesn't work, try another, and another, until one works.

3 Get information from experts.

Think About Reading

Write your answers.

1. What problems did wearers have with the first rubber overshoes?

2. What qualities did Charles Goodyear have that helped him find a way to use rubber?

3. In what ways do you think sneakers could be improved?

4. Why do you think the author includes the story about the rubber overshoes that didn't work?

5. What do Julie Lewis and Charles Goodyear have in common?

Write a Business Letter

Your class wants inventor Julie Lewis to give a talk on Careers Day. Write Ms. Lewis a business letter arranging the visit. Be sure to introduce yourself. Describe what you would like her to talk about, and give the date you want her to come. Be sure to include the heading, an inside address for Julie Lewis, and a closing.

Literature Circle

Some inventions spring from surprising materials. For example, Charles Goodyear found a way to use rubber and Julie Lewis turned garbage into shoes. Talk together about other unusual uses you can think of for used materials such as plastic, metal cans, cardboard, old tires. Then, brainstorm a list of possible uses for each.

AUTHOR
Steven Caney

Wouldn't it be great if someone invented a contraption that makes your bed for you every morning? That someone could be you—after you have read *Steven Caney's Invention Book.* Mr. Caney is a toy and game inventor who enthusiastically shares his ideas with young people. Where does he get his great ideas? He says, "It's from people."

MORE BOOKS BY
Steven Caney

- *Steven Caney's Toy Book*
- *Steven Caney's Invention Book*
- *Steven Caney's Kids' America*
- *Make Your Own Time Capsule*

How to
Make an Invention Diagram

Have you ever had an idea for an invention? Did you ever look at an everyday object and think, "I could improve that?" Inventors often write down their ideas when they think of them. Later, they may decide to develop an idea by making a diagram of it.

What is an invention diagram? An invention diagram is a drawing of an invention with each of its parts labeled, and a list of materials needed to make it. The diagram includes a description of what the invention can do.

Nathan Matter:
The Handy Helper

The name of the inventor

The name of the invention

flexible magnet

velcro fastens it to wrist

magnetic bracelet
holds nails and tacks

Matthew McCurdy's
Crayons for Keeps

long bolt

handle pushes crayon out

hard nylon dowel

crayon

Clearly labeled parts

Description of the invention's function

protects crayons from breaking

157

1 Make a List

Jot down ideas for inventions or product improvements that you would like to see. Don't worry if your ideas seem silly—how about motorized sneakers, or sunglasses with a built-in video camera? Write down as many ideas as you can.

TOOLS

- pencil, paper, ruler
- colored markers

2 Design Your Invention

Look over your ideas and choose the one you like best. Think of different ways to design your invention. For example, if your invention is a talking watch, one design idea might include a talking cartoon head on the watch. A different design idea would be a digital watch that would announce the time and date every hour. Write down at least three different design ideas for your invention.

3 Draw a Diagram

Pick your favorite design idea and make a diagram of it. You may want to draw a picture of the whole thing and then a closeup of one of its important parts. Or you could show what your invention looks like on both the outside and the inside. Be sure to label each part of your invention. Underneath the diagram, list the materials you need to build it.

Tip Make some quick sketches of your invention before you draw your finished diagram.

4 Add Finishing Touches

Write a brief description of what your invention does. Don't forget to name it. Share your invention diagram with your classmates.

If You Are Using a Computer ...

Keep track of your invention ideas by typing them in the journal format. You also can experiment with font sizes and styles to make labels for your diagram.

THINK

Why is a diagram an important step in the process of developing an invention?

Julie Lewis
Inventor ▶

from

Homer Price By Robert McCloskey

THE DOUGHNUTS

ne Friday night in November Homer over-
heard his mother talking on the telephone to Aunt Agnes over
in Centerburg. "I'll stop by with the car in about half an
hour and we can go to the meeting together," she said,
because tonight was the night the Ladies' Club was meeting
to discuss plans for a box social and to knit and sew for the
Red Cross.

"I think I'll come along and keep Uncle Ulysses company
while you and Aunt Agnes are at the meeting," said Homer.

So after Homer had combed his hair and his mother had
looked to see if she had her knitting instructions and the right
size needles, they started for town.

Homer's Uncle Ulysses and Aunt Agnes have a very up-
and-coming lunchroom over in Centerburg, just across from
the court house on the town square. Uncle Ulysses is a man
with advanced ideas and a weakness for labor-saving devices.

He equipped the lunchroom with automatic
toasters, automatic coffee maker, automatic
dishwasher, and an automatic doughnut maker.
All just the latest thing in labor-saving devices.

Aunt Agnes would throw up her hands and sigh every time Uncle Ulysses bought a new labor-saving device. Sometimes she became unkindly disposed toward him for days and days. She was of the opinion that Uncle Ulysses just frittered away his spare time over at the barbershop with the sheriff and the boys, so, what was the good of a labor-saving device that gave you more time to fritter?

When Homer and his mother got to Centerburg, they stopped at the lunchroom, and after Aunt Agnes had come out and said, "My, how that boy does grow!" which was what she always said, she went off with Homer's mother in the car. Homer went into the lunchroom and said, "Howdy, Uncle Ulysses!"

"Oh, hello, Homer. You're just in time," said Uncle Ulysses. "I've been going over this automatic doughnut machine, oiling the machinery and cleaning the works . . . wonderful things, these labor-saving devices."

"Yep," agreed Homer, and he picked up a cloth and started polishing the metal trimmings while Uncle Ulysses tinkered with the inside workings.

"Opfwo-oof!!" sighed Uncle Ulysses and, "Look here, Homer, you've got a mechanical mind. See if you can find where these two pieces fit in. I'm going across to the barbershop for a spell, 'cause there's somethin' I've got to talk to the sheriff about. There won't be much business here until the double feature is over and I'll be back before then."

Then as Uncle Ulysses went out the door he said, "Uh, Homer, after you get the pieces in place, would you mind mixing up a batch of doughnut batter and putting it in the machine? You could turn the switch and make a few doughnuts to have on hand for the crowd after the movie . . . if you don't mind."

"O.K." said Homer, "I'll take care of everything."

A few minutes later a customer came in and said, "Good evening, Bud."

Homer looked up from putting the last piece in the doughnut machine and said, "Good evening, Sir, what can I do for you?"

"Well, young feller, I'd like a cup o' coffee and some doughnuts," said the customer.

"I'm sorry, Mister, but we won't have any doughnuts for about half an hour, until I can mix some dough and start this machine. I could give you some very fine sugar rolls instead."

"Well, Bud, I'm in no real hurry so I'll just have a cup o' coffee and wait around a bit for the doughnuts. Fresh doughnuts are always worth waiting for is what I always say."

"O.K.," said Homer, and he drew a cup of coffee from Uncle Ulysses' superautomatic coffee maker.

"Nice place you've got here," said the customer.

"Oh, yes," replied Homer, "this is a very up-and-coming lunchroom with all the latest improvements."

"Yes," said the stranger, "must be a good business. I'm in business too. A traveling man in outdoor advertising. I'm a sandwich man. Mr. Gabby's my name."

"My name is Homer. I'm glad to meet you, Mr. Gabby. It must be a fine profession, traveling and advertising sandwiches."

"Oh no," said Mr. Gabby, "I don't advertise sandwiches. I just wear any kind of an ad, one sign on front and one sign on behind, this way . . . Like a sandwich. Ya know what I mean?"

"Oh, I see. That must be fun, and you travel too?" asked Homer as he got out the flour and the baking powder.

"Yeah, I ride the rods between jobs, on freight trains, ya know what I mean?"

"Yes, but isn't that dangerous?" asked Homer.

"Of course there's a certain amount a risk, but you take any method a travel these days it's all dangerous. Ya know what I mean? Now take airplanes for instance . . ."

Just then a large shiny black car stopped in front of the lunchroom and a chauffeur helped a lady out of the rear door. They both came inside and the lady smiled at Homer and said, "We've stopped for a light snack. Some doughnuts and coffee would be simply marvelous."

Then Homer said, "I'm sorry, Ma'm, but the doughnuts won't be ready until I make this batter and start Uncle Ulysses' doughnut machine."

"Well now aren't *you* a clever young man to know how to make *doughnuts*!"

"Well," blushed Homer, "I've really never done it before, but I've got a recipe to follow."

"Now, young man, you simply must allow me to help. You know, I haven't made doughnuts for years, but I know the best recipe for doughnuts. It's marvelous, and we really must use it."

"But, Ma'm . . ." said Homer.

"Now just *wait* till you taste these doughnuts," said the lady. "Do you have an apron?" she asked, as she took off her fur coat and her rings and her jewelry and rolled up her sleeves. "Charles," she said to the chauffeur, "hand me that baking powder, that's right, and, young man, we'll need some nutmeg."

So Homer and the chauffeur stood by and handed things and cracked the eggs while the lady mixed and stirred. Mr. Gabby sat on his stool, sipped his coffee, and looked on with great interest.

"There!" said the lady when all of the ingredients were mixed. "Just *wait* till you taste these doughnuts!"

"It looks like an awful lot of batter," said Homer as he stood on a chair and poured it into the doughnut machine with the help of the chauffeur. "It's about *ten* times as much as Uncle Ulysses ever makes."

"But wait till you taste them!" said the lady with an eager look and a smile.

Homer got down from the chair and pushed a button on the machine marked, *Start.* Rings of batter started dropping into the hot fat. After a ring of batter was cooked on one side, an automatic gadget turned it over and the other side would cook. Then another automatic gadget gave the doughnut a little push and it rolled neatly down a little chute, all ready to eat.

"That's a simply *fascinating* machine," said the lady as she waited for the first doughnut to roll out.

"Here, young man, *you* must have the first one. Now isn't that just *too* delicious!? Isn't it simply marvelous?"

"Yes, Ma'm, it's very good," replied Homer as the lady handed doughnuts to Charles and to Mr. Gabby, and asked if they didn't think they were simply divine doughnuts.

"It's an old family recipe!" said the lady with pride.

Homer poured some coffee for the lady and her chauffeur and for Mr. Gabby, and a glass of milk for himself. Then they all sat down at the lunch counter to enjoy another few doughnuts apiece.

"I'm so glad you enjoy my doughnuts," said the lady. "But now, Charles, we really must be going. If you will just take this apron, Homer, and put two dozen doughnuts in a bag to take along, we'll be on our way. And, Charles, don't forget to pay the young man." She rolled down her sleeves and put on her jewelry; then Charles managed to get her into her big fur coat.

"Good night, young man, I haven't had so much fun in years. I *really* haven't," said the lady, as she went out the door and into the big shiny car.

"Those are sure good doughnuts," said Mr. Gabby as the car moved off.

"You bet!" said Homer. Then he and Mr. Gabby stood and watched the automatic doughnut machine make doughnuts.

After a few dozen more doughnuts had rolled down the little chute, Homer said, "I guess that's about enough doughnuts to sell to the aftertheater customers. I'd better turn the machine off for a while."

Homer pushed the button marked *Stop* and there was a little click, but nothing happened. The rings of batter kept right on dropping into the hot fat, and an automatic gadget kept right on turning them over, and another automatic gadget kept right on giving them a little push, and the doughnuts kept right on rolling down the little chute, all ready to eat.

"That's funny," said Homer, "I'm sure that's the right button!" He pushed it again but the automatic doughnut maker kept right on making doughnuts.

"Well I guess I must have put one of those pieces in backwards," said Homer.

"Then it might stop if you pushed the button marked *Start*," said Mr. Gabby.

Homer did, and the doughnuts still kept rolling down the little chute, just as regular as a clock can tick.

"I guess we could sell a few more doughnuts," said Homer, "but I'd better telephone Uncle Ulysses over at the barbershop." Homer gave the number, and while he waited for someone to answer he counted thirty-seven doughnuts roll down the little chute.

Finally someone answered "Hello! This is the sarberbhop, I mean the barbershop."

"Oh, hello, Sheriff. This is Homer. Could I speak to Uncle Ulysses?"

"Well, he's playing pinochle right now," said the sheriff. "Anythin' I can tell 'im?"

"Yes," said Homer. "I pushed the button marked *Stop* on the doughnut machine, but the rings of batter keep right on dropping into the hot fat, and an automatic gadget keeps right on turning them over, and another automatic gadget keeps giving them a little push, and the doughnuts keep right on rolling down the little chute! It won't stop!"

"O.K. Wold the hire, I mean, hold the wire and I'll tell 'im." Then Homer looked over his shoulder and counted another twenty-one doughnuts roll down the little chute, all ready to eat. Then the sheriff said, "He'll be right over . . . Just gotta finish this hand."

"That's good," said Homer. "G'by, Sheriff."

The window was full of doughnuts by now, so Homer and Mr. Gabby had to hustle around and start stacking them on plates and trays and lining them up on the counter.

"Sure are a lot of doughnuts!" said Homer.

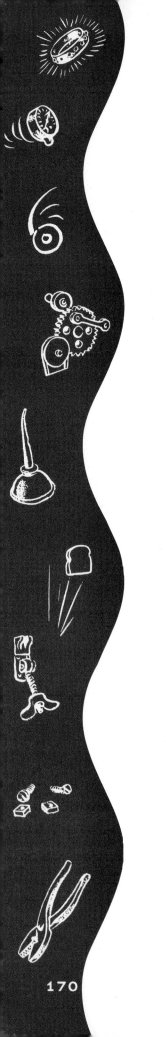

"You bet!" said Mr. Gabby. "I lost count at twelve hundred and two, and that was quite a while back."

People had begun to gather outside the lunchroom window, and someone was saying, "There are almost as many doughnuts as there are people in Centerburg, and I wonder how in tarnation Ulysses thinks he can sell all of 'em!"

Every once in a while somebody would come inside and buy some, but while somebody bought two to eat and a dozen to take home, the machine made three dozen more.

By the time Uncle Ulysses and the sheriff arrived and pushed through the crowd the lunchroom was a calamity of doughnuts! Doughnuts in the window, doughnuts piled high on the shelves, doughnuts stacked on plates, doughnuts lined up twelve deep all along the counter, and doughnuts still rolling down the little chute, just as regular as a clock can tick.

"Hello, Sheriff, hello, Uncle Ulysses, we're having a little trouble here," said Homer.

"Well, I'll be dunked!!" said Uncle Ulysses.

"Dernd ef you won't be when Aggy gits home," said the sheriff.

"Mighty fine doughnuts though. What'll you do with 'em all, Ulysses?"

Uncle Ulysses groaned and said, "What will Aggy say? We'll never sell 'em all."

Then Mr. Gabby, who hadn't said anything for a long time, stopped piling doughnuts and said, "What you need is an advertising man. Ya know what I mean? You got the doughnuts, ya gotta create a market . . . Understand? . . . It's balancing the demand with the supply . . . That sort of thing."

"Yep!" said Homer. "Mr. Gabby's right. We have to enlarge our market. He's an advertising sandwich man, so if we hire him, he can walk up and down in front of the theater and get the customers."

"You're hired, Mr. Gabby!" said Uncle Ulysses.

Then everybody pitched in to paint the signs and to get Mr. Gabby sandwiched between. They painted "SALE ON DOUGHNUTS" in big letters on the window too.

Meanwhile the rings of batter kept right on dropping into the hot fat, and an automatic gadget kept right on turning them over, and another automatic gadget kept right on giving them a little push, and the doughnuts kept right on rolling down the little chute, just as regular as a clock can tick.

"I certainly hope this advertising works," said Uncle Ulysses, wagging his head. "Aggy'll certainly throw a fit if it don't."

The sheriff went outside to keep order, because there was quite a crowd by now—all looking at the doughnuts and guessing how many thousand there were, and watching new ones roll down the little chute, just as regular as a clock can tick. Homer and Uncle Ulysses kept stacking doughnuts. Once in a while somebody bought a few, but not very often.

Then Mr. Gabby came back and said, "Say, you know there's not much use o' me advertisin' at the theater. The show's all over, and besides almost everybody in town is out front watching that machine make doughnuts!"

"Zeus!" said Uncle Ulysses. "We must get rid of these doughnuts before Aggy gets here!"

"Looks like you will have ta hire a truck ta waul 'em ahay, I mean haul 'em away!!" said the sheriff, who had just come in. Just then there was a noise and a shoving out front, and the lady from the shiny black car and her chauffeur came pushing through the crowd and into the lunchroom.

"Oh, gracious!" she gasped, ignoring the doughnuts, "I've lost my diamond bracelet, and I know I left it here on the counter," she said, pointing to a place where the doughnuts were piled in stacks of two dozen.

"Yes, Ma'm, I guess you forgot it when you helped make the batter," said Homer.

Then they moved all the doughnuts around and looked for the diamond bracelet, but they couldn't find it anywhere. Meanwhile the doughnuts kept rolling down the little chute, just as regular as a clock can tick.

After they had looked all around, the sheriff cast a suspicious eye on Mr. Gabby, but Homer said, "He's all right, Sheriff, he didn't take it. He's a friend of mine."

Then the lady said, "I'll offer a reward of one hundred dollars for that bracelet! It really *must* be found! . . . it *really* must!"

"Now don't you worry, lady," said the sheriff. "I'll get your bracelet back!"

"Zeus! This is terrible!" said Uncle Ulysses. "First all of these doughnuts and then on top of all that, a lost diamond bracelet . . ."

Mr. Gabby tried to comfort him, and he said, "There's always a bright side. That machine'll probably run outta batter in an hour or two."

If Mr. Gabby hadn't been quick on his feet Uncle Ulysses would have knocked him down, sure as fate.

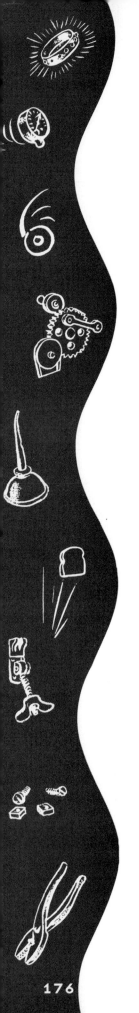

FRESH DOUGHNUTS
2 FOR 5¢
WHILE THEY LAST
$100.00 PRIZE
FOR FINDING
A BRACELET
INSIDE A DOUGHNUT
P.S. YOU HAVE TO GIVE THE
BRACELET BACK

Then while the lady wrung her hands and said, "We must find it we *must*!" and Uncle Ulysses was moaning about what Aunt Agnes would say, and the sheriff was eyeing Mr. Gabby, Homer sat down and thought hard.

Before twenty more doughnuts could roll down the little chute he shouted, "SAY! I know where the bracelet is! It was lying here on the counter and got mixed up in the batter by mistake! The bracelet is cooked inside one of these doughnuts!"

"Why . . . I really believe you're right," said the lady through her tears. "Isn't that *amazing*? Simply *amazing*!"

"I'll be durn'd!" said the sheriff.

"OhH-h!" moaned Uncle Ulysses. "Now we have to break up all of these doughnuts to find it. Think of the *pieces*! Think of the *crumbs*! Think of what *Aggy* will say!"

"Nope," said Homer. "We won't have to break them up. I've got a plan."

So Homer and the advertising man took some cardboard and some paint and printed another sign. They put this sign in the window, and the sandwich man wore two more signs that said the same thing and walked around in the crowd out front.

THEN . . . The doughnuts began to sell! *Everybody* wanted to buy doughnuts, *dozens* of doughnuts!

And that's not all. Everybody bought coffee to dunk the doughnuts in too. Those that didn't buy coffee bought milk or soda. It kept Homer and the lady and the chauffeur and Uncle Ulysses and the sheriff busy waiting on the people who wanted to buy doughnuts.

When all but the last couple of hundred doughnuts had been sold, Rupert Black shouted, "I GAWT IT!!" and sure enough . . . there was the diamond bracelet inside of his doughnut!

Then Rupert went home with a hundred dollars, the citizens of Centerburg went home full of doughnuts, the lady and her chauffeur drove off with the diamond bracelet, and Homer went home with his mother when she stopped by with Aunt Aggy.

As Homer went out of the door he heard Mr. Gabby say, "Neatest trick of merchandising I ever seen," and Aunt Aggy was looking skeptical while Uncle Ulysses was saying, "The rings of batter kept right on dropping into the hot fat, and the automatic gadget kept right on turning them over, and the other automatic gadget kept right on giving them a little push, and the doughnuts kept right on rolling down the little chute just as regular as a clock can tick—they just kept right on a-comin', an' a-comin', an' a-comin', an' a comin'."

from **A Ring of Tricksters**

THE
ANIMALS
SHARE

by

VIRGINIA HAMILTON

illustrated by

BARRY MOSER

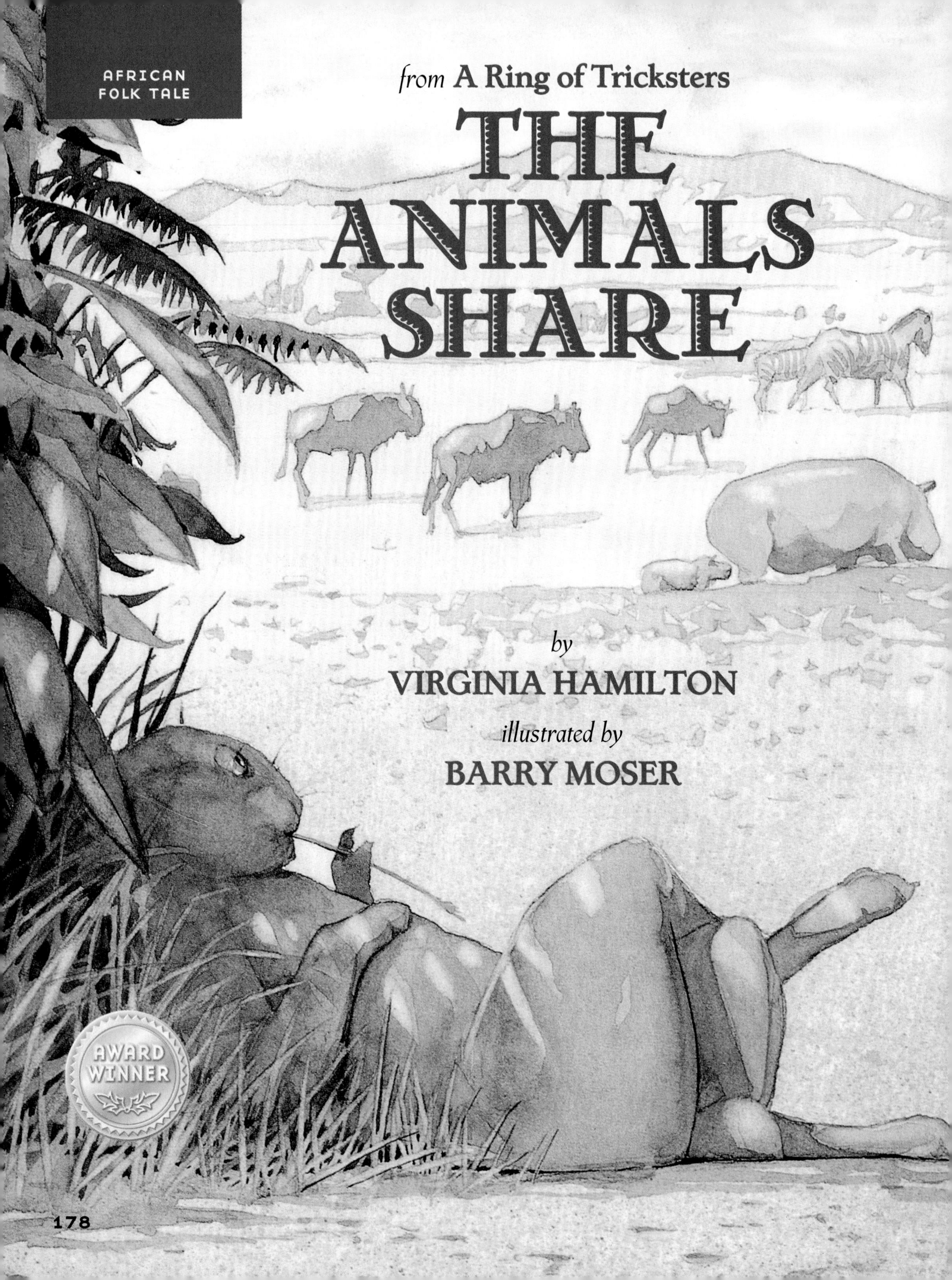

AWARD
WINNER

KING LION called all the animals together. "No rain falls," he told them. "The lakes are dry. There is no water for you. So you must dig a well."

The animals grumbled until King Lion swished his tail for silence.

King Lion roared, "All must do their part and take their turn!"

But Shulo, the hare, said to himself, "I won't waste my time digging. Let the others do it." He ran off by himself.

All the other animals gathered to do their share. They came from all over the country. And they danced as they trotted to the place chosen for the well. They thought by dancing they would kick up the ground. And that would be their way of digging.

The animals lined up, singing, one by one:

> *"I'm coming, joggy-jog trot,*
> *kuputu, kuputu,*
> *the dirt is flying!"*

Njiou Elephant danced and sang, said:

> *"I give my place to you,*
> *Nyati Buffalo!"*

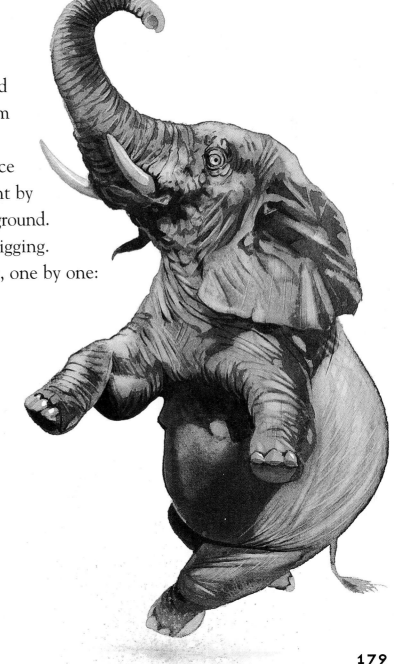

Nyati danced, then gave his place to Shelen, the Bush-buck. And so it went, until all had sung and danced. But no seeping wet came. There was no water anywhere.

But then, see, the animals thought they had been digging. Yet their dancing had only packed the earth down harder. So they had a meeting. King Lion called on Hamba, the tortoise. Hamba was old and very wise.

"The water is *inside* the earth," Hamba said. And he dug down far beneath, far into the ground. There, he found water!

All the animals were happy. King Lion was very much pleased. But he knew they could not trust Shulo, the hare. "Shulo has done nothing," King Lion said. "But we know he will come in the night to take some water. Each night, one of you must watch the well."

Bongo, the hyena, spoke out. "I will watch the first night."

Of course, Shulo was already planning how he could take the water.

He filled his calabash with honey and went to the well. There he spied Bongo. Shulo started talking to himself: "My calabash is full of something so sweet, anybody who tastes it won't get a second taste unless he's tied up."

"Ho, Shulo!" said Bongo. "Give me a taste of the sweets in your calabash." Shulo dipped a stick in the calabash and smeared just a little honey across Bongo's lips.

Bongo licked his jaws. "More!" he cried. "Tie me up, Shulo, for I must have a second taste."

So Shulo tied up Bongo, front and hind feet. He gave no second taste. Instead, he went to the well and drank all he wanted. He filled his water gourds. He jumped in the water and splashed around. And he left the well muddy and dirty.

All the animals took their turns, and it happened every night that each one was tricked by Shulo, the hare. He carried full water gourds home. And through the long drought, his family had plenty to drink.

At last, it was Hamba Tortoise's turn to watch by the well. Hamba went down in the water and lay quietly on the bottom.

"So they've all given up!" laughed Shulo, when he came to the well and found no one there. "This well is mine without any digging!" He put his gourds down and jumped into the water.

But something caught at Shulo's foot. Next, something held him tight so he could not get away.

What a fix Shulo was in! He said, "Is that you, Hamba? I know it is! I've got something for you that's so very sweet. I'll let you have a taste." Shulo hoped Hamba would open his mouth.

Hamba never said a word. He held Shulo until daylight came. When all of the animals came to the well to drink, there was Shulo, caught at last. The animals seized Shulo and took him to King Lion. "You would not help to dig the well," said King Lion. "You stole the well water and made the well all muddy. You must not live another day!"

"Oh, no!" cried Shulo. "Oh, my great king! If I must die, let me sing one song, let me dance one dance!"

"There can be no harm in that," King Lion thought. He was merciful and granted Shulo his wish.

The hare began to clap his hands. He danced and sang:

"You, oh hare,

going away.

Returning when?

Tomorrow!"

All the animals began to beat time to the music. They clapped and sang with Shulo, his song was so delightful. Soon they stomped their feet in the dance. And in a little while, dust rose up from the dry earth and made a thick cloud around them.

Long time, when tired out, the animals stopped and lay down. A fine dance! They couldn't see one another for the dust. And when it cleared? Where was Shulo, the hare?

Gone, long gone, with his gourds all full. No one, not even King Lion, knows where he went. Or if he will return—tomorrow!

THINK ABOUT READING

Answer the questions in the story map.

CHARACTERS

1. Who are the story's main characters?

SETTING

2. Where does the story take place?

PROBLEM

3. What trouble does the lady cause when she tries to help Homer make doughnuts?

4. What does the machine do that causes even more problems?

EVENTS

5. What do Homer and Mr. Gabby do with all the doughnuts?

6. What happens to the lady's bracelet?

SOLUTION

7. What is Homer's plan to solve both the problem of the doughnuts and the problem of the bracelet?

8. What happens as a result of Homer's plan?

WRITE A TV NEWSCAST

You are a TV reporter on location at the Centerburg doughnut shop. Write an eyewitness report about what happened to Homer. Remember, every word counts. Be sure to introduce yourself. Then tell the most important and colorful details about the runaway doughnut machine.

LITERATURE CIRCLE

Homer Price in "The Doughnuts" and Shulo in "The Animals Share" are both clever characters. Talk about what would happen if the two characters met. What advice do you think Shulo would give Homer about solving problems? What might Homer say to Shulo? How would each character feel about the other one. Why?

AUTHOR AND ILLUSTRATOR
ROBERT McCLOSKEY

As a child, Robert McCloskey spent hours taking apart machines and putting them back together. He says, "The inventor's life was for me—that is, until I started making drawings." In fact, he wrote his first book because he wanted something to illustrate. Mr. McCloskey can take up to three years to complete a book. Why does it take so long? The answer is simple. He often does 20 or 30 different drawings before he has one that satisfies him.

MORE BOOKS BY
ROBERT McCLOSKEY

- *Centerburg Tales*
- *Henry Reed, Inc.*
- *Henry Reed's Baby-Sitting Service*

WINGS

written by
JANE YOLEN

illustrated by
DENNIS NOLAN

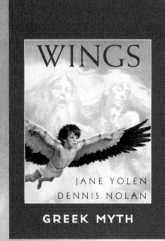

WINGS

JANE YOLEN
DENNIS NOLAN

GREEK MYTH

AWARD WINNER

ONCE IN ANCIENT GREECE, when the gods dwelt on a high mountain overseeing the world, there lived a man named Daedalus who was known for the things he made.

He invented the axe, the bevel, and the awl. He built statues that were so lifelike they seemed ready to move. He designed a maze whose winding passages opened one into another as if without beginning, as if without end.

But Daedalus never understood the labyrinth of his own heart. He was clever but he was not always kind. He was full of pride but he did not give others praise. He was a maker—but he was a taker, too.

The gods always punish such a man.

Athens was the queen of cities and she had her princes. Daedalus was one. He was a prince and he was an artist, and he was proud of being both.

The very elements were his friends, and the people of Athens praised him.

"The gods will love you forever, Daedalus," they cried out to him as he walked through the city streets.

The gods listened and did not like to be told what to do.

A man who hears only praise becomes deaf. A man who sees no rival to his art becomes blind. Though he grew rich and he grew famous in the city, Daedalus also grew lazy and careless. And one day, without thought for the consequences, he caused the death of his young nephew, Prince Talos, who fell from a tall temple.

Even a prince cannot kill a prince. The king of Athens punished Daedalus by sending him away, away from all he loved: away from the colorful pillars of the temples, away from the noisy, winding streets, away from the bustling shops and stalls, away from his smithy, away from the sound of the dark sea. He would never be allowed to return.

And the gods watched the exile from on high.

Many days and nights Daedalus fled from his past. He crossed strange lands. He crossed strange seas. All he carried with him was a goatskin flask, the clothes on his back, and the knowledge in his hands. All he carried with him was grief that he had caused a child's death and grief that Athens was now dead to him.

He traveled a year and a day until he came at last to the island of Crete, where the powerful King Minos ruled.

The sands of Crete were different from his beloved Athens, the trees in the meadow were different, the flowers and the houses and the little, dark-eyed people were different. Only the birds seemed the same to Daedalus, and the sky—the vast, open, empty road of the sky.

But the gods found nothing below them strange.

Daedalus knew nothing of Crete but Crete knew much of Daedalus, for his reputation had flown on wings before him. King Minos did not care that Daedalus was an exile or that he had been judged guilty of a terrible crime.

"You are the world's greatest builder, Daedalus," King Minos said. "Build me a labyrinth in which to hide a beast."

"A cage would be simpler," said Daedalus.

"This is no ordinary beast," said the King. "This is a monster. This is a prince. His name is Minotaur and he is my wife's own son. He has a bull's head but a man's body. He eats human flesh. I cannot kill the queen's child. Even a king cannot kill a prince. And I cannot put him in a cage. But in a maze such as you might build, I could keep him hidden forever."

Daedalus bowed his head, but he smiled at the king's praise. He built a labyrinth for the king with countless corridors and winding ways. He devised such cunning passages that only he knew the secret pathway to its heart—he, and the Minotaur who lived there.

Yet the gods marked the secret way as well.

191

For many years Daedalus lived on the island of Crete, delighting in the praise he received from king and court. He made hundreds of new things for them. He made dolls with moving parts and a dancing floor inlaid with wood and stone for the princess Ariadne. He made iron gates for the king and queen wrought with cunning designs. He grew fond of the little dark-eyed islanders, and he married a Cretan wife. A son was born to them whom Daedalus named Icarus. The boy was small like his mother but he had his father's quick, bright ways.

Daedalus taught Icarus many things, yet the one Daedalus valued most was the language of his lost Athens. Though he had a grand house and servants to do his bidding, though he had a wife he loved and a son he adored, Daedalus was not entirely happy. His heart still lay in Athens, the land of his youth, and the words he spoke with his son helped keep the memory of Athens alive.

One night a handsome young man came to Daedalus's house, led by a lovesick Princess Ariadne. The young man spoke with Daedalus in that Athenian tongue.

"I am Theseus, a prince of Athens, where your name is still remembered with praise. It is said that Daedalus was more than a prince, that he had the gods in his hands. Surely such a man has not forgotten Athens."

Daedalus shook his head. "I thought Athens had forgotten me."

"Athens remembers and Athens needs your help, O prince," said Theseus.

"Help? What help can I give Athens, when I am so far from home?"

"Then you do not know . . . ," Theseus began.

"Know what?"

"That every seven years Athens must send a tribute of boys and girls to King Minos. He puts them into the labyrinth you devised and the monster Minotaur devours them there."

Horrified, Daedalus thought of the bright-eyed boys and girls he had known in Athens. He thought of his own dark-eyed son asleep in his cot. He remembered his nephew, Talos, whose eyes had been closed by death. "How can I help?"

"Only you know the way through the maze," said Theseus. "Show me the way that I may slay the monster."

"I will show you," said Daedalus thoughtfully, "but Princess Ariadne must go as well. The Minotaur is her half-brother. He will not hurt her. She will be able to lead you to him, right into the heart of the maze."

The gods listened to the plan and nodded gravely.

Daedalus drew them a map and gave Princess Ariadne a thread to tie at her waist, that she might unwind it as they went and so find the way back out of the twisting corridors.

Hand in hand, Theseus and Ariadne left and Daedalus went into his son's room. He looked down at the sleeping boy.

"I am a prince of Athens," he whispered. "I did what must be done."

If Icarus heard his father's voice, he did not stir. He was dreaming still as Ariadne and Theseus threaded their way to the very center of the maze. And before he awakened, they had killed the Minotaur and fled from Crete, taking the boys and girls of Athens with them. They took all hope of Daedalus's safety as well.

Then the gods looked thoughtful and they did not smile.

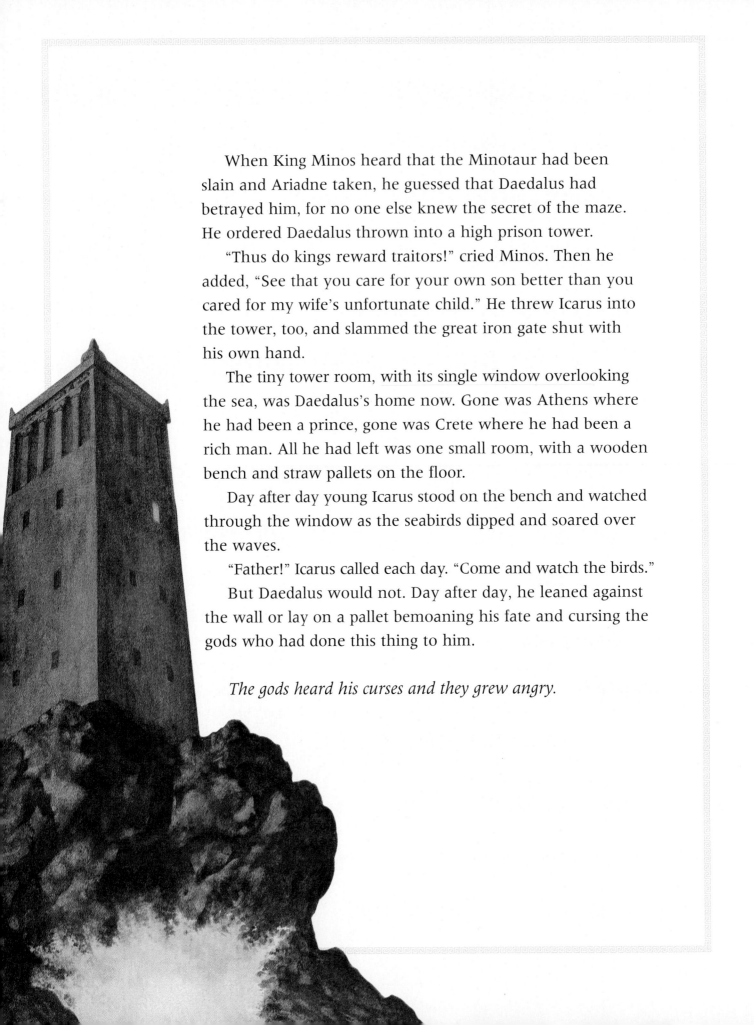

When King Minos heard that the Minotaur had been slain and Ariadne taken, he guessed that Daedalus had betrayed him, for no one else knew the secret of the maze. He ordered Daedalus thrown into a high prison tower.

"Thus do kings reward traitors!" cried Minos. Then he added, "See that you care for your own son better than you cared for my wife's unfortunate child." He threw Icarus into the tower, too, and slammed the great iron gate shut with his own hand.

The tiny tower room, with its single window overlooking the sea, was Daedalus's home now. Gone was Athens where he had been a prince, gone was Crete where he had been a rich man. All he had left was one small room, with a wooden bench and straw pallets on the floor.

Day after day young Icarus stood on the bench and watched through the window as the seabirds dipped and soared over the waves.

"Father!" Icarus called each day. "Come and watch the birds."

But Daedalus would not. Day after day, he leaned against the wall or lay on a pallet bemoaning his fate and cursing the gods who had done this thing to him.

The gods heard his curses and they grew angry.

One bright day Icarus took his father by the hand, leading him to the window.

"Look, Father," he said, pointing to the birds. "See how beautiful their wings are. See how easily they fly."

Just to please the boy, Daedalus looked. Then he clapped his hands to his eyes. "What a fool I have been," he whispered. "What a fool. Minos may have forbidden me sea and land, but he has left me the air. Oh, my son, though the king is ever so great and powerful, he does not rule the sky. It is the gods' own road and I am a favorite of the gods. To think a child has shown me the way!"

Every day after that, Daedalus and Icarus coaxed the birds to their windows with bread crumbs saved from their meager meals. And every day gulls, gannets, and petrels, cormorants and pelicans, shearwaters and grebes, came to the sill. Daedalus stroked the feeding birds with his clever hands and harvested handfuls of feathers. And Icarus, as if playing a game, grouped the feathers on the floor in order of size, just as his father instructed.

But it was no game. Soon the small piles of feathers became big piles, the big piles, great heaps. Then clever Daedalus, using a needle he had shaped from a bit of bone left over from dinner and thread pulled out of his own shirt, sewed together small feathers, overlapping them with the larger, gently curving them in great arcs. He fastened the ends with molded candle wax and made straps with the leather from their sandals.

At last Icarus understood. "Wings, Father!" he cried, clapping his hands together in delight. "Wings!"

At that the gods laughed, and it was thunder over water.

They made four wings in all, a pair for each of them. Icarus had the smaller pair, for he was still a boy. They practiced for days in the tower, slipping their arms through the straps, raising and lowering the wings, until their arms had grown strong and used to the weight. They hid the wings beneath their pallets whenever the guards came by.

At last they were ready. Daedalus kneeled before his son.

"Your arms are strong now, Icarus," he said, "but do not forget my warning."

The boy nodded solemnly, his dark eyes wide. "I must not fly too low or the water will soak the feathers. I must not fly too high or the sun will melt the wax."

"Remember," his father said. "Remember."

The gods trembled, causing birds to fall through the bright air.

Daedalus climbed onto the sill. The wings made him clumsy but he did not fall. He helped Icarus up.

First the child, then the man, leaped out into the air. They pumped once and then twice with their arms. The wind caught the feathers of the wings and pushed them upward into the Cretan sky.

Wingtip to wingtip they flew, writing the lines of their escape on the air. Some watchers below took them for eagles. Most took them for gods.

As they flew, Daedalus concentrated on long, steady strokes. He remembered earlier days, when the elements had been his friends: fire and water and air. Now, it seemed, they were his friends once more.

But young Icarus had no such memories to steady his wings. He beat them with abandon, glorying in his freedom. He slipped away from his father's careful pattern along a wild stream of wind.

"Icarus, my son—remember!" Daedalus cried out.

But Icarus spiraled higher and higher still. He did not hear his father's voice. He heard only the music of the wind; he heard only the sighing of the gods.

He passed the birds. He passed the clouds. He passed into the realm of the sun. Too late he felt the wax run down his arms; too late he smelled the singe of feathers. Surprised, he hung solid in the air. Then, like a star in nova, he tumbled from the sky, down, down, down into the waiting sea.

And the gods wept bitterly for the child.

"Where are you, my son?" Daedalus called. He circled the water, looking desperately for some sign. All he saw were seven feathers afloat on the sea, spinning into different patterns with each passing wave.

Weeping, he flew away over the dark sea to the isle of Sicily. There he built a temple to the god Apollo, for Apollo stood for life and light and never grew old but remained a beautiful boy forever. On the temple walls Daedalus hung up his beautiful wings as an offering to the bitter wisdom of the gods.

AWARD WINNER

Dreams

by Langston Hughes
illustrated by Paul Jermann

Hold fast to dreams
For if dreams die
Life is a broken-winged bird
That cannot fly.

Hold fast to dreams
For when dreams go
Life is a barren field
Frozen with snow.

THINK ABOUT READING

Answer the questions in the story map.

CHARACTER

1. Who is the main character?

SETTING

2. Where and when does the story take place?

BEGINNING

3. What is Daedalus's punishment for causing his nephew's death?

MIDDLE

4. Why does King Minos ask Daedalus to build a labyrinth?

5. How does Daedalus help Theseus and Ariadne?

6. How does King Minos punish Daedalus for betraying him?

7. How do Daedalus and Icarus escape from the tower?

ENDING

8. What happens to Icarus when he flies too close to the sun?

WRITE A BOOK REVIEW

Write a review of *Wings* for your school newspaper. Be sure to mention the title, author, and illustrator. Then briefly tell your readers who the main character is, and summarize the story. Finally, give your opinion. Would you recommend Jane Yolen's Greek myth to your classssmates? Why or why not? You may even wish to give the book a rating.

LITERATURE CIRCLE

Talk about Daedalus, the main character in *Wings*. What kind of person is he? What do you learn about him from his actions? Discuss what you learn about him from the other characters in the story. How do you think Langston Hughes, the poet of "Dreams," would feel about Daedalus's actions?

AUTHOR
JANE YOLEN

Jane Yolen, author, storyteller, and music composer, is full of ideas, and she has written over 150 books to prove it. Many of her books, including *Wings*, have been inspired by folklore. Although she has won numerous awards for her writing, she says, "My best reward is when I hear from the boys and girls who read my books." To young writers Yolen gives this advice: "It's important to keep your sense of wonder, your sense of curiosity, and your sense of exploration."

MORE BOOKS BY
JANE YOLEN

- *Camelot*
- *Favorite Folktales from Around the World*
- *Owl Moon*
- *The Emperor and the Kite*

How to Market Your Invention

Do market research and decide on a name for your invention.

Once an inventor patents an invention, the next step is to market it. Selling a product is just one part of marketing. Naming a product, packaging it, and advertising it are also part of the marketing process. Market research plays an important part, too. Companies test products by asking potential customers for their opinions of the new product. Then they use this research to choose a name for their product.

Put on a
Jet Pak and
Take Off!

Brainstorm an Inventive Idea

Think of an invention. If you need to get your imagination working, make a wish list. For example, you might write "I wish I could fly." Now think of inventions that would make it possible for you to fly. Would sneakers with wings and a motor be a good idea? a backpack with rocket jets? a hat with a propeller? Write down several wishes and the inventive ideas that would make them come true. After you're done, look back over your list and choose the one you like the most.

- Try using alliteration or rhyme when creating a name.
- Say the names aloud to hear how they sound.

TOOLS

- notebook and pencil
- colored markers
- posterboard
- glue
- clipboard (optional)

2 Name Your Invention

Once you think of your inventive idea, it's time to give it a name. What do you want the name to say about your product? Is your invention scientific? You may want a name with a technical or scientific sounding prefix. For example, the prefixes *therma-* and *micro-* sound scientific. An invention that is meant to be fun, rather than serious, should have a name that sounds fun. Use adjectives to liven up the name of your invention. Make a list of several possible names, and then pick three of them.

Name Chart of Inventions

Boomeroom	maybe
Jet Pak	good
Wing Pack	good

How Am I Doing?

Take a minute to ask yourself these questions:

• Have I thought of several names for my invention?

• Have I used the information from my notes to help me choose a name?

Do Market Research

Take the three names you've chosen, and show them to at least six people. After they have read the names, ask them to describe what they think your invention does. Find out which name they like the best. Be sure to take notes. You may also want to look at products already being sold that are like your invention. Which product has the best name? Do you like the design of the package it comes in?

What do you like about the name and the way the product is presented? Using your market research, decide on the best name for your invention. If you want, you can also design a logo for your product.

4 Launch Your Invention

Now that you've named your invention, you're ready to launch it. Think about what kind of company would want to manufacture your invention. Ask some of your classmates to play the part of executives in a company. Then present your invention to them. Here are some things to include in your presentation.

- Make a poster with a colorful picture, the name of your invention, and some sentences describing what your product does. If you designed a logo, put that on the poster, too.

- Use the market research that you did. Tell the audience the good things that people said about your invention.

- Show a model of your invention, if you want to build one.

At the end of the presentation ask the audience for questions and suggestions.

If You Are Using a Computer ...

Create your poster with the sign or poster format. Type the name of your invention using a large, fun font. You may wish to add a border and clip art to your poster. Then print it out and hang it up for everyone to see.

JET PAK

CONGRATULATIONS
You've learned that most problems have a solution. As you face new challenges, be sure to remember the problem-solving skills you've learned.

Julie Lewis
Inventor ▶

DISCOVERY TEAMS

THEME

When we work
as a team, we learn
new things about
our world.

UNIT 3

Welcome to

LITERACY PLACE

Space Center

When we work as
a team, we learn new
things about our world.

THE BEST NEW THING

by Isaac Asimov

illustrated by Tom Leonard

ada lived on a little world, far out in space. Her father and her mother and her brother, Jonathan, lived there too. So did other men and women.

Rada was the only little girl on the little world. Jonny was the only little boy. They had lived there all their lives. Rada's father and other men worked on the spaceships. They made sure everything was all right before the spaceships went on their way back to Earth or to other planets. Rada and Jonny would watch them come and go.

They had a special place where they could stand and watch the ships come down. The ships came down slower and slower and then they stopped.

Rada and Jonny had to wear their space suits when they watched. There was no air on the little world, but inside their suits there was air and it was warm. Over their heads they wore a glass ball that they could see through.

When men and women came out of the spaceships, they would see Rada and Jonny. Then they would say, "Think of that! Children live here."

One of the men said, "Have you lived here all your life?"

Rada said, "Yes, I have. We both have."

The man said, "Would you like to see Earth someday? It is a big world."

Jonny asked, "Are things different on Earth?"

"Well, the sky is blue," said the man.

"I have never seen a blue sky," said Rada. "The sky is always black here."

"On Earth, it is blue, except at night," said the man. "It is warm on Earth and there is air everywhere. You don't have to wear a space suit on Earth."

Rada said, "That must be nice. I will ask my father if I can go to Earth."

She jumped high to see where her father was. She jumped very high, higher than the man—much higher than the man. When she was that high, she could see all around the spaceship. She did not see her father, so she knew he must be inside the spaceship.

She pushed a little button on her suit. Some air came out fast. It went s-s-s-s. That made her go down again. She came down very near the man.

The man said, "You do that very well."

Jonny said, "I can do it, too. See?"

He jumped high—and then made himself come down headfirst. He landed very softly.

The man laughed and said, "That is well done, too, but you could not do that on Earth."

Rada said, "Why not?"

"On Earth," said the man, "you can only jump a little way. Earth is so big, it holds you down. If you jump up, Earth pulls you down right away. And you could roll down any slanting place."

Then the man had to go into the spaceship again. Rada and Jonny waited for their father.

When their father came, Rada and Jonny went underground with him. Rada and Jonny and their father and mother lived inside the little world, in large, comfortable rooms.

It was warm and nice inside their home. There were books and toys and good things to eat. And there was air for them to breathe, so they could take off their big, clumsy space suits. Jonny and Rada liked to run around with not many clothes on. Of course, even indoors they couldn't run without bouncing high into the air, because the little world was too little to pull them down.

Jonny said, "Daddy, is it true that you don't have to wear a space suit on Earth?"

His father said, "Yes, it is. There is air on Earth, just like the air that we have to manufacture here so we can breathe in these rooms."

Jonny said, "And is the sky really blue there?"

"That's right," his father answered. "And there are white things in the sky called clouds. Sometimes drops of water come from the sky. That is rain."

Rada thought about this for a minute, and then she said, "If the ground has water on it, doesn't that make it slippery?"

Her father laughed, and then he said, "The rain doesn't stay on top of the ground. It sinks into the ground and helps to make the grass grow."

Rada knew about grass, because her father and mother had told her about it. But she liked to hear about it over and over again. So she said, "Tell me about grass again, Daddy."

"Grass is like a green carpet that grows on the ground. It is soft and very beautiful," he said.

"I would like to see it," said Rada. "And I would like to feel it too. Will we go to Earth someday, Daddy?"

"Oh yes, Rada," her father said. "Perhaps we can go soon."

Rada was so happy to hear this that she wanted to put her arms about her father. She walked up the wall to be near his head.

Rada could do that on her little world, because that world was too little to pull her down. She could walk on the wall or anywhere because her shoes were made to stick to everything.

When she walked on the wall, the wall was under her feet just like a floor. Her head was near her father's head now and she put her arms around him.

"Thank you, Daddy," she said.

Her father hugged her and said, "You know, if you were on Earth, you could not walk on the wall. Earth would pull you down."

Rada's mother came into the room. She pushed down on the floor with her feet. That made her move up. She came to a stop near the top of the room by pushing the air with her hand.

She held two containers. She said, "Rada! Jonny! Here is your milk."

When she let go of the containers, they stayed in the air.

"Oh good, I'm thirsty," Rada said. She pushed the wall with her feet and moved to the container. She opened the container and put a straw into the opening.

Jonny moved up into the air and came near the other container. He said, "I don't want to use a straw, Mommy. May I roll the milk into a ball?"

"All right, but be careful not to get any on your clothes," his mother said.

Jonny opened the container and shook it. The milk floated out and made a soft white ball. Some of it made little tiny balls. Jonny pushed the tiny balls with his finger and they all went back into the big white ball.

He pushed the air with his hands and moved his head very near the ball. He put his lips to it and sucked it in. It was fun to drink milk that way.

His father said "If you drank milk that way on Earth, it would get all over your clothes. You will have to remember many things like that when you are on Earth."

"Have I ever been there, Daddy?" asked Rada.

"Oh yes," said her father, "but you can't remember it because you were only a baby when you came here with Mommy and me. And Jonny wasn't even born. Now it will soon be time to go back to Earth. We will take you with us."

Rada moved to her father and put her head on top of his. Her feet were in the air. Jonny had finished his milk and he was moving around and around his father, pushing the air to make himself go.

"Can you see the stars on Earth, Daddy?" asked Rada. On their little world, they could always see the stars because the sky was always dark.

"Yes, you can," said her father. "Part of the time."

Rada and Jonny talked a long time about Earth. They could hardly sleep that night. They kept thinking about Earth.

There were so many new things on Earth to think about. There was air that was everywhere. There were the blue sky and the rain, the wind and the flowers. And there were birds and animals.

The next day their father showed them pictures of some of the new things. They saw that the ground could be flat in some places and hilly in others. Soon they would see and feel all these things for themselves.

There would be other boys and girls to play with on Earth. There would be so many new things to see and do.

But there was one new thing Rada especially wanted to do. She told Jonny about it and he wanted to do it too. They didn't tell their father or mother. It was something they had never done in all their lives. On Earth, they were going to find out what it felt like.

Rada and Jonny had to make themselves strong for living on Earth.

Her mother said, "Now, Rada, Earth is a big world. It will pull at you hard. You must be strong so that you can walk in spite of all that pull."

Jonny said, "Yes, Rada, you have to be as strong as I am."

But Mother said, "You will have to be stronger than you are now, too, Jonny."

There were springs on the wall in the exercise room. Rada and Jonny had to pull on them. They stood on the wall and pulled on the springs. They pulled and pulled. It took all their strength to move the springs.

"Pull hard the way I do," said Jonny. He was breathing fast from all that pulling.

Rada said, "When we get strong, we can go to Earth. We will see grass and flowers and trees. Most of all, we will find out about the new thing."

Jonny said, "Don't tell anybody."

They pulled very hard.

Their father was happy. "You are both getting very strong," he said. "You will like it on Earth."

One day a spaceship came and their father said, "This is the ship that will take us to Earth."

They all put on their space suits. Their father was ready to go. So was their mother. But Rada and Jonny were ready first.

Rada felt a little bit sorry. She would miss her little world. When they were getting into the spaceship, she turned and said, "Goodbye, little world. Maybe I will see you again someday." Then she jumped very high so she could see almost all of their side of the little world.

"Good-bye," she said again. "It is time for me to go to Earth now."

Jonny called her from the spaceship. "Come on, slowpoke. We're all waiting for you."

On the spaceship they went to their little room. It had chairs with seatbelts.

Their father said, "Let me put the seatbelts around you, children. They must hold you when the spaceship starts to move."

He fastened their seatbelts so they couldn't move. Then their father and mother sat in their own chairs and fastened their own seatbelts. The chairs were very soft.

Then the spaceship started to move. There was a big noise all through the ship and Rada and Jonny were pushed against the soft, soft chair. They were pushed harder and harder but the seatbelts kept everything all right.

"I'm not frightened," said Jonny. "Are you frightened, Rada?"

"Just a little bit," said Rada. She could see the little world as the ship moved away from it. The little world was smaller than ever. Soon it was just a dot and then all Rada could see were the stars.

"Can we see Earth, Daddy?" Jonny asked.

"It looks like a star from here. It's that bright one there," said his father.

"Look at Earth, Rada," said Jonny. He was very excited.

Rada looked at the bright star and was happy. Soon she would be on Earth and would know about the new thing. She knew Jonny was thinking about it, too.

"Wake up, Rada," said her father. "We are coming down to Earth. Jonny is awake already."

Rada opened her eyes. "Can we get out of the ship now, Daddy?"

"Soon, Rada," said her father. "You must wait a little while."

Rada looked out the window. Down below she could see a big, big world. She had never seen anything so very, very big. It was green and brown and lots of other colors too. She could see water, too, and that was blue.

Above all the green and brown and blue and other colors of the Earth was the sky.

Jonny said, "How big everything is!"

And Rada said, "How pretty everything is!"

They could hardly wait.

When the ship stopped, Rada took off her belt. She was the first one to get out of the chair. Jonny was second.

228

Jonny tried to walk. "The floor is holding my foot," he said.

"Pull harder," said his father.

Jonny did and at last he succeeded in lifting his foot from the floor.

"Aren't we going to put on our space suits?" asked Rada.

"Don't forget, we don't have to put on space suits on Earth," said her father.

"Oh, yes," said Rada. "That's one of the new things." She and Jonny were waiting for another new thing, too. They squeezed each other's hands but they didn't say anything.

They went down and down and down inside the ship to get to a little door that would let them out on the Earth. It was hard to walk, but they were beginning to get used to it.

The door opened and they all walked out. There was flat paving all around the spaceship, as there had been on the little world. But at the edge of the paving there was grass. There had been no grass on the little world.

"My," said Mother, "doesn't the air smell sweet?"

"Oh, yes," said Rada. She could feel the air moving. That was the wind. It blew her dress and her hair.

It was warm and the sun was very big and yellow.

Jonny said, "Look how big the sun is." The sun had looked much smaller from their little world.

"Don't look right at the sun," his father said quickly. "That would hurt your eyes."

"What is that sound?" asked Rada.

"It is a bird singing," said her mother.

Rada had never heard a bird singing. She had never felt the wind. She had never seen such a big sun and such bright sunlight.

These were all new things.

Now it was time for the best new thing of all. Now she would find out what it was really like.

She said, "Come on, Jonny."

Jonny said, "Look at the grass. And there's a little hill just like the one in the pictures. Let's try it."

Rada said, "Look, Mother. See how I can run."

It was hard to run because Earth pulled at her legs. She ran with all her might to the grassy hill. Jonny was running, too.

Jonny said, "I can run faster than you." But they reached the grass together. Both were breathing hard from running.

Then they came to the little hill and they climbed to the top. That was even harder than walking, but they made it. They looked at each other and laughed, and then they both lay down on the grass and rolled down the hill. When they reached the bottom, they stood up, laughing and breathing hard.

Their father and mother came to them.

"Are you hurt, children?" their father asked.

"You should not run like that till you are used to Earth's pull," said their mother.

"Oh, but we wanted to," said Rada. "We are so happy because we know, now, about the new thing. It is something we had never done before."

"What new thing?" asked her father.

"We rolled down the hill," said Rada. "We could never do that before, because our own little world never pulled us. But it was really fun. I think it's the best new thing of all."

"Yes," said Jonny, "that is the best new thing of all."

And they ran up to the top of the hill to try it again.

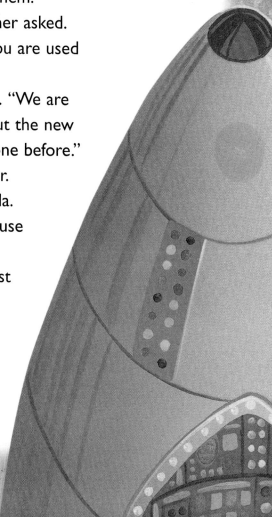

230

MENTOR

Dr. Mae Jemison

Astronaut

An astronaut reaches for the stars.

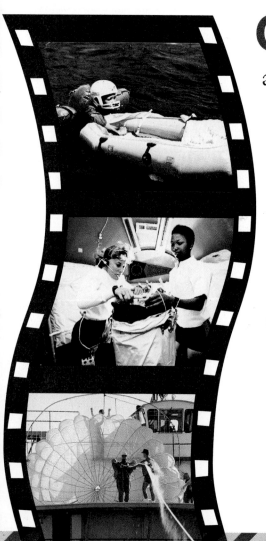

On September 12, 1992, a team of astronauts boarded the space shuttle *Endeavor*. Mission Control gave the final ten-second countdown: 3...2...1... Then the rockets ignited, and the shuttle zoomed into outer space. On board was Dr. Mae Jemison— physician, chemical engineer, and astronaut.

PROFILE

Name: Dr. Mae Jemison

Occupation: doctor, chemical engineer, astronaut, entrepreneur

Languages: English, Russian, Japanese, and Swahili

Hobbies: dance, weight training, reading history, photography

Childhood dream: to travel through outer space

QUESTIONS
for Dr. Mae Jemison

Find out why Dr. Jemison became an astronaut.

Q A space mission involves a lot of people working together. Would you say that teamwork is an important part of the process?

A I think teamwork is important in anything that you do. To be an astronaut means working with a team. Each astronaut has a job to do while in space, and those jobs can be complicated. But the bulk of the work is done by the people who stay on the ground—the scientists and engineers who get the shuttle ready. We're all part of the same team.

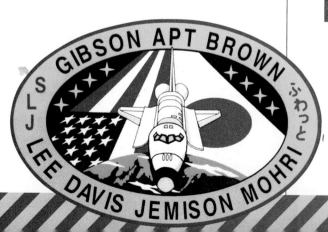

Q What was your job during the space shuttle flight?

A I was the science mission specialist. My job was to be the representative of the scientists on the ground who had designed the experiments. I was their eyes, ears, and hands. I did experiments to find out how the human body adapts to weightlessness.

Q When did you decide that you wanted to become an astronaut?

A As a child, I watched the Gemini and Apollo launches on television in the 1960s. When I watched the astronauts walk on the moon, I knew that I would go into space one day.

234

Q When did you start working toward your goal of joining the space program?

A I started working toward my goal when I was still in school. I got my degree in chemical engineering and then went on to become a doctor. In 1985 I decided to apply to NASA's astronaut program. I was accepted in 1987.

Q What advice would you give to kids who want to become astronauts?

A There are not enough spaces for everyone to become an astronaut. But all kinds of people are involved in making space exploration work, so remember you can always be involved. My advice is to find something that you like to do. Don't be limited by others who have a limited imagination.

Dr. Mae Jemison's Tips
for Working Together as a Team

1 Share your ideas with the others on your team.

2 Remember that everyone is a part of the team.

3 Be willing to compromise.

Think About Reading

Write your answers.

1. What is the new thing that Jonny and Rada most want to do when they reach Earth?

2. Why do you think Rada and Jonny are the only children on the small planet?

3. If you lived in Rada and Jonny's world, what would you like most about it? What would you like least?

4. *The Best New Thing* is a science fiction story. What parts of the story have to do with science?

5. If Dr. Mae Jemison lived in Rada and Jonny's world, what jobs do you think she might do? Explain your answer.

Write a Radio Advertisement

- Your job is to find a family who wants to live and work on the little world. Write a radio advertisement that will persuade listeners to move there. In your advertisement, tell why the little world is a great place to live. Describe what the housing is like. Encourage families to sign up for the move. You may want to tape record your advertisement, too.

Literature Circle

The Best New Thing is a science fiction story partially set in outer space. Discuss other science fiction books, comics, TV shows, or films you know that also have a space setting. Record the titles on a concept web about outer space stories. Then compare the stories to *The Best New Thing*. In what ways were they alike and different? Which parts of these science fiction stories did you like the best?

AUTHOR
Isaac Asimov

As a boy, Isaac Asimov loved to read the science fiction magazines sold in his father's candy store. Asimov wrote his first story when he was only eleven years old. During his lifetime, he wrote almost 500 science and science fiction books—more than any other author. He once said, "I'm on fire to explain, and happiest when it's something reasonably intricate, which I can make clear step by step." Isaac Asimov died in 1992.

MORE BOOKS ABOUT
Outer Space

- *Living in Space* by Larry Kettelkamp
- *The Outer Space Mystery (Boxcar Children)* by Gertrude Chandler Warner
- *Star Walk* by Seymour Simon

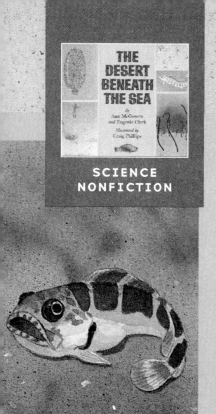

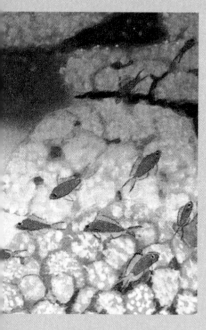

FROM

THE DESERT BENEATH THE SEA

By
Ann McGovern
and Eugenie Clark

Illustrated by
Craig Phillips

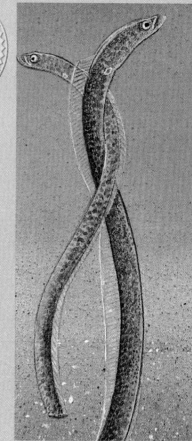

How Marine Biologists Study the Undersea Desert

Marine biologist Eugenie Clark is known as the Shark Lady. She studies sharks all over the world. But she is also interested in the tiny creatures who live in the desert beneath the sea.

A scientist like Eugenie Clark studies fish in many different ways. As a young girl, she studied fish in an aquarium at home. Now she goes on expeditions to observe the creatures in their homes in the sea. She goes scuba diving to study their behavior firsthand. Many people enjoy diving with her—students, her grown children, other scientists and diving friends, including author Ann McGovern.

Eugenie and Ann have a lot of fun on these expeditions. But they work hard, too.

They learn to lie quietly on the sea bottom, careful not to disturb the creatures they are studying.

Ann takes notes for her books and Eugenie records her findings. They write with a pencil tied to a plastic slate or on special underwater paper held to a clipboard with two rubber bands.

Eugenie and her scuba-diving friends watch how the creatures behave . . . how they act alone and with other sand dwellers . . . how they fight, feed, and mate . . . how the seasons and the sun and moon and currents affect them. They study the creatures at sunrise, at dusk, and in the dark of night.

Eugenie also studies the kind of water and sand in which the creatures live. She spends many hours in libraries and museums all over the world. She reads information by other scientists.

Back in her lab at the University of Maryland where she is a professor of Zoology, Eugenie does further study. She examines fish preserved in alcohol by *dissecting*, or cutting them open. She studies tiny parts of them under microscopes.

She counts the rays in each fin and the scales on their bodies. She measures many parts of the fish.

She examines what remains in the fishes' stomachs to find out what they eat. Sometimes she has to play detective. From only a few fish scales or bones, she tries to figure out the kind of food that was eaten.

In a notebook, she records all her information, called *data*. This data can also be put into a computer, revealing other fish facts. As she writes her findings, she analyzes and studies the computer images.

Her data is published in scientific magazines and books for other scientists to read. Sometimes she writes for popular magazines, like *National Geographic*. Her stories are illustrated with beautiful photographs.

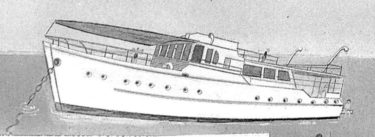

If You Joined an Underwater Expedition

Suppose you were a scuba diver and were invited to take part in an underwater study. You would be one of fourteen people—including Ann McGovern—who volunteered to live on a dive boat for a week to study the sand tilefish of the Caribbean Sea.

The leaders of the expedition—Eugenie Clark and Joan Rabin—would give you jobs to do. You would help them try to find answers to many questions about the sand tilefish.

How deep down do these fish build their burrows? What are they made of? Does each fish build its burrow alone or with other tilefishes? Why are the tops of burrows built so big? Is it to show off? Is it to build an artificial reef to attract their food?

Coral reefs around the world are being damaged in shallow waters where people drop their trash—sometimes right in the tilefish's territory. How does the tilefish react to this?

Your first job would be to scuba dive to locate the sand tilefish. Its pale color makes it hard to spot when it hovers above the sandy bottom. You would learn to tell males from females. Males are larger and develop streamers on their tails. They behave differently from females.

Tilefish homes, called *burrows*, are easy to locate because of the mountains of coral rubble piled on top. Some of them are over eight feet across. Juvenile tilefish build small burrows. Once you find a burrow, you mark it with a plastic marker with your initials and a number. All week, you would study that area and the tilefish that live there. You would see that only one tilefish lives in each burrow.

You would measure the size of the roof mounds and the distances between them. You use a compass and a cotton string that is knotted in measured lengths. After each scuba dive, you give your information to Eugenie or Joan. They record your observations in a scientific way. They make detailed drawings and maps of the whole area. Your observations would be part of a scientific study.

Another job would be to help Joan *excavate*, or take apart, a large roof mound. These are made mostly of pieces of broken coral. A tilefish can easily build its burrow and roof mound again.

First Joan divides the large mound into four parts with her diving knife, the way you might divide a pie. One quarter, or *quadrant*, would be studied. You pick up the coral pieces carefully and put them into your collecting bag. When the bag is filled, a lift bag is inflated to bring the heavy rubble up to the boat.

The coral rubble is weighed and sorted. You would work on the back deck, sorting the hundreds of coral rubble pieces by size and shape and texture. The job might take all afternoon. Your back would get very tired, bending over the piles of rubble on the deck. Mixed in with the coral rubble, you might find surprises—fish teeth, bits of glass, and other trash.

A photographer takes pictures of the tilefish underwater. Now he photographs the rubble on the deck.

You would learn many things on this expedition. You would see tilefish at different depths—from eight feet to 168 feet! You would see groups of little yellowhead jawfish that make their burrows nearby. You might wonder why the jawfish live so close to the tilefish. Scientists wonder, too—but no one has been able to come up with a scientific reason, so far.

On many dives, you would see a tilefish pick up a piece of coral in its mouth. It would swim up to a big mound. Yet the tilefish makes its mound even bigger by adding another piece of coral on top! Scientists are still investigating the reasons why tilefish keep building.

Divers check up on the fish at night, too. When the sun sets, the tilefish cover the openings to their burrows by fanning the sand with their tails. Then they dive through the soft, new sand that closes over them. Here they sleep until morning, protected from danger.

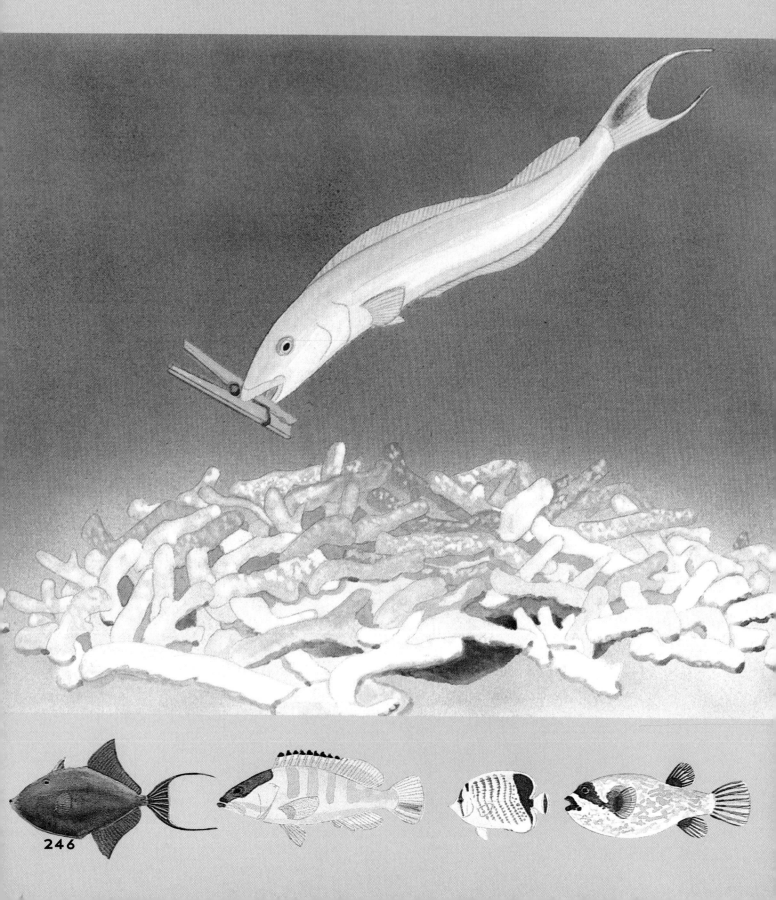

Joan and Eugenie want to see what happens if a burrow entrance is blocked. They ask you to help. Tilefish move objects by carrying them or dragging them with their mouths. At the entrance of one burrow, you place a red plastic checker. At the second, you block the entrance with a golf ball. You put a clothespin in front of the last burrow.

You watch to see if the tilefish moves them. The red checker doesn't completely block the entrance so the tilefish simply ignores it and slips in and out of the burrow.

The golf ball is too round and smooth for the tilefish to get hold of in its mouth, so it does not use that burrow opening again.

And the clothespin? The tilefish can pick it up easily and move it to the top of its burrow.

Probably the most important fact you would learn is that sand tilefish can make a home out of almost anything. If there is no coral around, they use pieces of a light bulb, parts of shipwrecks, bits of glass, a fishnet or a clothespin—even little pieces of diving equipment. They seem to use anything that might have dropped into the sea.

Sometimes sand tilefish make their home in plastic pipes or under wooden boards that are lying on the sandy bottom. It seems they can live in almost any kind of shelter.

A Mystery Fish

One day, Eugenie and her friend David Shen were diving in the Red Sea. They were studying razorfish when David noticed a strange fish swimming by. David had never seen such a fish before.

It looked like a tiny jawfish with a big head and four dark patches on its back. It was a female with her belly bulging with eggs. He took many pictures of the fish.

David motioned to Eugenie. She swam over to the mystery fish. She, too, had never seen anything like it. They collected it in a plastic bag and brought it to the surface. They kept it alive in a bucket of seawater and brought it to David Fridman at the aquarium. Surely he would be able to identify the fish.

But David Fridman didn't know what it was, either. By chance, a scientist from a museum in Germany happened to be visiting the Red Sea. He got very excited when he saw the strange little fish and asked to take it back to his museum.

It turned out to be a new species. He preserved the fish by pickling it in a jar with special chemicals. He described it in a scientific paper and named it *Stalix davidsheni,* after David Shen.

David Shen says today, "I often wonder what that little fish was doing, swimming over the sand. It was not the usual jawfish behavior. Jawfish usually build their burrows in sand and rubble. They almost never wander far from their homes. Was this rare fish looking for its mate?"

Since that day in 1984, no other *Stalix davidsheni* has been seen, but Eugenie and David keep looking.

David Shen joined Eugenie and Ann McGovern on a Red Sea trip in 1980 because he wanted to learn about fish. It was his first expedition. Since then he has become an expert underwater photographer, and some of his pictures have been on magazine covers.

David has also become an expert on many kinds of fish. He became fascinated with the desert beneath the sea and produced a movie about it. He helped Eugenie map the largest colony of garden eels in the world. He knows fish by their scientific names.

If you help scientists, like David does, perhaps some day, you, too, will have a fish named after you!

THE JASON PROJECT

Passport to Adventure

The Jason Project is named after a character in Greek mythology. In Greek myths, Jason was the first great explorer to sail the seas. His ship was called the Argo, so the sea-going members of the Jason Project are called "argonauts."

250

icture this. You are at the controls of a deep-sea submersible. Your robot-like vehicle has dived down more than a mile under the ocean's surface. All around you, the sea is pitch black, except where your vehicle's floodlights pierce the darkness. You can see tiny, brightly colored sea animals dancing through the light beams.

Cautiously, you steer your way into a deep undersea canyon. You enter what seems to be a mysterious new planet. All around you, giant tube worms sway. Huge crabs crawl by in slow motion. You are at the bottom of the ocean, seeing what few humans have ever seen.

Finally, it's time for you to leave. You turn over the controls to another pilot. Then you turn around. Watching you are your classmates, teachers, and a big audience. You are not underwater at all. You have just been on an electronic field trip as a member of the Jason Project team!

The Jason Project gives students all over the world a chance to be part of an underwater discovery team. The project is the brainchild of Dr. Robert Ballard, an oceanographer and deep-sea explorer, who discovered and visited the wreck of the *Titanic*. After making his famous discovery in a manned submersible, Ballard got thousands of letters from students. "I realized that we could put this incredible robot technology to work to excite students about the thrills of scientific discovery," he says.

Ballard has set up a team of scientists, computer experts, and explorers to work with young people interested in underwater exploration. A complex communications network allows students to become part of Ballard's discovery team.

This is how it works. Scientists aboard a research ship send a remote-operated robot vehicle named *Jason* down into the ocean depths. Pictures from the robot are transmitted from the research ship to a satellite. From there, they are beamed to auditoriums across the United States.

Lucky students in the audience become "pilots" and sit at control panels where they can talk to the scientists and drive the robot vehicle. The audiences can watch on huge screens set up in the auditoriums. A few young people are even luckier! For each expedition of the Jason Project, several student "argonauts" are chosen. They accompany the scientists on board the research ship and become members

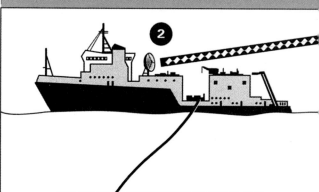

DIAGRAM OF THE JASON PROJECT TRANSMISSION
Baja California Sur

❶ Video signals originate from JASON 6,000 feet below the research vessel in the Sea of Cortez. ❷ Audio, video and data signals are collected at multiple sites and converted to compressed digital video aboard ship.

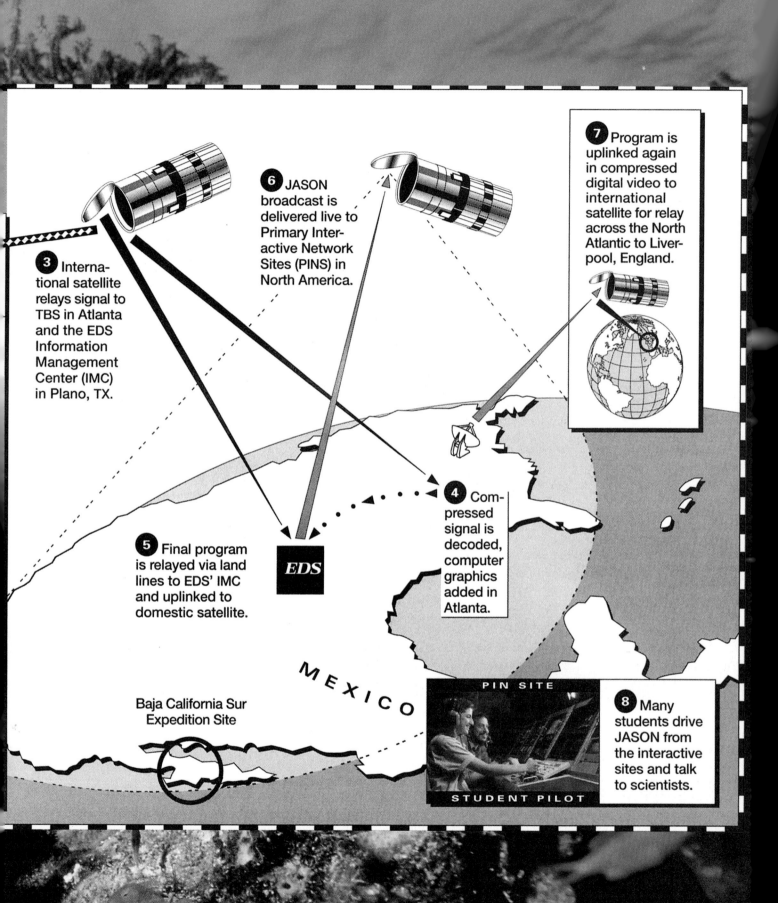

3 International satellite relays signal to TBS in Atlanta and the EDS Information Management Center (IMC) in Plano, TX.

6 JASON broadcast is delivered live to Primary Interactive Network Sites (PINS) in North America.

7 Program is uplinked again in compressed digital video to international satellite for relay across the North Atlantic to Liverpool, England.

5 Final program is relayed via land lines to EDS' IMC and uplinked to domestic satellite.

EDS

4 Compressed signal is decoded, computer graphics added in Atlanta.

Baja California Sur Expedition Site

MEXICO

PIN SITE
STUDENT PILOT

8 Many students drive JASON from the interactive sites and talk to scientists.

TEAMWORK TIPS

It definitely takes teamwork to make the Jason Project work. Two team members, Ernie Radowick and Christina Torruella give these tips for successful teamwork:

 HAVE A MISSION EVERYONE BELIEVES IN. **The mission of the Jason Project is to excite students about science and technology and get them involved in scientific discovery. "The feedback we get from students is my biggest satisfaction," says Radowick.**

 KEEP FOCUSED. **"Everyone should have a specific task," says Torruella. "The danger is spreading yourself too thin," she warns. "Ask yourself, what do I have to do to accomplish my job. Then do it."**

 MAKE THE SUCCESS OF THE PROJECT YOUR GOAL. **"The key is dedicated people who are willing to do whatever it takes for the project to succeed," says Radowick.**

 ENJOY WHAT YOU DO. **Torruella gives this advice: "If you enjoy what you are doing, you will always succeed."**

THE JASON PROJECT
EXPEDITIONS

The Jason Project has embarked on fantastic journeys all over the globe. Over the years, several million students have joined scientists in and out of the water. Here are some of the Jason Project's most exciting destinations.

JASON I—MAY 1989
In the Mediterranean Sea, the Jason team examined an ancient Roman ship that sank over 1,600 years ago and sent a robot vehicle to photograph it.

JASON III—DECEMBER 1991
Journeying to the Galápagos Islands in the Pacific Ocean, the Jason scientists studied animals, birds, and marine life found nowhere else on earth.

JASON VI—FEBRUARY 1995
The Jason team traveled to the Big Island of Hawaii, witnessed the largest surface lava flow in 25 years, and studied wildlife.

JASON VIII—APRIL/MAY 1997
These expeditions focused on geysers, glaciers, and volcanic activity in Yellowstone Park and Iceland. In Yellowstone, a special video camera, lowered into a hot pool, recorded organisms that live in near-boiling water.

JASON X—MARCH 1999
Scientists travelled to rain forests in Colorado, Washington state, and Peru's Amazon River region. In the Amazon, they climbed into the canopy 100 feet above the forest floor and studied the wet and wild ecosystem.

THINK ABOUT READING

Write your answers.

1. What methods do Eugenie and Ann use to study fish?

2. What skills does a member of an underwater scientific expedition need?

3. If you could go on an expedition, which job would you like to do? Use details from the selection to support your answer.

4. What clues in the selection show that Eugenie and Ann feel a deep respect for creatures of the sea?

5. In what ways is the Jason Project like Ann and Eugenie's diving expeditions?

WRITE A SCIENCE LOG ENTRY

You are joining Ann McGovern and Eugenie Clark on a diving expedition. Write an entry in your science log about one of your dives. Tell the time and the date. Record what you did on the dive, the job you performed, and what you observed. You may wish to include a diagram or drawing in your entry.

LITERATURE CIRCLE

Talk about the different expeditions of the Jason Project that are listed at the end of the selection. If you could participate in one of them, which one would you choose? Why? Which ones do you think would interest Eugenie Clark most? Why?

AUTHORS
ANN McGOVERN
AND
EUGENIE CLARK

Ann McGovern has been diving for over 30 years. She says, "You don't have to know how to scuba dive or travel around the world to be a writer. Everything that you want to write about is in you."

As a child, Eugenie Clark spent weekends watching sharks at the New York City aquarium. Today people call her "The Shark Lady" because she has made so many discoveries about these fish.

MORE BOOKS ABOUT
OCEAN LIFE

- *Night Dive*
  by Ann McGovern
- *Beneath Blue Waters*
  by Deborah Kovacs
- *Watch Out for Sharks*
  by Caroline Arnold

WORKSHOP

How to Make an Exploration Map

When explorers travel to far-off places, they are finding new routes and discovering geographical features that may not have been recorded before. Explorers often mark their routes on special exploration maps.

What is an exploration map? An exploration map shows an explorer's route through a certain area. It also includes the usual information shown on a map: natural features such as mountains, volcanoes, and rivers; and features created by people, such as roads and borders.

N
W · E
S

0 200 400 600 m

ASIA

Mongolia

Gobi Desert

China

Loyang

(Persia)

Hormuz

Himalayas

Tibet

Yangtze

Ganges

Chittagong

India

Calicut

Maldive Islands

INDIAN OCEAN

KEY TO MAP
- - - Main Silk Route
· · · Main Spice Route
——— Cheng Ho

Sumatra

SOUTH CHINA SEA

Borneo

Java

Many maps use symbols such as arrows and colored lines to stand for different routes.

Important places like oceans and mountains are included on the map.

The map legend tells what the symbols on the map represent.

The green line shows the routes traveled by the explorer Cheng Ho.

1   Choose a Place

Break into teams and brainstorm a list of ideas for your map. Think of places you've visited, places you've learned about through books or movies, or local places of interest. Each team member should make a suggestion. Take a team vote to find out which place is the most popular.

TOOLS

- paper and pencil
- colored markers
- tracing paper
- ruler
- reference books

2   Research Your Place

- Find maps or pictures of the place that your team selected. As a group, study the maps or pictures and decide what parts you want to include.

- Draw the outline of the map. Then sketch in some of the important features.

- Each team member can draw his or her own route on the map. Have each person use a different color.

- Add landmarks to help guide you on your way.

3 Create Map Symbols

With your group, create symbols that will show important features on your map. For example, you may wish to use blue lines for rivers and dotted lines for borders. Make the symbols look like the things they represent, such as trees to show a forest or ships to show a harbor. Add these symbols to your map's legend. A map legend is a list of the symbols that appear on the map. Next to each symbol is an explanation of what it stands for.

Tips
- Choose a place you all want to learn more about.
- Sketch the map in pencil first, in case you need to make changes.
- Research the place you want to map. You never know what interesting facts you'll discover.

4 Finish and Display Your Map

When your team is satisfied with the map, use colored markers to draw the final outline, features, and routes. Working with your team, display the map. Explain to the class why you selected your route and what they would see if they took that route.

If You Are Using a Computer . . .

Create your map on the computer, using the Paint Tools. Use clip art, such as arrows, to create the symbols for your map.

THINK

Why is it important to bring maps on an expedition?

Dr. Mae Jemison
Astronaut ▶

THE LOST LAKE

ALLEN SAY

REALISTIC
FICTION

THE LOST LAKE

by Allen Say

I went to live with Dad last summer.

Every day he worked in his room from morning to night, sometimes on weekends, too. Dad wasn't much of a talker, but when he was busy he didn't talk at all.

I didn't know anybody in the city, so I stayed home most of the time. It was too hot to play outside anyway. In one month I finished all the books I'd brought and grew tired of watching TV.

One morning I started cutting pictures out of old magazines, just to be doing something. They were pictures of mountains and rivers and lakes, and some showed people fishing and canoeing. Looking at them made me feel cool, so I pinned them up in my room.

Dad didn't notice them for two days. When he did, he looked at them one by one.

"Nice pictures," he said.

"Are you angry with me, Dad?" I asked, because he saved old magazines for his work.

"It's all right, Luke," he said. "I'm having this place painted soon anyway."

He thought I was talking about the marks I'd made on the wall.

That Saturday Dad woke me up early in the morning and told me we were going camping! I was wide awake in a second. He gave me a pair of brand-new hiking boots to try out. They were perfect.

In the hallway I saw a big backpack and a knapsack all packed and ready to go.

"What's in them, Dad?" I asked.

"Later," he said. "We have a long drive ahead of us."

In the car I didn't ask any more questions because Dad was so grumpy in the morning.

"Want a sip?" he said, handing me his mug. He'd never let me drink coffee before. It had lots of sugar in it.

"Where are we going?" I finally asked.

"We're off to the Lost Lake, my lad."

"How can you lose a lake?"

"No one's found it, that's how." Dad was smiling! "Grandpa and I used to go there a long time ago. It was our special place, so don't tell any of your friends."

"I'll never tell," I promised. "How long are we going to stay there?"

"Five days, maybe a week."

"We're going to sleep outside for a whole week?"

"That's the idea."

"Oh, boy!"

We got to the mountains in the afternoon.

"It's a bit of a hike to the lake, son," Dad said.

"I don't mind," I told him. "Are there any fish in the lake?"

"Hope so. We'll have to catch our dinner, you know."

"You didn't bring any food?"

"Of course not. We're going to live like true outdoorsmen."

"Oh . . ."

Dad saw my face and started to laugh. He must have been joking. I didn't think we were going very far anyway, because Dad's pack was so heavy I couldn't even lift it.

Well, Dad was like a mountain goat. He went straight up the trail, whistling all the while. But I was gasping in no time. My knapsack got very heavy and I started to fall behind.

Dad stopped for me often, but he wouldn't let me take off my pack. If I did I'd be too tired to go on, he said.

It was almost suppertime when we got to the lake.

The place reminded me of the park near Dad's apartment.
He wasn't whistling or humming anymore.

"Welcome to the *Found* Lake," he muttered from the side
of his mouth.

"What's wrong, Dad?"

"Do you want to camp with all these people around us?"

"I don't mind."

"Well, I do!"

"Are we going home?"

"Of course not!"

He didn't even take off his pack. He just turned and started to walk away.

Soon the lake was far out of sight.

Then it started to rain. Dad gave me a poncho and it kept me dry, but I wondered where we were going to sleep that night. I wondered what we were going to do for dinner. I wasn't sure about camping anymore.

I was glad when Dad finally stopped and set up the tent. The rain and wind beat against it, but we were warm and cozy inside. And Dad had brought food. For dinner we had salami and dried apricots.

"I'm sorry about the lake, Dad," I said.

He shook his head. "You know something, Luke? There aren't any secret places left in the world anymore."

"What if we go very far up in the mountains? Maybe we can find our own lake."

"There are lots of lakes up here, but that one was special."

"But we've got a whole week, Dad."

"Well, why not? Maybe we'll find a lake that's not on the map."

"Sure, we will!"

We started early in the morning. When the fog cleared we saw other hikers ahead of us. Sure enough, Dad became very glum.

"We're going cross-country, partner," he said.

"Won't we get lost?"

"A wise man never leaves home without his compass."

So we went off the trail. The hills went on and on. The mountains went on and on. It was kind of lonesome. It seemed as if Dad and I were the only people left in the world.

And then we hiked into a big forest.

At noontime we stopped by a creek and ate lunch and drank ice-cold water straight from the stream. I threw rocks in the water, and fish, like shadows, darted in the pools.

"Isn't this a good place to camp, Dad?"

"I thought we were looking for our lake."

"Yes, right . . ." I mumbled.

The forest went on and on.

"I don't mean to scare you, son," Dad said. "But we're in bear country. We don't want to surprise them, so we have to make a lot of noise. If they hear us, they'll just go away."

What a time to tell me! I started to shout as loudly as I could. Even Dad wouldn't be able to beat off bears. I thought about those people having fun back at the lake. I thought about the creek, too, with all those fish in it. That would have been a fine place to camp. The Lost Lake hadn't been so bad either.

It was dark when we got out of the forest. We built a fire and that made me feel better. Wild animals wouldn't come near a fire. Dad cooked beef stroganoff and it was delicious.

Later it was bedtime. The sleeping bag felt wonderful. Dad and I started to count the shooting stars, then I worried that maybe we weren't going to find our lake.

"What are you thinking about, Luke?" Dad asked.

"I didn't know you could cook like that," I said.

Dad laughed. "That was only freeze-dried stuff. When we get home, I'll cook you something really special."

"You know something, Dad? You seem like a different person up here."

"Better or worse?"

"A lot better."

"How so?"

"You talk more."

"I'll have to talk more often, then."

That made me smile. Then I slept.

Dad shook me awake. The sun was just coming up, turning everything all gold and orange and yellow. And there was the lake, right in front of us.

For a long time we watched the light change on the water, getting brighter and brighter. Dad didn't say a word the whole time. But then, I didn't have anything to say either.

After breakfast we climbed a mountain and saw our lake below us. There wasn't a sign of people anywhere. It really seemed as if Dad and I were all alone in the world.

I liked it just fine.

from
MATTHEW HENSON
ARCTIC EXPLORER

All the Way There

by
Sean Dolan

*B*y the end of the 1800s, many people had tried to reach the North Pole but failed. The most famous attempt, made by Adolphus Greeley's team, came the closest. Commander Robert Peary and his aide Matthew Henson had also led many unsuccessful expeditions. Against all odds, they continued their effort to reach their goal—the top of the world.

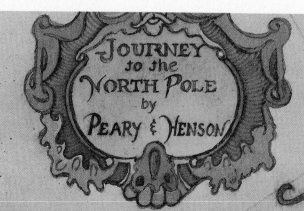

JOURNEY
to the
NORTH POLE
by
PEARY & HENSON

ATLA

In 1905, Peary set off on a new expedition, and Henson was with him. This time, a new ship, the *Roosevelt,* succeeded in smashing its way through the Arctic ice. Sledding over extremely treacherous ice, Henson and Peary came within 175 miles of the Pole. This was the closest that anyone had ever come. They returned to the United States both frustrated and certain that next time they would make it.

Peary and Henson's sixth polar expedition departed from Long Island, New York, on July 6, 1908. With the two men this time were four other adventurers. All of them were younger than the 42-year-old Henson, but Henson knew that his vast experience would more than make up for the youthful high spirits of his comrades.

This time the expedition had good luck right from the beginning. The weather was just cold enough to keep the surface frozen with a minimum of breaks in the ice, but not too cold to work and travel in. Henson wrote in his diary that he had never seen such smooth sea ice, and the group made rapid progress. After every five days, Peary sent one of the members of his party back to the ship. The final assault on the Pole would be made by just Peary, one other member of his expedition, and a couple of Eskimos. In this way, only a small load of supplies would have to be carried the entire length of the journey. But who Peary would ask to join him at the Pole remained a mystery.

The explorers continued on, averaging a very fast 16 miles a day. On March 28, 1909, they passed the farthest point north they had ever reached. Two days later, Peary asked the third remaining member of the expedition to return to the ship. Matthew Henson would go with him to the North Pole.

The next day, April 1, Peary, Henson, and four Eskimos, Seegloo, Ootah, Eginwah, and Ooqueah, began their final dash for the Pole, which was now 130 miles away. Because of his crippled feet Peary was traveling slowly, but Henson drove his lead team at a furious pace. On the morning of April 6, Henson woke up Seegloo and Ootah. "Ahdoolo! . . . Ahdoolo!" he called, a little more urgently than usual. They were just 35 miles from the Pole.

At Peary's orders, Henson and the two Eskimos forged ahead. They were supposed to stop just short of the Pole to let Peary catch up. That afternoon, when Henson stopped for a rest, he realized that he had made a mistake. If his calculation was correct, he had not only reached the Pole, but gone beyond it! He backtracked a little bit and waited for Peary. The commander of the expedition took out his instruments, took his readings, and announced in a matter-of-fact voice that at last, after so many years of hardship, they had reached their destination. Henson explained to Ootah, "We have found what we hunt." The Eskimo shrugged his shoulders, still unable to fully understand these strange outsiders from another part of the world. "There is nothing here," Ootah said. "Only ice."

An Eskimo family in Greenland converses and plays outside its tent, which is made from the skins of seals. During the summer, Eskimos often lived in tents instead of in igloos.

North Pole

Arctic Ocean

ELLESMERE IS.

GREENLAND

Iceland

Baffin Island

Hudson Bay

Henson and Peary's successful route to the North Pole.

With an American flag in his hand, Henson climbed to the top of a nearby pressure ridge. Peary snapped his picture. Then Henson helped set up camp. After a long night's sleep, the expedition headed home. Henson's exploring days were over.

The rest of Matthew Henson's life was frustrating in many ways. Peary was treated as a national hero, but Henson was slighted. Racist reporters asked Peary why he had allowed a Negro to accompany him to the North Pole. Peary, who was unwilling to share the credit for his achievement, made things worse with his answer. He had been forced to take Henson with him all the way, he said, because Henson was too ignorant to make it back to the ship on his own. This was completely unfair, of course, for many times it had been only Henson's courage and intelligence that saved the expedition from disaster. While Peary received large fees for giving lectures and was granted a rich pension from the government, Henson was forced to park cars in a Brooklyn garage to earn his living.

But Matthew Henson was not the kind of man to let bitterness ruin his life. He later got a good job with the U.S. Customs Bureau, and he lived a long, rich, full life until he died in 1955, at the age of 88. During his final years he took satisfaction in his own knowledge of all that he had achieved. If any doubted him, there was always the picture Peary had taken at the North Pole.

PEARY & HENSON

ATLA

That photograph showed Matthew Henson, a black American, with the flag of his country in his hand at the top of the world. And anyone who doubted his achievements could always ask the Eskimos, who for years afterward told legends about a very great man named Miy Paluk. The Eskimos even added a new word to their language: The word *ahdoolo* came to stand for a very special kind of courage. It was used not only to mean bravery and endurance, but to mean the ability to face even the hardest work and the greatest challenge with hope and good spirits. It is a fitting word with which to remember Matthew Henson.

Triumph at the Pole: Atop an icy hill near the North Pole, Henson and his Eskimo friends hoist the American flag and several other banners.

THINK ABOUT READING

Answer the questions in the story map.

SETTING

1. Where does the story begin?

2. How does the story's setting change?

CHARACTERS

3. Who are the main characters in *The Lost Lake*?

BEGINNING

4. Why is the narrator cutting pictures out of old magazines?

5. What is Dad's surprise on Saturday morning?

MIDDLE

6. What does the narrator discover about Dad as they begin the hike?

7. How does Dad feel when they reach the first lake? Why?

8. What do the two characters do the next morning?

ENDING

9. What do the narrator and his father discover after camping the second night?

10. How does the narrator feel? Why?

WRITE A SENSORY DESCRIPTION

Write a description of the "lost lake" from the boy's viewpoint. Tell how the lake looks as the sun is rising. Describe the colors you see. Include other sensory details about the setting. What is the early morning temperature? What aromas do you smell? Are there any sounds? As you write your description, use colorful adjectives and vivid verbs to help a reader experience the lake.

LITERATURE CIRCLE

The Lost Lake and "All the Way There" are both about adventures in the wilderness. One is fiction and one is biography. Compare the two adventures and how they are written. Discuss which kind of writing you find more exciting and tell why. Which kind of writing would you recommend to a friend? List your ideas on a chart.

AUTHOR/ILLUSTRATOR
ALLEN SAY

Allen Say began drawing as a child in Yokohama, Japan. After moving to the United States, he worked as a photographer but never stopped drawing and painting. Eventually he began to write and illustrate his own stories—many of them based on his own experiences. He says, "All good artists have an excellent memory. You cannot imagine without memory." *The Lost Lake* is proof of Allen Say's own imagination and good memory. It was inspired by a camping trip he once took.

MORE BOOKS BY
ALLEN SAY

- *Grandfather's Journey*
- *The Bicycle Man*
- *A River Dream*

from

Sarah,
Plain and Tall

by
Patricia MacLachlan

illustrated by
Allen Garns

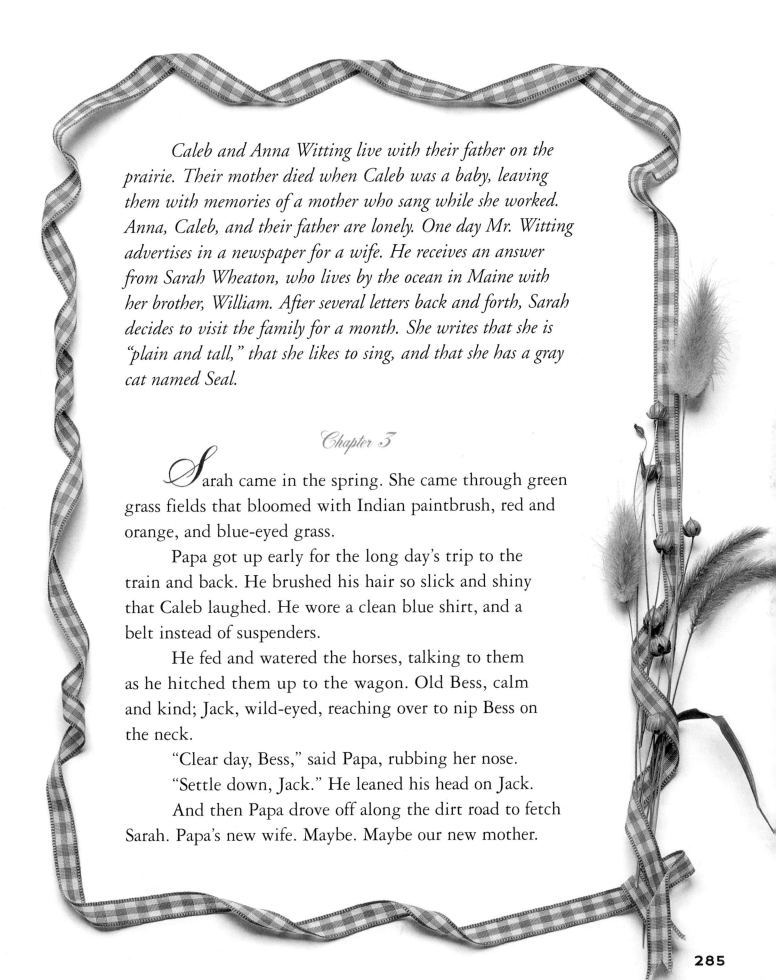

Caleb and Anna Witting live with their father on the prairie. Their mother died when Caleb was a baby, leaving them with memories of a mother who sang while she worked. Anna, Caleb, and their father are lonely. One day Mr. Witting advertises in a newspaper for a wife. He receives an answer from Sarah Wheaton, who lives by the ocean in Maine with her brother, William. After several letters back and forth, Sarah decides to visit the family for a month. She writes that she is "plain and tall," that she likes to sing, and that she has a gray cat named Seal.

Chapter 3

Sarah came in the spring. She came through green grass fields that bloomed with Indian paintbrush, red and orange, and blue-eyed grass.

Papa got up early for the long day's trip to the train and back. He brushed his hair so slick and shiny that Caleb laughed. He wore a clean blue shirt, and a belt instead of suspenders.

He fed and watered the horses, talking to them as he hitched them up to the wagon. Old Bess, calm and kind; Jack, wild-eyed, reaching over to nip Bess on the neck.

"Clear day, Bess," said Papa, rubbing her nose.

"Settle down, Jack." He leaned his head on Jack.

And then Papa drove off along the dirt road to fetch Sarah. Papa's new wife. Maybe. Maybe our new mother.

Gophers ran back and forth across the road, stopping to stand up and watch the wagon. Far off in the field a woodchuck ate and listened. Ate and listened.

Caleb and I did our chores without talking. We shoveled out the stalls and laid down new hay. We fed the sheep. We swept and straightened and carried wood and water. And then our chores were done.

Caleb pulled on my shirt.

"Is my face clean?" he asked. "Can my face be *too* clean?" He looked alarmed.

"No, your face is clean but not too clean," I said.

Caleb slipped his hand into mine as we stood on the porch, watching the road. He was afraid.

"Will she be nice?" he asked. "Like Maggie?"

"Sarah will be nice," I told him.

"How far away is Maine?" he asked.

"You know how far. Far away, by the sea."

"Will Sarah bring some sea?" he asked.

"No, you cannot bring the sea."

The sheep ran in the field, and far off the cows moved slowly to the pond, like turtles.

"Will she like us?" asked Caleb very softly.

I watched a marsh hawk wheel down behind the barn.

He looked up at me.

"Of course she will like us." He answered his own question. "We are nice," he added, making me smile.

We waited and watched. I rocked on the porch and Caleb rolled a marble on the wood floor. Back and forth. Back and forth. The marble was blue.

We saw the dust from the wagon first, rising above the road, above the heads of Jack and Old Bess. Caleb climbed up onto the porch roof and shaded his eyes.

"A bonnet!" he cried. "I see a yellow bonnet!"

The dogs came out from under the porch, ears up, their eyes on the cloud of dust bringing Sarah. The wagon passed the fenced field, and the cows and sheep looked up, too. It rounded the windmill and the barn and the windbreak of Russian olive that Mama had planted long ago. Nick began to bark, then Lottie, and the wagon clattered into the yard and stopped by the steps.

"Hush," said Papa to the dogs.

And it was quiet.

Sarah stepped down from the wagon, a cloth bag in her hand. She reached up and took off her yellow bonnet, smoothing back her brown hair into a bun. She was plain and tall.

"Did you bring some sea?" cried Caleb beside me.

"Something from the sea," said Sarah, smiling. "And me." She turned and lifted a black case from the wagon. "And Seal, too."

Carefully she opened the case, and Seal, gray with white feet, stepped out. Lottie lay down, her head on her paws, staring. Nick leaned down to sniff. Then he lay down, too.

"The cat will be good in the barn," said Papa. "For mice."

Sarah smiled. "She will be good in the house, too."

Sarah took Caleb's hand, then mine. Her hands were large and rough. She gave Caleb a shell—a moon snail, she called it—that was curled and smelled of salt.

"The gulls fly high and drop the shells on the rocks below," she told Caleb. "When the shell is broken, they eat what is inside."

"That is very smart," said Caleb.

"For you, Anna," said Sarah, "a sea stone."

And she gave me the smoothest and whitest stone I had ever seen.

"The sea washes over and over and around the stone, rolling it until it is round and perfect."

"That is very smart, too," said Caleb. He looked up at Sarah. "We do not have the sea here."

Sarah turned and looked out over the plains.

"No," she said. "There is no sea here. But the land rolls a little like the sea."

My father did not see her look, but I did. And I knew that Caleb had seen it, too. Sarah was not smiling. Sarah was already lonely. In a month's time the preacher might come to marry Sarah and Papa. And a month was a long time. Time enough for her to change her mind and leave us.

Papa took Sarah's bags inside, where her room was ready with a quilt on the bed and blue flax dried in a vase on the night table.

Seal stretched and made a small cat sound. I watched her circle the dogs and sniff the air. Caleb came out and stood beside me.

"When will we sing?" he whispered.

I shook my head, turning the white stone over and over in my hand. I wished everything was as perfect as the stone. I wished that Papa and Caleb and I were perfect for Sarah. I wished we had a sea of our own.

Chapter 4

The dogs loved Sarah first. Lottie slept beside her bed, curled in a soft circle, and Nick leaned his face on the covers in the morning, watching for the first sign that Sarah was awake. No one knew where Seal slept. Seal was a roamer.

Sarah's collection of shells sat on the windowsill.

"A scallop," she told us, picking up the shells one by one, "a sea clam, an oyster, a razor clam. And a conch shell. If you put it to your ear you can hear the sea."

She put it to Caleb's ear, then mine. Papa listened, too.
Then Sarah listened once more, with a look so sad and
far away that Caleb leaned against me.

"At least Sarah can hear the sea," he whispered.

Papa was quiet and shy with Sarah, and so was I.
But Caleb talked to Sarah from morning until the light
left the sky.

"Where are you going?" he asked. "To do what?"

"To pick flowers," said Sarah. "I'll hang some of
them upside down and dry them so they'll keep some
color. And we can have flowers all winter long."

"I'll come, too!" cried Caleb. "Sarah said winter,"
he said to me. "That means Sarah will stay."

Together we picked flowers, paintbrush and clover
and prairie violets. There were buds on the wild roses
that climbed up the paddock fence.

"The roses will bloom in early summer," I told
Sarah. I looked to see if she knew what I was thinking.
Summer was when the wedding would be. *Might* be.
Sarah and Papa's wedding.

We hung the flowers from the ceiling in little
bunches. "I've never seen this before," said Sarah. "What
is it called?"

"Bride's bonnet," I told her.

Caleb smiled at the name.

"We don't have this by the sea," she said. "We have
seaside goldenrod and wild asters and woolly ragwort."

"Woolly ragwort!" Caleb whooped. He made up a song.

"Woolly ragwort all around,
Woolly ragwort on the ground.
Woolly ragwort grows and grows,
Woolly ragwort in your nose."

Sarah and Papa laughed, and the dogs lifted their heads and thumped their tails against the wood floor. Seal sat on a kitchen chair and watched us with yellow eyes.

We ate Sarah's stew, the late light coming through the windows. Papa had baked bread that was still warm from the fire.

"The stew is fine," said Papa.

"Ayuh." Sarah nodded. "The bread, too."

"What does 'ayuh' mean?" asked Caleb.

"In Maine it means yes," said Sarah. "Do you want more stew?"

"Ayuh," said Caleb.

"Ayuh," echoed my father.

After dinner Sarah told us about William. "He has a gray-and-white boat named *Kittiwake*." She looked out the window. "That is a small gull found way off the shore where William fishes. There are three aunts who live near us. They wear silk dresses and no shoes. You would love them."

"Ayuh," said Caleb.

"Does your brother look like you?" I asked.

"Yes," said Sarah. "He is plain and tall."

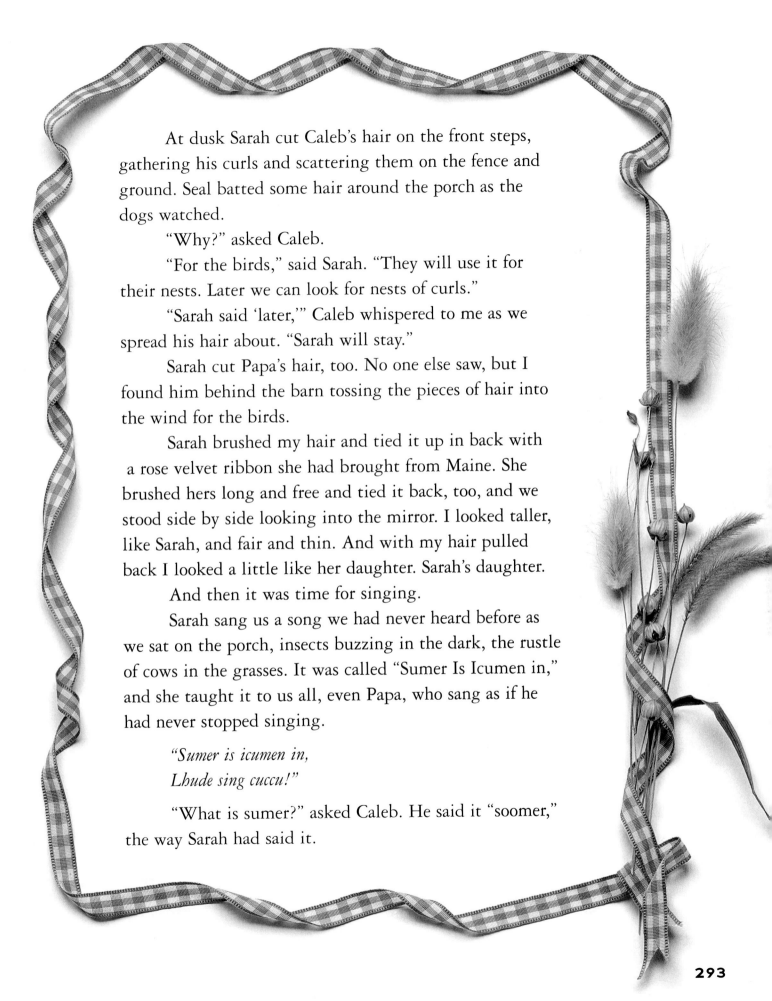

At dusk Sarah cut Caleb's hair on the front steps, gathering his curls and scattering them on the fence and ground. Seal batted some hair around the porch as the dogs watched.

"Why?" asked Caleb.

"For the birds," said Sarah. "They will use it for their nests. Later we can look for nests of curls."

"Sarah said 'later,'" Caleb whispered to me as we spread his hair about. "Sarah will stay."

Sarah cut Papa's hair, too. No one else saw, but I found him behind the barn tossing the pieces of hair into the wind for the birds.

Sarah brushed my hair and tied it up in back with a rose velvet ribbon she had brought from Maine. She brushed hers long and free and tied it back, too, and we stood side by side looking into the mirror. I looked taller, like Sarah, and fair and thin. And with my hair pulled back I looked a little like her daughter. Sarah's daughter.

And then it was time for singing.

Sarah sang us a song we had never heard before as we sat on the porch, insects buzzing in the dark, the rustle of cows in the grasses. It was called "Sumer Is Icumen in," and she taught it to us all, even Papa, who sang as if he had never stopped singing.

"Sumer is icumen in,
Lhude sing cuccu!"

"What is sumer?" asked Caleb. He said it "soomer," the way Sarah had said it.

"Summer," said Papa and Sarah at the same time. Caleb and I looked at each other. Summer was coming.

"Tomorrow," said Sarah, "I want to see the sheep. You know, I've never touched one."

"Never?" Caleb sat up.

"Never," said Sarah. She smiled and leaned back in her chair. "But I've touched seals. Real seals. They are cool and slippery and they slide through the water like fish. They can cry and sing. And sometimes they bark, a little like dogs."

Sarah barked like a seal. And Lottie and Nick came running from the barn to jump up on Sarah and lick her face and make her laugh. Sarah stroked them and scratched their ears and it was quiet again.

"I wish I could touch a seal right now," said Caleb, his voice soft in the night.

"So do I," said Sarah. She sighed, then she began to sing the summer song again. Far off in a field, a meadowlark sang, too.

Chapter 5

The sheep made Sarah smile. She sank her fingers into their thick, coarse wool. She talked to them, running with the lambs, letting them suck on her fingers. She named them after her favorite aunts, Harriet and Mattie and Lou. She lay down in the field beside them and sang "Sumer Is Icumen in," her voice drifting over the meadow grasses, carried by the wind.

She cried when we found a lamb that had died, and she shouted and shook her fist at the turkey buzzards that came from nowhere to eat it. She would not let Caleb or me come near. And that night, Papa went with a shovel to bury the sheep and a lantern to bring Sarah back. She sat on the porch alone. Nick crept up to lean against her knees.

After dinner, Sarah drew pictures to send home to Maine. She began a charcoal drawing of the fields, rolling like the sea rolled. She drew a sheep whose ears were too big. And she drew a windmill.

"Windmill was my first word," said Caleb. "Papa told me so."

"Mine was flower," I said. "What was yours, Sarah?"

"Dune," said Sarah.

"Dune?" Caleb looked up.

"In Maine," said Sarah, "there are rock cliffs that rise up at the edge of the sea. And there are hills covered with pine and spruce trees, green with needles. But William and I found a sand dune all our own. It was soft and sparkling with bits of mica, and when we were little we would slide down the dune into the water."

Caleb looked out the window.

"We have no dunes here," he said.

Papa stood up.

"Yes we do," he said. He took the lantern and went out the door to the barn.

"We do?" Caleb called after him.

He ran ahead, Sarah and I following, the dogs
close behind.

Next to the barn was Papa's mound of hay for bedding,
nearly half as tall as the barn, covered with canvas to keep
the rain from rotting it. Papa carried the wooden ladder
from the barn and leaned it against the hay.

"There." He smiled at Sarah. "Our dune."

Sarah was very quiet. The dogs looked up at her,
waiting. Seal brushed against her legs, her tail in the air.
Caleb reached over and took her hand.

"It looks high up," he said. "Are you scared, Sarah?"

"Scared? Scared!" exclaimed Sarah. "You bet I'm
not scared."

She climbed the ladder, and Nick began to bark.
She climbed to the very top of the hay and sat, looking

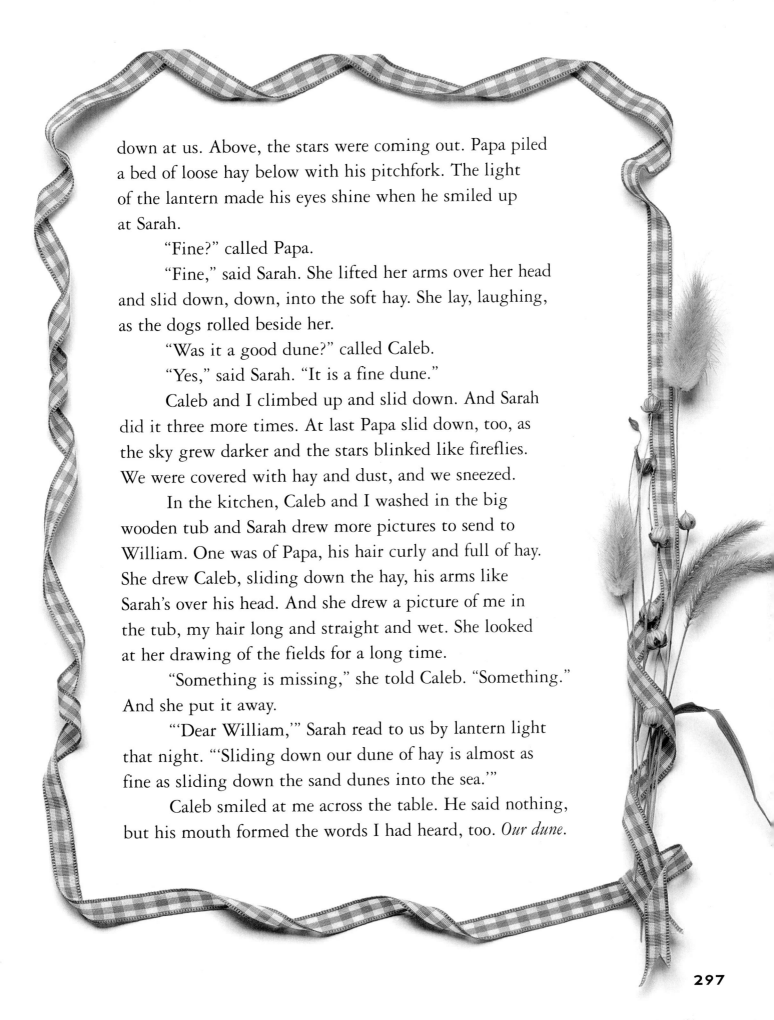

down at us. Above, the stars were coming out. Papa piled a bed of loose hay below with his pitchfork. The light of the lantern made his eyes shine when he smiled up at Sarah.

"Fine?" called Papa.

"Fine," said Sarah. She lifted her arms over her head and slid down, down, into the soft hay. She lay, laughing, as the dogs rolled beside her.

"Was it a good dune?" called Caleb.

"Yes," said Sarah. "It is a fine dune."

Caleb and I climbed up and slid down. And Sarah did it three more times. At last Papa slid down, too, as the sky grew darker and the stars blinked like fireflies. We were covered with hay and dust, and we sneezed.

In the kitchen, Caleb and I washed in the big wooden tub and Sarah drew more pictures to send to William. One was of Papa, his hair curly and full of hay. She drew Caleb, sliding down the hay, his arms like Sarah's over his head. And she drew a picture of me in the tub, my hair long and straight and wet. She looked at her drawing of the fields for a long time.

"Something is missing," she told Caleb. "Something." And she put it away.

"'Dear William,'" Sarah read to us by lantern light that night. "'Sliding down our dune of hay is almost as fine as sliding down the sand dunes into the sea.'"

Caleb smiled at me across the table. He said nothing, but his mouth formed the words I had heard, too. *Our dune.*

Chapter 6

The days grew longer. The cows moved close to the pond, where the water was cool and there were trees.

Papa taught Sarah how to plow the fields, guiding the plow behind Jack and Old Bess, the reins around her neck. When the chores were done we sat in the meadow with the sheep, Sarah beside us, watching Papa finish.

"Tell me about winter," said Sarah.

Old Bess nodded her head as she walked, but we could hear Papa speak sharply to Jack.

"Jack doesn't like work," said Caleb. "He wants to be here in the sweet grass with us."

"I don't blame him," said Sarah. She lay back in the grass with her arms under her head. "Tell me about winter," she said again.

"Winter is cold here," said Caleb, and Sarah and I laughed.

"Winter is cold everywhere," I said.

"We go to school in winter," said Caleb. "Sums and writing and books," he sang.

"I am good at sums and writing," said Sarah. "I love books. How do you get to school?"

"Papa drives us in the wagon. Or we walk the three miles when there is not too much snow."

Sarah sat up. "Do you have lots of snow?"

"Lots and lots and lots of snow," chanted Caleb, rolling around in the grass. "Sometimes we have to dig our way out to feed the animals."

"In Maine the barns are attached to the houses sometimes," said Sarah.

Caleb grinned. "So you could have a cow to Sunday supper?"

Sarah and I laughed.

"When there are bad storms, Papa ties a rope from the house to the barn so no one will get lost," said Caleb.

I frowned. I loved winter.

"There is ice on the windows on winter mornings," I told Sarah. "We can draw sparkling pictures and we can see our breath in the air. Papa builds a warm fire, and we bake hot biscuits and put on hundreds of sweaters. And if the snow is too high, we stay home from school and make snow people."

Sarah lay back in the tall grasses again, her face nearly hidden.

"And is there wind?" she asked.

"Do you like wind?" asked Caleb.

"There is wind by the sea," said Sarah.

"There is wind here," said Caleb happily. "It blows the snow and brings tumbleweeds and makes the sheep run. Wind and wind and wind!" Caleb stood up and ran like the wind, and the sheep ran after him. Sarah and I watched him jump over rock and gullies, the sheep behind him, stiff legged and fast. He circled the field, the sun making the top of his hair golden. He collapsed next to Sarah, and the lambs pushed their wet noses into us.

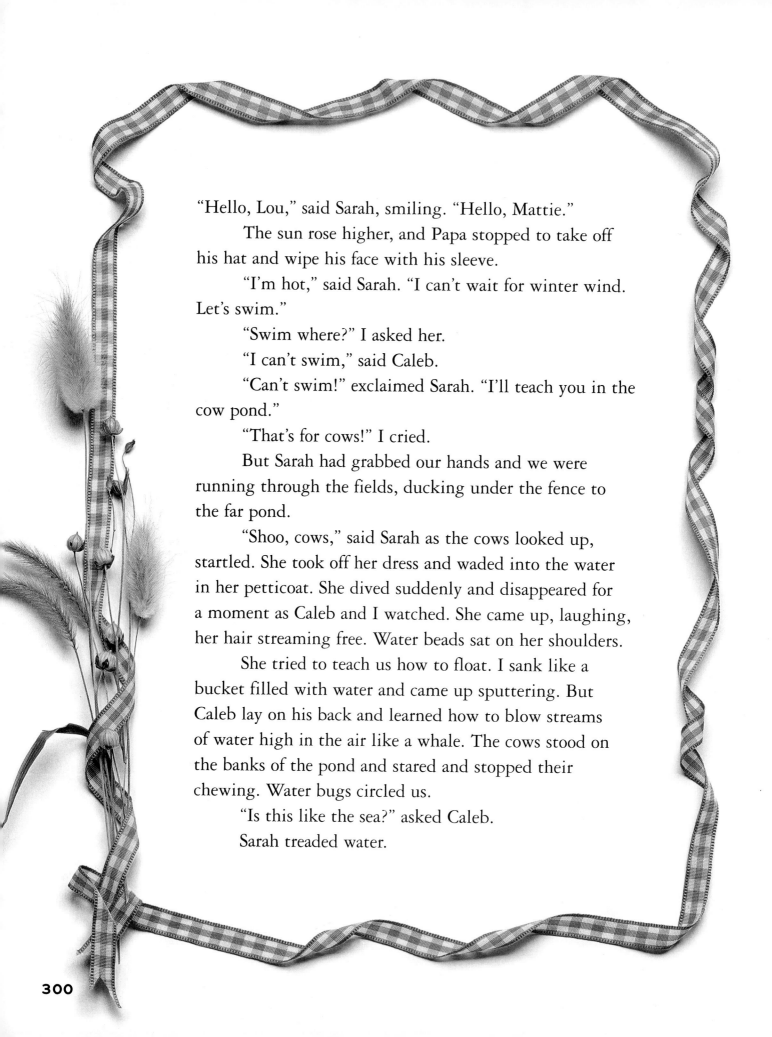

"Hello, Lou," said Sarah, smiling. "Hello, Mattie."

The sun rose higher, and Papa stopped to take off his hat and wipe his face with his sleeve.

"I'm hot," said Sarah. "I can't wait for winter wind. Let's swim."

"Swim where?" I asked her.

"I can't swim," said Caleb.

"Can't swim!" exclaimed Sarah. "I'll teach you in the cow pond."

"That's for cows!" I cried.

But Sarah had grabbed our hands and we were running through the fields, ducking under the fence to the far pond.

"Shoo, cows," said Sarah as the cows looked up, startled. She took off her dress and waded into the water in her petticoat. She dived suddenly and disappeared for a moment as Caleb and I watched. She came up, laughing, her hair streaming free. Water beads sat on her shoulders.

She tried to teach us how to float. I sank like a bucket filled with water and came up sputtering. But Caleb lay on his back and learned how to blow streams of water high in the air like a whale. The cows stood on the banks of the pond and stared and stopped their chewing. Water bugs circled us.

"Is this like the sea?" asked Caleb.

Sarah treaded water.

"The sea is salt," said Sarah. "It stretches out as far as you can see. It gleams like the sun on glass. There are waves."

"Like this?" asked Caleb, and he pushed a wave at Sarah, making her cough and laugh.

"Yes," she said. "Like that."

I held my breath and floated at last, looking up into the sky, afraid to speak. Crows flew over, three in a row. And I could hear a killdeer in the field.

We climbed the bank and dried ourselves and lay in the grass again. The cows watched, their eyes sad in their dinner-plate faces. And I slept, dreaming a perfect dream. The fields had turned to a sea that gleamed like sun on glass. And Sarah was happy.

Chapter 7

The dandelions in the fields had gone by, their heads soft as feathers. The summer roses were opening.

Our neighbors, Matthew and Maggie, came to help Papa plow up a new field for corn. Sarah stood with us on the porch, watching their wagon wind up the road, two horses pulling it and one tied in back. I remembered the last time we had stood here alone, Caleb and I, waiting for Sarah.

Sarah's hair was in thick braids that circled her head, wild daisies tucked here and there. Papa had picked them for her.

Old Bess and Jack ran along the inside of the fence, whickering at the new horses.

"Papa needs five horses for the big gang plow," Caleb told Sarah. "Prairie grass is hard."

Matthew and Maggie came with their two children and a sackful of chickens. Maggie emptied the sack into the yard and three red banty chickens clucked and scattered.

"They are for you," she told Sarah. "For eating."

Sarah loved the chickens. She clucked back to them and fed them grain. They followed her, shuffling and scratching primly in the dirt. I knew they would not be for eating.

The children were young and named Rose and Violet, after flowers. They hooted and laughed and chased the chickens, who flew up to the porch roof, then the dogs, who crept quietly under the porch. Seal had long ago fled to the barn to sleep in cool hay.

Sarah and Maggie helped hitch the horses to the plow, then they set up a big table in the shade of the barn, covering it with a quilt and a kettle of flowers in the middle. They sat on the porch while Caleb and Matthew and Papa began their morning of plowing. I mixed biscuit dough just inside the door, watching.

"You are lonely, yes?" asked Maggie in her soft voice.

Sarah's eyes filled with tears. Slowly I stirred the dough.

Maggie reached over and took Sarah's hand.

"I miss the hills of Tennessee sometimes," she said.

Do not miss the hills, Maggie, I thought.

"I miss the sea," said Sarah.

Do not miss the hills. Do not miss the sea.

I stirred and stirred the dough.

"I miss my brother William," said Sarah. "But he is married. The house is hers now. Not mine any longer. There are three old aunts who all squawk together like crows at dawn. I miss them, too."

"There are always things to miss," said Maggie. "No matter where you are."

I looked out and saw Papa and Matthew and Caleb working. Rose and Violet ran in the fields. I felt something brush my legs and looked down at Nick, wagging his tail.

"I would miss you, Nick," I whispered. "I would." I knelt down and scratched his ears. "I miss Mama."

"I nearly forgot," said Maggie on the porch. "I have something more for you."

I carried the bowl outside and watched Maggie lift a low wooden box out of the wagon.

"Plants," she said to Sarah. "For your garden."

"My garden?" Sarah bent down to touch the plants.

"Zinnias and marigolds and wild feverfew," said Maggie. "You must have a garden. Wherever you are."

Sarah smiled. "I had a garden in Maine with dahlias and columbine. And nasturtiums the color of the sun when it sets. I don't know if nasturtiums would grow here."

"Try," said Maggie. "You must have a garden."

We planted the flowers by the porch, turning over the soil and patting it around them, and watering. Lottie and Nick came to sniff, and the chickens walked in the dirt, leaving prints.

In the fields, the horses pulled the plow up and down under the hot summer sun.

Maggie wiped her face, leaving a streak of dirt.

"Soon you can drive your wagon over to my house and I will give you more. I have tansy."

Sarah frowned. "I have never driven a wagon."

"I can teach you," said Maggie. "And so can Anna and Caleb. And Jacob."

Sarah turned to me.

"Can you?" she asked. "Can you drive a wagon?"

I nodded.

"And Caleb?"

"Yes."

"In Maine," said Sarah, "I would walk to town."

"Here it is different," said Maggie. "Here you will drive."

Way off in the sky, clouds gathered. Matthew and Papa and Caleb came in from the fields, their work done. We all ate in the shade.

"We are glad you are here," said Matthew to Sarah. "A new friend. Maggie misses her friends sometimes."

Sarah nodded. "There is always something to miss, no matter where you are," she said, smiling at Maggie.

Rose and Violet fell asleep in the grass, their bellies full of meat and greens and biscuits. And when it was time to go, Papa and Matthew lifted them into the wagon to sleep on blankets.

Sarah walked slowly behind the wagon for a long time, waving, watching it disappear. Caleb and I ran to bring her back, the chickens running wildly behind us.

"What shall we name them?" asked Sarah, laughing as the chickens followed us into the house.

I smiled. I was right. The chickens would not be for eating.

And then Papa came, just before the rain, bringing Sarah the first roses of summer.

Chapter 8

The rain came and passed, but strange clouds hung in the northwest, low and black and green. And the air grew still.

In the morning, Sarah dressed in a pair of overalls and went to the barn to have an argument with Papa. She took apples for Old Bess and Jack.

"Women don't wear overalls," said Caleb, running along behind her like one of Sarah's chickens.

"This woman does," said Sarah crisply.

Papa stood by the fence.

"I want to learn how to ride a horse," Sarah told him. "And then I want to learn how to drive the wagon. By myself."

Jack leaned over and nipped at Sarah's overalls. She fed him an apple. Caleb and I stood behind Sarah.

"I can ride a horse, I know." said Sarah. "I rode once when I was twelve. I will ride Jack." Jack was Sarah's favorite.

Papa shook his head. "Not Jack," he said. "Jack is sly."

"I am sly, too," said Sarah stubbornly.

Papa smiled. "Ayuh," he said, nodding. "But not Jack."

"Yes, Jack!" Sarah's voice was very loud.

"I can teach you how to drive a wagon. I have already taught you how to plow."

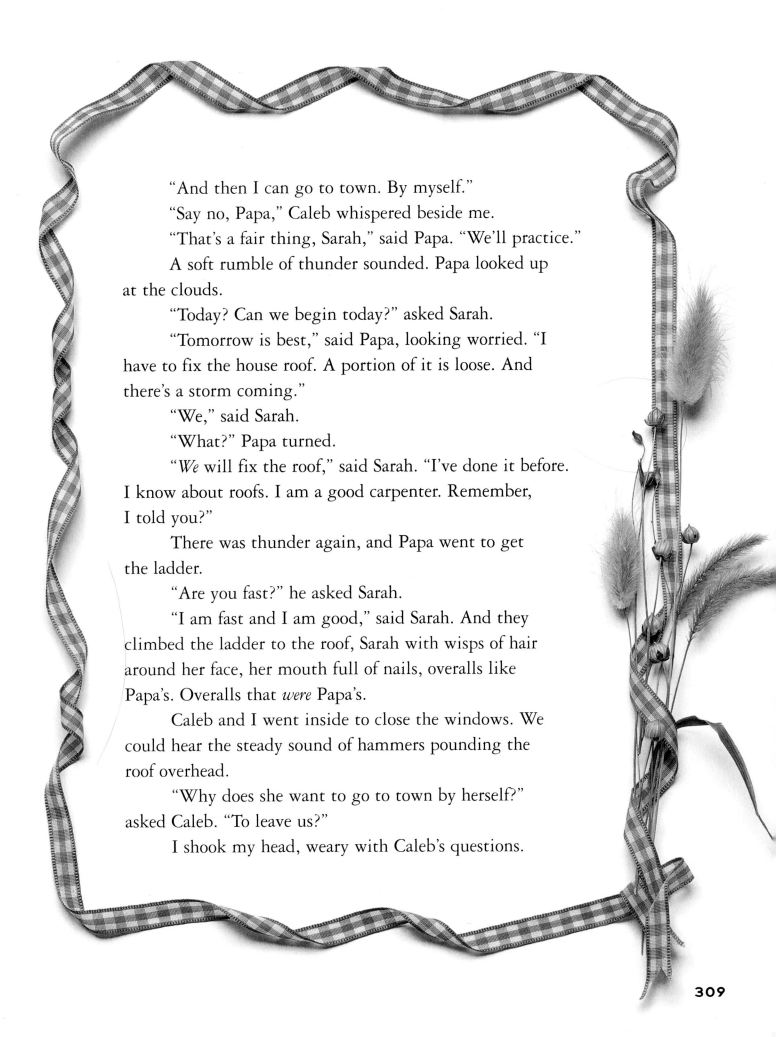

"And then I can go to town. By myself."

"Say no, Papa," Caleb whispered beside me.

"That's a fair thing, Sarah," said Papa. "We'll practice."

A soft rumble of thunder sounded. Papa looked up at the clouds.

"Today? Can we begin today?" asked Sarah.

"Tomorrow is best," said Papa, looking worried. "I have to fix the house roof. A portion of it is loose. And there's a storm coming."

"We," said Sarah.

"What?" Papa turned.

"*We* will fix the roof," said Sarah. "I've done it before. I know about roofs. I am a good carpenter. Remember, I told you?"

There was thunder again, and Papa went to get the ladder.

"Are you fast?" he asked Sarah.

"I am fast and I am good," said Sarah. And they climbed the ladder to the roof, Sarah with wisps of hair around her face, her mouth full of nails, overalls like Papa's. Overalls that *were* Papa's.

Caleb and I went inside to close the windows. We could hear the steady sound of hammers pounding the roof overhead.

"Why does she want to go to town by herself?" asked Caleb. "To leave us?"

I shook my head, weary with Caleb's questions.

Tears gathered at the corners of my eyes. But there was no time to cry, for suddenly Papa called out.

"Caleb! Anna!"

We ran outside and saw a huge cloud, horribly black, moving toward us over the north fields. Papa slid down the roof, helping Sarah after him.

"A squall!" he yelled to us. He held up his arms and Sarah jumped off the porch roof.

"Get the horses inside," he ordered Caleb. "Get the sheep, Anna. And the cows. The barn is safest."

The grasses flattened. There was a hiss of wind, a sudden pungent smell. Our faces looked yellow in the strange light. Caleb and I jumped over the fence and found the animals huddled by the barn. I counted the sheep to make sure they were all there, and herded them into a large stall. A few raindrops came, gentle at first, then stronger and louder, so that Caleb and I covered our ears and stared at each other without speaking. Caleb looked frightened and I tried to smile at him. Sarah carried a sack into the barn, her hair wet and streaming down her neck, Papa came behind, Lottie and Nick with him, their ears flat against their heads.

"Wait!" cried Sarah. "My chickens!"

"No, Sarah!" Papa called after her. But Sarah had already run from the barn into a sheet of rain. My father followed her. The sheep nosed open their stall door and milled around the barn, bleating. Nick crept under my arm, and a lamb, Mattie with the black face, stood close to me, trembling. There was a soft paw on my lap, then a gray body. Seal. And then, as the thunder pounded and the wind rose and there was the terrible crackling of lightning close by, Sarah and Papa stood in the barn doorway, wet to the skin. Papa carried Sarah's chickens. Sarah came with an armful of summer roses.

Sarah's chickens were not afraid, and they settled like small red bundles in the hay. Papa closed the door at last, shutting out some of the sounds of the storm. The barn was eerie and half lighted, like dusk without a lantern. Papa spread blankets around our shoulders and Sarah unpacked a bag of cheese and bread and jam. At the very bottom of the bag were Sarah's shells.

Caleb got up and went over to the small barn window.

"What color is the sea when it storms?" he asked Sarah.

"Blue," said Sarah, brushing her wet hair back with her fingers. "And gray and green."

Caleb nodded and smiled.

"Look," he said to her. "Look what is missing from your drawing."

Sarah went to stand between Caleb and Papa by the window. She looked a long time without speaking. Finally, she touched Papa's shoulder.

"We have squalls in Maine, too," she said. "Just like this. It will be all right, Jacob."

Papa said nothing. But he put his arm around her, and leaned over to rest his chin in her hair. I closed my eyes, suddenly remembering Mama and Papa standing that way, Mama smaller than Sarah, her hair fair against Papa's shoulder. When I opened my eyes again, it was Sarah standing there. Caleb looked at me and smiled and smiled until he could smile no more.

We slept in the hay all night, waking when the wind was wild, sleeping again when it was quiet. And at dawn there was the sudden sound of hail, like stones tossed against the barn. We stared out the window, watching the ice marbles bounce on the ground. And when it was over we opened the barn door and walked out into the early-morning light. The hail crunched and melted beneath our feet. It was white and gleaming for as far as we looked, like sun on glass. Like the sea.

Chapter 9

It was very quiet. The dogs leaned down to eat the hailstones. Seal stepped around them and leaped up on the fence to groom herself. A tree had blown over near the cow pond. And the wild roses were scattered on the ground, as if a wedding had come and gone there. "I'm glad I saved an armful" was all that Sarah said.

Only one field was badly damaged, and Sarah and Papa hitched up the horses and plowed and replanted during the next two days. The roof had held.

"I told you I know about roofs," Sarah told Papa, making him smile.

Papa kept his promise to Sarah. When the work was done, he took her out into the fields, Papa riding Jack who was sly, and Sarah riding Old Bess. Sarah was quick to learn.

"Too quick," Caleb complained to me as we watched from the fence. He thought a moment. "Maybe she'll fall off and have to stay here. Why?" he asked, turning to me. "Why does she have to go away alone?"

"Hush up, Caleb," I said crossly. "Hush up."

"I could get sick and make her stay here," said Caleb.

"No."

"We could tie her up."

"No."

And Caleb began to cry, and I took him inside the barn where we could both cry.

Papa and Sarah came to hitch the horses to the wagon, so Sarah could practice driving. Papa didn't see Caleb's tears, and he sent him with an ax to begin chopping up the tree by the pond for firewood. I stood and watched Sarah, the reins in her hands, Papa next to her in the wagon. I could see Caleb standing by the pond, one hand shading his eyes, watching, too. I went into the safe darkness of the barn then, Sarah's chickens scuttling along behind me.

"Why?" I asked out loud, echoing Caleb's question.

The chickens watched me, their eyes small and bright.

The next morning Sarah got up early and put on her blue dress. She took apples to the barn. She loaded a bundle of hay on the wagon for Old Bess and Jack. She put on her yellow bonnet.

"Remember Jack," said Papa. "A strong hand."

"Yes, Jacob."

"Best to be home before dark," said Papa. "Driving a wagon is hard if there's no full moon."

"Yes, Jacob."

Sarah kissed us all, even my father, who looked surprised.

"Take care of Seal," she said to Caleb and me. And with a whisper to Old Bess and a stern word to Jack, Sarah climbed up in the wagon and drove away.

"Very good," murmured Papa as he watched. And after a while he turned and went out into the fields.

Caleb and I watched Sarah from the porch. Caleb took my hand, and the dogs lay down beside us. It was sunny, and I remembered another time when a wagon had taken Mama away. It had been a day just like this day. And Mama had never come back.

Seal jumped up to the porch, her feet making a small thump. Caleb leaned down and picked her up and walked inside. I took the broom and slowly swept the porch. Then I watered Sarah's plants. Caleb cleaned out the wood stove and carried the ashes to the barn, spilling them so that I had to sweep the porch again.

"I *am* loud and pesky," Caleb cried suddenly. "You said so! And she has gone to buy a train ticket to go away!"

"No, Caleb. She would tell us."

"The house is too small," said Caleb. "That's what it is."

"The house is not too small," I said.

I looked at Sarah's drawing of the fields pinned up on the wall next to the window.

"What is missing?" I asked Caleb. "You said you knew what was missing."

"Colors," said Caleb wearily. "The colors of the sea."

Outside, clouds moved into the sky and went away again. We took lunch to Papa, cheese and bread and lemonade. Caleb nudged me.

"Ask him. Ask Papa."

"What has Sarah gone to do?" I asked.

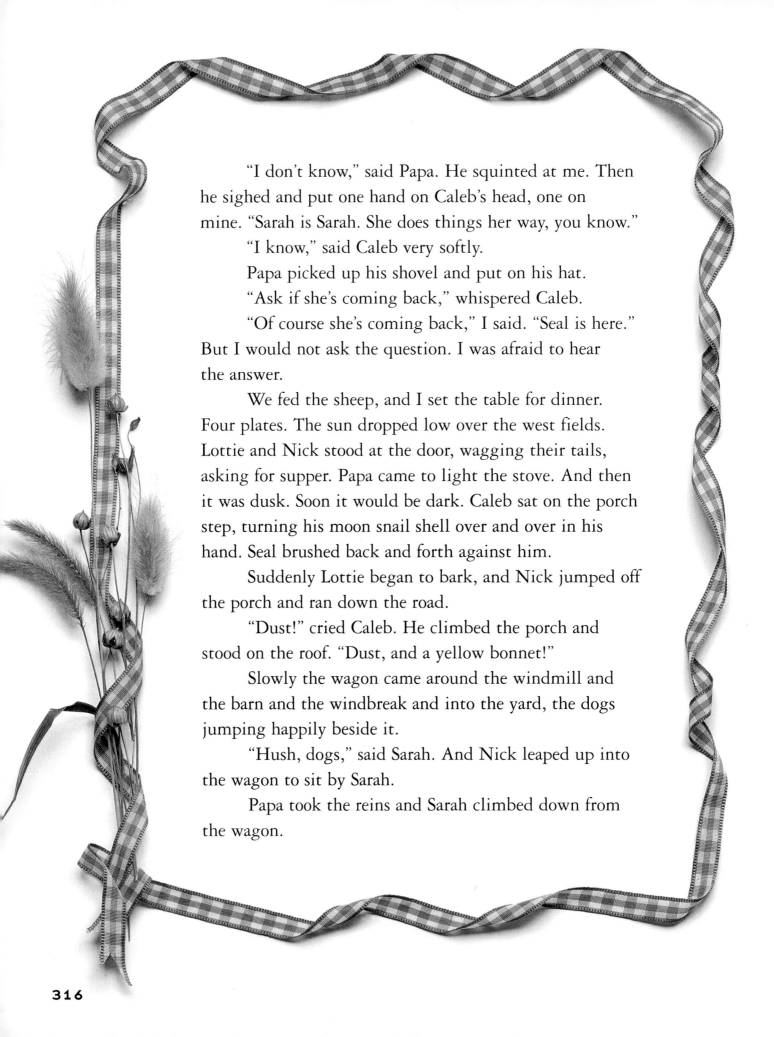

"I don't know," said Papa. He squinted at me. Then he sighed and put one hand on Caleb's head, one on mine. "Sarah is Sarah. She does things her way, you know."

"I know," said Caleb very softly.

Papa picked up his shovel and put on his hat.

"Ask if she's coming back," whispered Caleb.

"Of course she's coming back," I said. "Seal is here." But I would not ask the question. I was afraid to hear the answer.

We fed the sheep, and I set the table for dinner. Four plates. The sun dropped low over the west fields. Lottie and Nick stood at the door, wagging their tails, asking for supper. Papa came to light the stove. And then it was dusk. Soon it would be dark. Caleb sat on the porch step, turning his moon snail shell over and over in his hand. Seal brushed back and forth against him.

Suddenly Lottie began to bark, and Nick jumped off the porch and ran down the road.

"Dust!" cried Caleb. He climbed the porch and stood on the roof. "Dust, and a yellow bonnet!"

Slowly the wagon came around the windmill and the barn and the windbreak and into the yard, the dogs jumping happily beside it.

"Hush, dogs," said Sarah. And Nick leaped up into the wagon to sit by Sarah.

Papa took the reins and Sarah climbed down from the wagon.

Caleb burst into tears.

"Seal was very worried!" he cried.

Sarah put her arms around him, and he wailed into her dress. "And the house is too small, we thought! And I am loud and pesky!"

Sarah looked at Papa and me over Caleb's head.

"We thought you might be thinking of leaving us," I told her. "Because you miss the sea."

Sarah smiled.

"No," she said. "I will always miss my old home, but the truth of it is I would miss you more."

Papa smiled at Sarah, then he bent quickly to unhitch the horses from the wagon. He led them to the barn for water.

Sarah handed me a package.

"For Anna," she said. "And Caleb. For all of us."

The package was small, wrapped in brown paper with a rubber band around it. Very carefully I unwrapped it, Caleb peering closely. Inside were three colored pencils.

"Blue," said Caleb slowly, "and gray. And green."

Sarah nodded.

Suddenly Caleb grinned.

"Papa," he called. "Papa, come quickly! Sarah has brought the sea!"

We eat our night meal by candlelight, the four of us. Sarah has brought candles from town. And nasturtium seeds for her garden, and a book of songs to teach us. It is late, and Caleb is nearly sleeping by his plate and Sarah is smiling at my father. Soon there will be a wedding. Papa says that when the preacher asks if he will have Sarah for his wife, he will answer, "Ayuh."

Autumn will come, then winter, cold with a wind that blows like the wind off the sea in Maine. There will be nests of curls to look for, and dried flowers all winter long. When there are storms, Papa will stretch a rope from the door to the barn so we will not be lost when we feed the sheep and the cows and Jack and Old Bess. And Sarah's chickens, if they aren't living in the house. There will be Sarah's sea, blue and gray and green, hanging on the wall. And songs, old ones and new. And Seal with yellow eyes. And there will be Sarah, plain and tall.

Until I Saw the Sea

by Lilian Moore

Until I saw the sea
I did not know
that wind
could wrinkle water so.

I never knew
that sun
could splinter a whole sea of blue.

Nor
did I know before,
a sea breathes in and out
upon a shore.

High Cliff, Coast of Maine by Winslow Homer. National Museum of American Art

Summer Grass

by Carl Sandburg

Summer grass aches and whispers.

It wants something; it calls and sings; it pours
out wishes to the overhead stars.

The rain hears; the rain answers; the rain is slow
coming; the rain wets the face of the grass.

Wheat by Thomas Hart Benton. National Museum of American Art

Think About Reading

Answer the questions in the story map.

SETTING
1. Where does the story take place?

CHARACTERS
2. Who are the main characters in the story?

BEGINNING
3. Why is Sarah coming to visit Anna and Caleb's family?

MIDDLE
4. How do Anna and Caleb feel about Sarah's visit?

5. How can you tell that Sarah misses her home in Maine?

6. Why don't Caleb and Anna want Sarah to drive the wagon?

ENDING
7. What is in the package Sarah brings from town?

8. By the end of the story, how does Sarah feel about staying on the prairie?

Write a Journal Entry

Write a journal entry that Sarah might have written during her visit with Anna and Caleb's family. Choose one of the events described in the story. Tell what happens from Sarah's point of view, and describe how she feels about what happened. Be sure to use colorful adjectives and vivid verbs in the journal entry.

Literature Circle

The poems "Until I Saw the Sea" and "Summer Grass" may remind you of places in *Sarah, Plain and Tall*. Discuss how the poet's description of the sea is different from the ocean that Sarah describes. Tell how is it similar. Then compare the place described in "Summer Grass" with the prairie in the story. Record your ideas on a Venn diagram.

AUTHOR
Patricia MacLachlan

Patricia MacLachlan loves books—reading them and writing them. She says, "My greatest fear is being stuck somewhere without a book." Ms. MacLachlan's stories are often based on real events or people, but she always colors them with her imagination. She says, "I tend to write as if I were looking through a movie camera." Family stories about an ancestor who moved from Maine to the prairies inspired her to write her Newbery award winner, *Sarah, Plain and Tall*.

MORE BOOKS BY
Patricia MacLachlan

- *Skylark*
- *Journey*
- *Arthur, for the Very First Time*

How to Create a
Multimedia Presentation

Bring your team's journey to life with words and pictures.

If you rocketed into space, how could you share the excitement of the journey? One way is through a multimedia presentation. A multimedia presentation uses words, pictures, sound effects, and music to make an experience come alive. The idea for a presentation can start with a script. Then pictures, sound effects, lighting, models, and anything else can be added.

TAKE A TRIP THAT'S OUT OF THIS WORLD.

Tour the Solar System!
A Multimedia Presentation
- Light Show
- Sound Effects
- Dramatic Narration

Wednesday at 1:30 Room 4B

Explore Your Options

Your multimedia presentation will tell about an exciting place. So, first your team needs to choose a location. Pick a place that you want to learn more about. It can be as far away as Mars or as near as a location you can visit. Once you've chosen the place, it's time to gather facts and pictures for your show. Have each team member check a different source. Use atlases, travel books, magazines, encyclopedias, and newspapers. Team members can share their findings with the group.

TOOLS

- paper and pencil
- glue or tape
- colored markers
- magazine and newspaper pictures
- reference books and travel magazines
- tape recorder (optional)

Tips
- Use several different kinds of pictures and props in your show, such as original drawings, photographs, maps, and a globe.
- If you want to use a picture or map from a reference book, someone in the group can make a drawing or trace the original.
- If your pictures are small, mount them onto a posterboard. This will help them stand out.

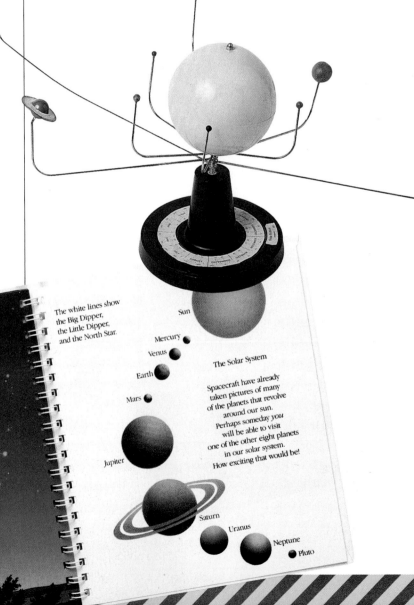

The white lines show the Big Dipper, the Little Dipper, and the North Star.

The Solar System

Sun

Mercury

Venus

Earth

Mars

Jupiter

Saturn

Uranus

Neptune

Pluto

Spacecraft have already taken pictures of many of the planets that revolve around our sun. Perhaps someday *you* will be able to visit one of the other eight planets in our solar system. How exciting that would be!

2   **Organize Your Material**

Gather the materials you'll need for your show. Here are some things you may want to include.

- Captions: Write captions under all the pictures. Decide as a group what the captions will say.

- A Script: If you want, write a script and include stage directions.

- Music and Sound Effects: If you can borrow a tape recorder, some members of your team can record music or sound effects.

- A Model: Create a model to use in your presentation.

How Am I Doing?

Before you put your presentation together, take a few minutes to answer these questions with your group.

- Did we pick exciting, colorful pictures?

- Have we found interesting facts to go with our pictures?

- Did we decide how to organize our presentation?

- Do we need a script to go with our presentation?

Put It All Together

As a team, decide how to present your show. Here are some ideas. Tape your pictures together on a long sheet of paper. Two team members can unroll the paper while another team member reads the captions or the script. Mount several pictures onto pieces of posterboard. Narrate your trip while playing your music or a sound effects tape, if you made one. If you want a spotlight, try using a flashlight and dimming the lights. Think of different ways to perform your show, and then choose one.

Our solar system is part of an enormous group of stars called a galaxy.

The closer a planet is to the Sun, the shorter the year. Mercury is the closest planet to the Sun and has a year that is 88 Earth-days long.

The Moon is much smaller and lighter than the Earth.

4 Present Your Multimedia Show

Before you perform your show in front of the class, you may want to rehearse it a few times. Every team member should take part in the performance. While you are rehearsing, you may think of other things to add to your performance. Remember to discuss any changes with the rest of the team. When it's time to perform, speak up so your classmates will hear you. At the end of your performance, don't forget to have your team take a bow.

If You Are Using a Computer ...

Create your multimedia presentation on the computer. Choose photographs and clip art to show each stage of your team's journey. Use the Record Tools to narrate your presentation. Have fun adding music and sound effects. Then present your journey on the computer, using the Slide Show Tools.

The sun is 900,000 miles across and the temperature at its center is 15 million degrees centigrade.

CONGRATULATIONS

You and your classmates are members of a discovery team. Practice your teamwork skills.

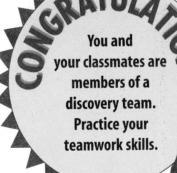

Dr. Mae Jemison
Astronaut ▶

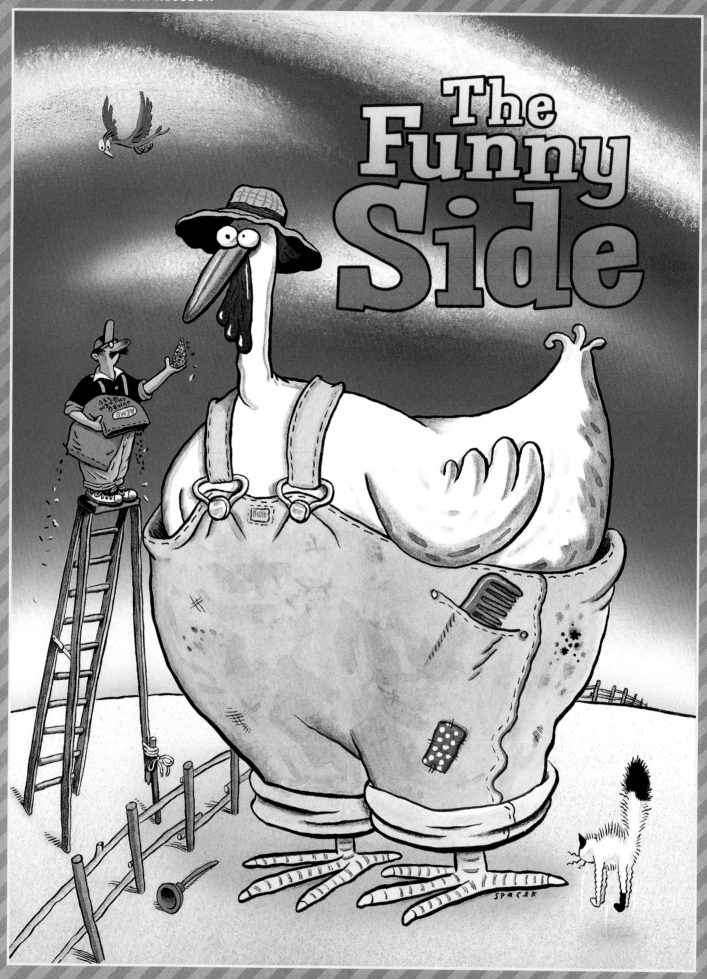

The Funny Side

THEME

Sometimes humor is the best way to communicate.

UNIT 4

Welcome to

LITERACY PLACE

Cartoonist's Studio

**Sometimes humor
is the best way
to communicate.**

FRACTURED
FAIRY TALE

AWARD
WINNER

Yours Truly, Goldilocks

by ALMA FLOR ADA

illustrated by LESLIE TRYON

Brick House
Woodsy Woods
April 7

Goldilocks McGregor
McGregor's Farm
Veggie Lane

Dear Goldilocks,

Thank you, thank you, thank you! The three of us had a great time at your birthday party.

It was a wonderful, wonderful, wonderful party. That is, all three of us think it was wonderful.

As you know, we have had a terrible time building our houses. Now that we are sure that no wolf can blow down our new house, no matter how hard he huffs and puffs, we would like to finally have a house warming party on April twenty-ninth. We would be very happy if you were our special guest. We are also sending invitations to Baby Bear, Little Red Riding Hood, and Peter Rabbit. We look forward to a wonderful day.

Love, love, love, your three friends,

Pig One, Pig Two, and Pig Three

Cottage in the Woods
Hidden Forest
April 9

Little Red Riding Hood
Cardinal Cottage
Riding Lane

Dearest Granddaughter,

You have such a wonderful imagination! Just to think . . .
a birthday party with bears, rabbits, and pigs. Well, well,
I imagine you and Goldilocks must have had fun with your
stuffed animals.

Goldilocks sounds like a very nice girl. I have known the
McGregor family for a long time. Years ago when I lived on
Riding Lane, I used to buy all my vegetables from them.
Mr. McGregor is a stern man but a wonderful gardener.

Give a kiss to your mother for me. I hope you can come to
see me again soon. I'll be here all day on the twelfth. Why
not then? But you must keep your promise to stay on the
trail this time. That encounter with the wolf was certainly
not imaginary.

Love,

Grandma

Majestic Tower
Hidden Lane
Wooden Heights
April 9

Wolfy Lupus
Wolf Lane
Oakshire

Dear Cousin Wolfy,

After my humiliation at their hands, my continued surveillance of the porcine trio and their friends has finally proven useful.

I have been led to believe that there will be a gathering at their house on the twenty-ninth of April for a house warming party. This means that a delicious bunch of morsels—that is, guests—will be attending and I have a stupendous plan to ensure that not all of them will return home.

A deep trench on Royal Road after the fork will force them to take Forest Trail. It will not be difficult for us to ambush them there.

After their party at that stubborn brick house, we will show them a true party in my majestic tower. What do you think?

Why don't you come to stay on the twenty-seventh? That will give us ample time for the necessary preparations.

Affectionately,

Fer O'Cious

Goldilocks McGregor

McGregor's Farm

Veggie Lane

Dearest Goldilocks,

Have you received an invitation from the three Pigs for their house warming party? After all the fun we had at your birthday it will be wonderful to all get together again. You certainly have interesting friends.

I wrote a long letter to my grandmother telling her all about your birthday party, and she doesn't believe it's true that Peter Rabbit, Baby Bear, and the three Pigs were there.

When I visit her the day after tomorrow I will take the invitation to the house warming party and tell her all about it in person, and she will see it is true.

Do you want to go together to the Pigs' party? My mother says it is okay if you want to come the day before and spend the night. And she will make us some of her special gingerbread cookies.

Your good friend,

LITTLE RED RIDING HOOD

McGregor's Farm
Veggie Lane
April 12

Little Red Riding Hood
Cardinal Cottage
Riding Lane

Dear Little Red Riding Hood,

Yes, I did receive the invitation and I would love to spend the night at your house and go together to the house warming party. Do you have any idea what one does at a house warming party? I know the Pigs have been trying to have one for a long time. Do you think we bring blankets to warm the house?

Baby Bear would like for us to go play hide-and-seek a week from Sunday. His cousins Teddy and Osito are visiting. Do you want to go? I love houses in the forest, don't you?

Be careful on your visit to your grandmother. My father says there definitely still are wolves around.

I have to write to the Pigs and Baby Bear, and I still need to water three rows of vegetables, so I must go now.

Your busy friend,

Goldilocks

Wolf Lane
Oakshire
April 13

Fer O'Cious
Majestic Tower
Hidden Lane
Wooden Heights

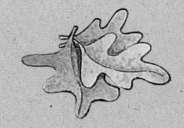

Dear Cousin Fer,

You are definitely right about the forthcoming event on April twenty-ninth. Yesterday, as I was trailing that appetizing-looking creature in red, she seemed to have gotten scared somehow. As she ran into her grandmother's house, she dropped an invitation on the path. Sure enough, those pigs of yours are inviting everyone to a house warming party. I am enclosing the foolish card for your perusal.

I found any mention to warming in their house somewhat distasteful, their description of their abode pretentious, and their reference to us rather offensive.

There is no question that I will join you in your efforts. I like your plan and I will be there on the twenty-seventh with ready paws and sharpened teeth!

Your affectionate cousin,

Wolfy

McGregor's Farm
Veggie Lane
April 13

Baby Bear
Bear House in the Woods
Hidden Meadow

Dear Baby Bear,

Your letter was very nice. I have always loved getting letters. Although right now I am getting so many, I can't find enough time to answer back. And my father is always after me to go water the vegetables.

I don't mind too much watering the lettuces and the carrots. They grow close to the well and I don't have to carry the watering can that far. But the spinach and the peas are much farther away and that full can gets heavy. I can't understand how anyone likes to eat that green stuff anyway.

I would love to go to your house to play hide-and-seek a week from Sunday and meet your cousins Teddy and Osito. I have already asked Little Red Riding Hood to come also.

Your very good and busy friend,

Goldilocks

McGregor's Farm

Veggie Lane

April 15

Pig One, Pig Two, and Pig Three

Brick House

Woodsy Woods

Dear Pig One, Pig Two, and Pig Three,

A house warming party sounds like a terrific idea! I love parties, but I have never been to a house warming one yet. How do we warm the house? Do you want us to bring blankets?

Little Bear would like to play hide-and-seek. Would you like to come to his house a week from today? His cousins Teddy and Osito will be there also.

Have you seen or heard from Peter Rabbit? I haven't heard anything from him, except that the one carrot I leave each night outside the hedge is always gone the next morning. Do you know if he is alright? Things are a lot quieter in my house since my father doesn't complain anymore about stolen vegetables, but I miss Peter! If you come to the Bears' house, please bring him along!

Your friend,

Goldilocks

347

Goldilocks McGregor

McGregor's Farm

Veggie Lane

Dear Goldilocks,

My friends the Pigs came by to see me yesterday, after you all played hide-and-seek at the Bears'. Sorry I couldn't be there.

They told me you were worried about me and I am sorry I have not written before. You see, I have been in bed now for almost three weeks with measles.

Your carrots have been wonderful. Flopsy, Mopsy, and Cotton-tail have been picking them up every morning at dawn. They did not get measles this time because they all had it last year. My mother has been feeding us carrot soup, carrot salad, and carrot cake. I love carrots! She has also been feeding me gallons of chamomile tea. You know my mother loves chamomile tea!

Now that the measles are all gone I will be able to go to the Pigs' party Sunday. See you there!

Thanks again for the carrots!

Your very dearest friend,

Peter Rabbit

P.S. The Pigs convinced my mother to allow Flopsy, Mopsy, and Cotton-tail to come to their party. They are dying to meet you!

Rabbit's Burrow

Hollow Oak

May 1

Mrs. Mother Bear

Bear House in the Woods

Hidden Meadow

Dear Mrs. Bear,

    I wanted my mother to help me write you a letter, but she says that if I can get into trouble all by myself, I should be able to write this letter all by myself.

    The first thing I want to say to you is THANK YOU VERY MUCH! Thank you for saving me from those two terrible wolves.

    As you know, it is usually not very easy for a wolf to catch a rabbit. And I could race those two and win easily anytime. But I was talking to Goldilocks about the party and didn't even see them coming. Before I knew it I was inside that ugly sack. I thought it was the end of all of us.

    They tell me you were terrific, and I wish I could have helped you instead of being inside that smelly sack. Thank you again for saving my life.

Gratefully yours,

Peter Rabbit

P.S. Although my mother wanted me to write the letter she is very thankful too. And it wouldn't surprise me at all if she planning something special to thank you.

Speedy Raccoon, Furrier
Forest Drive
Hidden Forest

Dear Mr. Raccoon:

My cousin Mr. Wolfy Lupus and I are in great need of your services again. Both of us have been the unfortunate victims at the paws of an angry mother bear.

Since we are both bedridden, would you be able to make a house call to take the necessary measurements?

I will be needing a new tail. I trust you will be able to provide one of an elegant deep gray color to match the rest of my beautiful fur. My cousin will require some large patches on the back as well as a supplementary ear.

To imagine that a bear would go to such lengths to defend a couple of little girls and some silly rabbits! We certainly did not mean to bother her bear cub at all.

We look forward to hearing from you at your earliest convenience since we would like to change our sorrowful state.

Sincerely,

Fer O'Cious

McGregor's Farm

Veggie Lane

May 1

Pig One, Pig Two, and Pig Three

Brick House

Woodsy Woods

Dear Pig One, Pig Two, and Pig Three,

Your house warming party was truly spectacular. I didn't know what a house warming party was all about before it started. It was great to realize that a house is warmed with friends, fun, and laughter.

As I am sure you know by now, several of us had a horrific experience on our way home after the party. It was very scary!

Little Red Riding Hood and I have been thinking we should all get together to plan how to thank Mother Bear for saving our lives and how to make sure those ugly wolves cannot hurt us.

Please begin thinking of wonderful ideas. When we decide a time and place to meet, we will let you know.

Enjoy your brick house!

Yours Truly,

Goldilocks

from

KISS A FROG!

by Rick & Ann Walton   illustrated by Rob Dunlavey

Q **When were clocks invented?**
A: Once upon a time.

Q **Why was Little Red Riding Hood suspicious when she saw the wolf's big nose?**
A: Because she knew that something smelled.

Q **What do you get when you cross Little Red Riding Hood with a bird?**
A: Robin Hood.

Q **What kind of locks won't keep people out of your house?**
A: Goldi-locks.

Q **Why didn't the three bears eat their porridge?**
A: Because they didn't have any mush-room.

Q **Why did the Baby Bear's chair break when Goldilocks sat on it?**
A: Because it couldn't bear her weight.

Q **What did the first little pig say when the Big Bad Wolf blew down his house?**
A: "That's the last straw!"

355

Think About Reading

Write your answers.

1. Who is going to the Three Little Pigs' house on April twenty-ninth? Why?

2. What happened to Fer O'Cious and Wolfy Lupus when they tried to capture Peter Rabbit after the Pigs' party?

3. How is *Yours Truly, Goldilocks* different from most fairy tales that you have read?

4. Why do you think Alma Flor Ada tells the story through letters between several different characters?

5. Why do you think author Alma Flor Ada and joke writers Rick and Ann Walton use fairy tale characters in their writing?

Write a Home Page Biography

Goldilocks is a celebrity, and she is planning to create an Internet web site about herself. Write a short biography of Goldilocks that will appear on her home page. Describe what she looks like and tell about her interests and hobbies. Include some important events in her life. Be sure to include the titles of any books or media in which she has starred.

Literature Circle

Yours Truly, Goldilocks is a fractured fairy tale. Discuss the elements that make it "fractured." Then think of other fractured fairy tales that you have read. Talk about how these special versions are similar to or different from the original stories. How are the characters changed? How is humor used in the writing and the illustrations? Record you ideas on a Venn diagram.

AUTHOR
Alma Flor Ada

As a girl growing up in Cuba, Alma Flor Ada loved stories of all kinds. In fact, she had many imaginary conversations with her favorite storybook characters. Years later Ms. Ada discovered letters from her grandfather to her grandmother and found that letters can tell a story. When she decided to write about much-loved fairy tale characters, she told their stories through letters.

MORE BOOKS BY
Alma Flor Ada

- *Dear Peter Rabbit*
- *The Gold Coin*
- *My Name is María Isabel*
- *Gathering the Sun: An Alphabet in Spanish and English*

from
The Hoboken Chicken Emergency

A Television Script
by Arthur Alsberg and Don Nelson
illustrated by Rick Brown

Based on the novel by
Daniel Manus Pinkwater

INTERIOR—BOBOWICZ LIVING ROOM—NIGHT

[POPPA snaps off the TV set as MOMMA enters, followed by
ARTHUR. He reaches into his pocket and pulls out twenty dollars,
which he hands to ARTHUR.]

POPPA

Arthur, that's for tomorrow morning. To pick
up a turkey at O'Brien's.

MOMMA

Carl . . . How can I fit a turkey in the ice box
for two weeks?

POPPA

I'm not taking any chances, and no mistakes
like last year, Arthur.

ARTHUR

Why couldn't we have something else?
Maybe meatloaf.

POPPA

In America, on Thanksgiving, it's turkey.
Every family in the neighborhood will want a
turkey—the Antonellis, the Glucksterns, the
Lings, [indicating himself] . . . and the
Bobowiczs. It's an American tradition.

ARTHUR

I'd rather have pizza.

POPPA

[firmly] When your grandparents were young and
still in Poland, if someone said "eat turkey" they'd
have to eat turkey. Here in America we have a
choice. [firmly] And the choice is turkey!

EXTERIOR—PARK AND PLAYGROUND—MORNING

[ARTHUR is trudging through the park where he sees three boys playing on
the swing, some distance from him.]

ARTHUR

[calling] Hey George! Hi, Benny!

[He waves, but the three boys continue swinging and don't even look over at
ARTHUR. ARTHUR waits a moment . . . maybe they didn't hear him.]

ARTHUR

[calling again] Mario! Want to come to the butcher
with me?

MARIO

[calling] I can't!

[The boys continue swinging, and ARTHUR turns and walks along the fence
and out of the park.]

EXTERIOR—HOBOKEN STREET—MORNING

[ARTHUR stands in front of O'Brien's Meat Market. He tries the door, but it
is locked. He peers through the window, but no one is inside. There is a sign
in the window of the door—CLOSED BECAUSE OF A DEATH IN THE FAMILY.]

[He finally turns away, wondering what to do. Suddenly some large feathers come floating down from above. They are accompanied by a clucking sound coming from off stage. ARTHUR looks around. The clucking is not like any clucking he has ever heard before. It's deeper and louder. ARTHUR looks up toward an apartment above the meat market.]

ANOTHER ANGLE

[The second story window of the apartment. PROFESSOR MAZZOCCHI, a wild-eyed, slightly frazzled older man is leaning out the window, backwards, as if preventing something from jumping out. He notices ARTHUR in the street below.]

PROFESSOR

[calling down] Nothing to fear. Everything's under control.

[The PROFESSOR then directs his attention into the room.]

PROFESSOR

[continuing] Back! Back, Number 73!

ANGLE ON ARTHUR

[He looks up at the PROFESSOR.]

ARTHUR

Are you the butcher?

ANGLE ON PROFESSOR

PROFESSOR

[indignantly] Butcher? Me? Doctor Frankenstein was a butcher! I am a scientist!

ANGLE ON ARTHUR

ARTHUR

I came to buy our Thanksgiving turkey, but they're closed.

ANGLE ON PROFESSOR

PROFESSOR

[his eyes widen] Money? You have some money?
Press the button next to the name "Professor Mazzocchi."

[The PROFESSOR is distracted for a moment as he pushes something back into the room with his foot. Then he turns back toward ARTHUR.]

PROFESSOR

[continuing; calling down] But hurry! They're going fast!

ANGLE ON ARTHUR

[ARTHUR considers the offer, then hurries over to the entrance to the apartment building. He looks at the card near the doorway. It reads: Professor Mazzocchi—Inventor of the chicken system—By appointment. ARTHUR presses the button. In a moment the buzzer sounds to release the door. ARTHUR pushes it and enters the building.]

INTERIOR—APARTMENT LOBBY—DAY

[ARTHUR starts up the stairs but is frozen by the sound of PROFESSOR MAZZOCCHI's voice.]

PROFESSOR (off stage)

[shouting] You will not get me evicted! My brother owns this building! I'm a scientist! If you people don't stop bothering me, I'll let the rooster loose again!

ARTHUR

[puzzled, calls] But you told me to come in.

PROFESSOR (off stage)

[realizes] Oh, it's you, my boy. Come right up. What are you waiting for?

INTERIOR HALL—TOP OF THE STAIRS—DAY

[The PROFESSOR, wearing an old bathrobe with dragons embroidered on it, greets ARTHUR as he comes up.]

PROFESSOR

The only people who ever come up here are neighbors to complain about my chickens. They don't want me to keep them.

ARTHUR

You keep chickens in your apartment?

PROFESSOR

A farm would be better, but my brother lets me stay here without paying any rent. Also, they are special chickens. I prefer to keep them under lock and key.

ARTHUR

I was supposed to get a turkey.

PROFESSOR

Do you have a large family?

ARTHUR

No, sir.

PROFESSOR

But your family has friends . . .

ARTHUR

Yes, sir. We live in a big apartment building.

PROFESSOR

Splendid! Perfect for number 73—my super chicken.

ARTHUR

My father wants a turkey.

PROFESSOR

In the spirit of Thanksgiving wouldn't your father rather feed his family and all his friends and neighbors for only . . . [stops] How much money have you got?

ARTHUR

Twenty dollars.

[ARTHUR takes the twenty dollar bill out of his pocket.]

PROFESSOR

[continuing] Just enough. Wait here.

[The PROFESSOR opens the door just enough to slide through it and closes it, leaving ARTHUR standing outside. ARTHUR stands patiently for a moment, then stirs uneasily as he hears the same loud, low clucking sound he'd heard before. Suddenly the door swings open and the PROFESSOR comes out of the apartment leading a huge chicken, taller than he is, on a leash. The CHICKEN has a look of wide-eyed innocence about her.]

PROFESSOR

The best poultry bargain on earth! One medium-sized super chicken—eight cents a pound. Here's Number 73, your two hundred and sixty-six pound super chicken.

ARTHUR

But I was supposed to get a turkey.

PROFESSOR

When I'm offering you a super chicken? Just look at this fine specimen. Good for roasting, frying, and barbecuing.

[At the sound of this the CHICKEN begins to tremble all over.]

ARTHUR

But what about my father?

PROFESSOR

Well, take it or leave it. I can always sell her to a Kiwanis picnic or the Coast Guard mess.

[ARTHUR hesitates. The CHICKEN seems to moan.]

PROFESSOR

She'll be mighty good eating.

[The CHICKEN looks over toward ARTHUR, almost pleading.]

ARTHUR

Well . . .

PROFESSOR

[quickly] A deal!

[He snaps the twenty dollars from ARTHUR's fingers and hands him
the leash.]

PROFESSOR

And I'll throw in the collar and leash.

[The PROFESSOR opens the door of his apartment and disappears.
ARTHUR stands there for a moment then looks up at the CHICKEN. The
CHICKEN shifts from foot to foot looking rather nervous. ARTHUR,
realizing his mistake, pounds on the apartment door.]

PROFESSOR (off stage)

[shouts] No refunds!

ARTHUR

Don't you have anything smaller?

PROFESSOR (off stage)

No refunds!

[ARTHUR shakes his head and looks up at the CHICKEN.]

ARTHUR

I hope Poppa likes bargains.

[He starts to lead the CHICKEN away.]

EXTERIOR—PARK AND PLAYGROUND—MORNING

[ARTHUR leads the CHICKEN along the walk as he searches the park for the three boys he had seen earlier. But the swings are empty, and no one is in sight. With a little shrug, ARTHUR accepts his lonely fate and crosses the street toward home, an old brick building with a fire escape on the outside.]

INTERIOR—APARTMENT BUILDING HALLWAY—DAY

[ARTHUR is leading the CHICKEN who follows him tamely as they climb the stairs to the second floor. ARTHUR starts down the hallway toward his apartment, then looks at the CHICKEN and stops. He has second thoughts.]

ARTHUR
[to CHICKEN] You better wait here.

[ARTHUR ties the CHICKEN to the banister and then goes to the door of his apartment. He stops and thinks for a moment. Then he enters.]

INTERIOR—BOBOWICZ LIVING ROOM—DAY

[MOMMA BOBOWICZ is vacuuming as ARTHUR enters. MOMMA looks up but continues vacuuming.]

MOMMA
What took you so long? I was starting to get worried.

ARTHUR
Are you in a good mood or a bad mood?

[ARTHUR'S MOTHER looks up at ARTHUR suspiciously then turns off the vacuum cleaner.]

MOMMA

Arthur. You didn't lose the twenty dollars?

ARTHUR

[defensively] No.

MOMMA

Good.

[ARTHUR'S MOTHER turns on the vacuum again and starts cleaning.]

ARTHUR

Not exactly.

[ARTHUR'S MOTHER turns the vacuum off again.]

MOMMA

Exactly what did you do?

ARTHUR

I got a chicken.

MOMMA

You what?

ARTHUR

You *are* in a bad mood.

MOMMA

[softening] Well, where is it?

ARTHUR

I left it in the hall. It only cost eight cents a pound.

MOMMA

That's very cheap. Are you sure there's nothing wrong with it? Maybe it isn't fresh?

ARTHUR

It's fresh all right.

[MOMMA BOBOWICZ opens the door to reveal the CHICKEN standing in the hallway tied to the banister. The CHICKEN looks toward her and clucks! MOMMA BOBOWICZ quickly closes the door and just stands there facing the closed door—speechless for a moment.]

MOMMA

There's a two hundred pound chicken in the hall!

ARTHUR

[nervously] Two hundred and sixty-six pounds.

[MOMMA BOBOWICZ is still looking at the door.]

MOMMA

Two hundred and sixty-six pounds of live chicken!
It's wearing a dog collar.

[MOMMA BOBOWICZ opens the door just a crack, peeks out, then quickly closes the door again.]

MOMMA

[continuing] It's there, all right.

[She turns toward ARTHUR accusingly.]

ARTHUR

[close to tears] I couldn't help it, Momma. I got it
from this old scientist. He was saying it was a
bargain, and I didn't know what to do.

[MOMMA BOBOWICZ looks at her son who is on the verge of tears. She then opens the door again and looks into the hall.]

<u>ANGLE ON HALL</u>

[The CHICKEN stands shifting from one foot to the other.]

<u>ANGLE ON LIVING ROOM</u>

[MOMMA closes the door again.]

ARTHUR

I thought we could call her "Henrietta."

MOMMA

We're not calling her anything! That twenty dollars
was for a turkey to eat, not a two hundred sixty-six
pound chicken to keep as a pet.

ARTHUR

[fighting the tears] But we can't take her back or that
old man is gonna feed her to the Coast Guard or
some people at a picnic. Momma, please.

[MOMMA BOBOWICZ looks at ARTHUR for a moment, thinking it over.
Then she opens the door again and looks out into the hallway.]

<u>ANGLE ON HALLWAY</u>

[The CHICKEN looks toward MOMMA and cocks its head.]

<u>ANGLE ON LIVING ROOM</u>

[MOMMA looks out toward the CHICKEN and softens a bit.]

MOMMA

She does seem friendly, in a dumb sort of way.

[ARTHUR senses his mother's change of attitude.]

ARTHUR

I'd feed her and walk her and take care of her. I
could train her so she'd cluck if burglars ever came.

MOMMA

Well . . .

ARTHUR

Please, Momma. She's a good chicken. And I'd do
everything.

MOMMA

Who's going to tell your father?

ARTHUR

You could do that.

[ARTHUR looks at his mother innocently. She shakes her head and smiles.
It's the signal for ARTHUR to hug her gratefully.]

INTERIOR—DINING ROOM—NIGHT

[ARTHUR is seated at the dinner table with his parents. POPPA BOBOWICZ
is definitely in a bad mood.]

POPPA

You think I make money just to throw it away?

ARTHUR

I'm sorry, Poppa. I didn't mean to.

MOMMA

It's such an unusual pet, Carl. And psychologists say
it's good for the children when the family has a pet.

POPPA

Dr. Freud should raise a family on my salary.

[ARTHUR gets up and hurries from the room.]

MOMMA

There'll still be time to get the turkey. Besides,
with what they're paying for pets these days, the
chicken's a bargain. [slyly] And everybody looks
for bargains. It's the American way.

POPPA

[seeing through it] The American way is a turkey on
the table at Thanksgiving, not a two hundred pound
chicken on a leash!

ANOTHER ANGLE TO INCLUDE ARTHUR AS HE ENTERS WITH
HENRIETTA ON THE LEASH.

ARTHUR

I'll take her back if that's what you want, Poppa.

[POPPA looks at MOMMA. She looks back, beseechingly.]

POPPA

[weakening] Well, we'll see.

[ARTHUR exchanges smiles with his mother. Then he pats HENRIETTA.
HENRIETTA looks down at a dinner plate with French fries on it. ARTHUR
holds one up for her to eat and she gobbles it down.]

POPPA

[sternly] And no feeding pets from the table.

[ARTHUR and his MOTHER react at the word "pets."]

INTERIOR—ARTHUR'S ROOM—NIGHT

[ARTHUR, in his pajamas, is standing on his bed as he talks to HENRIETTA who stands on the floor.]

                    ARTHUR
          I've never had a chicken for a pet before. I've
          never even had a pet. Poppa doesn't like pets. He
          says they're a lot of trouble. But maybe he'll
          change his mind.

[HENRIETTA just looks at ARTHUR and clucks.]

                    ARTHUR
          Come on. Jump up.

[HENRIETTA doesn't budge.]

                    ARTHUR
          [continuing] Up on the bed, Henrietta. Up on the bed!

[HENRIETTA turns absently and starts to walk away. ARTHUR turns and closes the closet door. Startled, HENRIETTA turns and jumps on the bed. The bed collapses. ARTHUR shakes his head in dismay.]

CAMERA TERMS

DISSOLVE   the gradual replacement of one shot with another
EXTERIOR   a view of an outdoor scene
INTERIOR   a view of an indoor scene
ANGLE   the camera's point of view as it films its subject

MENTOR

Robb Armstrong

Cartoonist

Making people laugh is all in a day's work.

Robb Armstrong is a cartoonist whose comic strip "Jump Start" appears in more than 250 newspapers worldwide and on the Internet. During the day, Armstrong is an art director at an advertising agency. Mornings, evenings, and weekends he draws his comic strip. He has deadlines each week, when all his strips for the following week have to be handed in. The Joe and Marcy characters in "Jump Start" may lead busy lives, but Armstrong is kept even busier creating them.

PROFILE

Name: Robb Armstrong

Occupation: cartoonist and art director

Favorite cartoon characters in fourth grade: Fred Flintstone and Snoopy

Childhood idol: Charles M. Schulz, creator of "Peanuts"

Cartoon created in fourth grade: "Praying Mantis Man," an African-American superhero

Funniest joke: "Never mind. It's so dumb, my wife leaves the room every time I tell it."

QUESTIONS
for Robb Armstrong

Find out how Robb Armstrong turned a talent for drawing into a career.

Q How did you become interested in being a cartoonist?

A I began drawing when I was four years old. Like many kids, I loved to draw, and I decided to stick with it. When I was 17, I sold some political cartoons to the *Philadelphia Tribune*. I thought I had found an easy career. It wasn't until later that I realized how much work it would take to be a professional cartoonist.

Q Did you continue to draw cartoons in college?

A When I went to Syracuse University, I worked on the school paper, *The Daily Orange*. I did a strip called "Hector." Having to draw a comic strip every day meant that I had to be organized and self-disciplined. The experience taught me a lot and helped me later in life.

Q Is it difficult to get a new comic strip published?

A It took me a good ten years to achieve any kind of success. The field of syndicated comics—comics which appear in newspapers all over the country—is very competitive. I finally got a yearlong development deal with United Features Syndicate. This meant I had a year in which to come up with a successful strip.

Q Why do you like to visit schools and talk about your career?

A I enjoy visiting schools almost as much as drawing. I want kids to know that they can have dreams. I tell them that everyone has a talent—that's the easy part. Building a talent, that's what takes hard work.

Robb Armstrong's Tips
for Cartoon Ideas

Q How did you think up the characters Joe and Marcy?

A My editor suggested I think about characters that I know best. Eventually, I drew the characters Joe and Marcy, a young black couple with busy careers. Joe might be a cop and Marcy a nurse, but they're a lot like me and my wife, Sherry.

Q Where do your ideas for jokes in the strip come from?

A Sometimes an idea comes from radio or TV. But I think the best ideas come from life.

1 Watch how people act in different situations.

2 Listen to the way people talk, the stories they tell one another. What makes them laugh?

3 Keep a list of things that you find funny. Can you create a joke from an item on your list?

381

Think About Reading

Write your answers.

1. Why does Poppa give Arthur twenty dollars?

2. Why do you think Arthur bought the super chicken?

3. How would you like to have a 226-pound chicken as a pet? Explain your answer.

4. *The Hoboken Chicken Emergency* is presented as a television script. Which scene from the script do you think would be funniest if you were watching it on TV? Give reasons for your choice.

5. Cartoonist Robb Armstrong thinks that "the best ideas come from life." In what ways does *The Hoboken Chicken Emergency* come from real life? How is it different?

Write a Television Guide Entry

The Hoboken Chicken Emergency is going to appear on television this week. Write an entry about this humorous program that will appear in a TV guide. Briefly tell what the program is about, but don't give away the ending. Tell who will enjoy the show and give reasons why this is the best show of the week.

Literature Circle

The Hoboken Chicken Emergency is a television script based on a novel. Discuss how the format of a television script is different from a novel. How do you learn about the characters in a TV show? How do you learn about them in a novel? Think of other television shows or movies that are based on books. Discuss how they are different from the original books. Discuss which versions of the stories you like best and tell why.

AUTHOR

Daniel Pinkwater

Daniel Pinkwater's writing career began when he was in school. He was always trying to get his friends to laugh out loud by writing them funny notes. Pinkwater had his first big break as a writer when he entered a short-story contest at school and won a magazine subscription. He says, "That's how I first learned that you could get things by writing." How does Pinkwater come up with story ideas? He uses what he calls "the greatest single and only formula for writing fiction: the two words *what if*."

MORE BOOKS BY
Daniel Pinkwater

- *Author's Day*
- *The Blue Moose*
- *Lizard Music*

How to
Write a Fractured Fairy Tale

The fairy godmother is a young girl instead of an older woman.

Many fairy tales begin with "Once upon a time" and end with "happily ever after." What would happen if you turned a fairy tale into a fractured fairy tale?

What is a fractured fairy tale? A fractured fairy tale is a fairy tale with a twist. For example, what would happen if the Three Little Pigs became Three Big Dinosaurs, or if Sleeping Beauty decided to go back to sleep? Sometimes changing the setting is enough to add a humorous twist to the story.

Instead of a ball at the palace, there's a party at a disco.

"Biff
To the

In this story, Cinderella is a boy called Prince Cinders.

Prince Cinders wears modern clothes.

"All your wishes shall be granted," cried the fairy. "Ziz Ziz Boom, Tic Tac Ta, This empty can shall be a car."

Bang Bong, Bo Bo Bo, disco you shall go!"

The fairy godmother turns an empty can into a car, instead of turning a pumpkin into a coach.

1 Choose a Fairy Tale

On your own, make a list of fairy tales that you've read or heard. If you need ideas, look through a book of fairy tales and skim the stories you know well. Read a few new ones, too. Then choose your favorite.

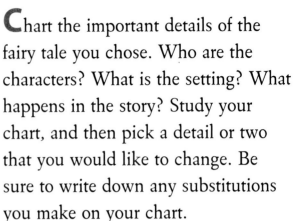

TOOLS

- book of fairy tales
- pencil and paper
- ruler

2 Make a Story Chart

Chart the important details of the fairy tale you chose. Who are the characters? What is the setting? What happens in the story? Study your chart, and then pick a detail or two that you would like to change. Be sure to write down any substitutions you make on your chart.

	Fairy Tale	My version
Characters	Goldilocks 3 Bears	Goldzilla The Bear Family (people)
Setting	House in woods	House in suburbs

3 Write Your Fractured Fairy Tale

If you like, begin with the traditional fairy tale opening, "Once upon a time. . . ." Use your story chart as an outline. Then rewrite the fairy tale in your own words, using your funny new twist. Are you smiling or laughing as you write? That's a sign that your audience will laugh, too. Be sure to use dialogue. It will make the story more lively.

Tips
- Change the time period of the story.
- Change the setting.
- Have a character in the fairy tale narrate the story.
- Change the characters in the story.
- Change the ending of the story.

4 Present Your Fairy Tale

When you've finished writing your fairy tale:

- Read it aloud to the class.
- Create a class book of fractured fairy tales.
- Work with a small group to turn some of the fractured fairy tales into a series of one-act plays. Invite another class to see your performance.

If You Are Using a Computer . . .

Type your fractured fairy tale on the computer, using the Sign format. Choose a border and clip art to illustrate your story.

THINK

Why does a fairy tale become humorous when you change an important part of the story?

Robb Armstrong
Cartoonist ▶

AWARD
WINNER

"**Y**ou've got fifteen minutes to make up your mind," Mom said. She put the red toothbrush and the green toothbrush on the table, side by side. "If you haven't decided by the time Violet gets here, I'll do the deciding."

My old toothbrush had been yellow, and its bristles were soft and bent. These two looked pretty good. Maybe the red would be best. I sat down at the table and studied them.

Two minutes later Violet Deever walked in, big smile on her face like she owned the world.

"What're you doing?" she asked.

"Nothing."

She saw the toothbrushes on the table. She reached for one, but I pushed her hand away.

by **Larry Callen**

illustrated by **Tim Spransy**

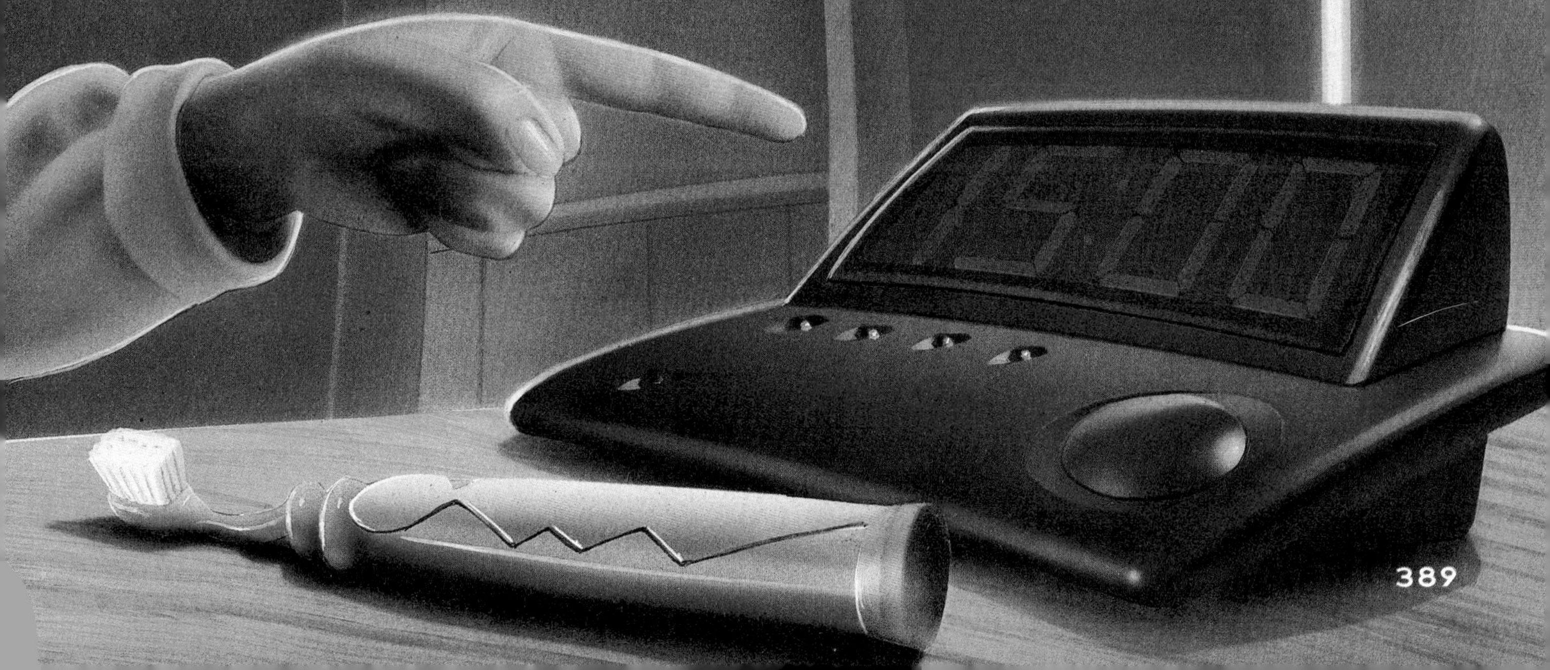

"Pat, stop that," she said. "I asked your mother to buy me a toothbrush. One of those is mine."

Mom heard her and shouted from the kitchen that I had asked first so I had first choice.

"Twelve minutes left to decide, Pat."

"Oh," said Deever. She sat down on the other side of the table and studied the toothbrushes.

"They're both nice, aren't they?" she asked. "You know which one you're going to take yet?"

"Whichever one I want," I said. I wasn't going to have her trying to make me take the one *she* didn't want.

"Maybe you ought to take the red one," she said, touching the end of the red handle. "It's very nice. The bristles look very straight."

Then a sly look crossed her face and I knew she was playing one of her games again. She was going to try and trick me. Well, this time I wasn't going to be tricked. This time I would do the tricking.

"Deever, don't touch them. Mom said I had first choice, and that means first touching, too."

I looked closely at the green one. If she wanted me to take the red one, she must've seen something special about the green one. Or maybe she just liked the color best.

The green one looked a little bit longer than the red one. But maybe it was just where I was sitting. I moved them closer together to compare size.

"It doesn't seem right that you can touch them and I can't," she said. "One of them is going to be mine, isn't it? Well, I don't want you touching my toothbrush. A toothbrush is a very personal thing, Pat. People don't go around touching other people's toothbrushes."

All her talk was getting in the way of my deciding which one I wanted.

"Mom, make Violet stop talking. I can't think when she is talking."

Deever looked at her wristwatch. "You've got only ten more minutes to decide, Pat."

Now she was really trying to get me confused.

"Mom, do I really have only ten more minutes?"

But Mom didn't answer, and Deever smiled and pointed to her watch. Then she drew a little circle around the red toothbrush with her finger. She didn't say a word, but she might as well have.

I looked at the toothbrushes and then I looked at her. She kept telling me the red one was best. She wanted me to think she wanted the green one. But suppose it was one of her tricks? Maybe it was the red one she wanted. Well, two could play at that game.

"I haven't really decided yet, but I think that I might just take the green one," I said.

The expression on her face didn't change a whit. Not an eyelid flickered. She stared me in the eye, daring me to guess what she was thinking.

"You have nine minutes left, Pat," she said.

But I wasn't going to be rushed into anything. I stood up and went to the kitchen for a glass of water. Mom was slicing tomatoes and cucumbers and celery for a salad.

"Mom, do I *have* to decide in fifteen minutes?"

"Decide about what, dear?"

"Aw, Mom. You know. The toothbrush. Violet is sitting right there, trying to get me to take the one she doesn't want."

Now Mom was washing lettuce at the sink.

"I can't see what difference the color of a toothbrush makes, Pat. Just pick one and be done with it."

But she didn't understand. I went back into the dining room. And I saw right away that Deever had moved both brushes. The green one had been closest to where I was sitting. Now the red one was closest.

"A fly lit on it," she said.

"What?"

"I wouldn't take the green one if I were you, Pat. While you were gone a fly lit on it. Maybe it laid some eggs. How would you like brushing your teeth with a bunch of fly eggs?"

"I'm not listening to that kind of stuff, Deever. I'm picking the one I want. Not the one you *don't* want."

"Know what color fly eggs are, Pat?"

I was looking at the toothbrushes. The bristles of both were snowy white. It looked like there might be a fleck of something on the bristles of the green one, but it surely wasn't fly eggs. Maybe dust is all.

"They are green. That's what color fly eggs are."

I flicked the bristles of the green toothbrush with my finger and whatever was on them disappeared. But if I took the green one, I would wash it with scalding water anyway.

The screen door slammed in the kitchen and I could hear my brother, E.J., asking Mom if he had time to take a shower before dinner. Then he rushed into the dining room. When he saw us, he slowed.

"What are you two doing?" he asked.

"Pat is selecting a toothbrush," said Deever. "He has been at it for exactly seven minutes so far."

E.J. wasn't interested in what we were doing. He kept on walking. A minute later he came back into the room, holding his own toothbrush.

"Mom," he called, "I think I need a toothbrush worse than anybody. Could I have one of those on the table?"

"I get one," I told him. "Mom says Violet gets the other."

"But if you *could* have one, E.J., which one would you take?" asked Deever.

He stopped at the table and stared down at the two brushes.

"That all the colors there are? Mine is orange. I'd like another orange one."

"Don't you think Pat ought to take the red one?" asked Deever.

E.J. didn't answer. When he had gotten a promise out of Mom to buy him an orange toothbrush, he headed back to the shower.

"I think he secretly wants the red brush, Patrick," said Deever. "But you have first choice."

I'd already wasted more than half of my time and I still didn't know which one I wanted. I like red. It's a bright, kind of loud color. I wouldn't want red clothes, except maybe a tie. Dad's got a red sport coat that he wore one time only, and then swore he would never wear again because everybody kept making jokes about it. But a toothbrush is different. I never heard a toothbrush joke in my whole life.

"Pat, have you ever broken a tooth?" asked Deever.

I was just getting started on my thinking and she got me distracted again.

Mom's not going to fool around. At the end of the fifteen minutes, she's going to decide who gets what color.

"The reason I asked, Pat, is that when you break a tooth, it means a friend will die. I had that happen to me when I was only six years old. It wasn't exactly a person-friend. It was a hamster. But it broke my heart. You know what my hamster's name was, Pat?"

"Deever, will you please let me think?"

She says I ought to take the red one. She knows I'm not going to take the one she wants me to. That means she knows I'll take the green one. And that means she wants the red one. If she just keeps quiet a little bit longer, I'll have this thing puzzled out.

"Red is a very lucky color, Pat. Did you know it can even help you if you have a poor memory? All you have to do is tie a red string around a finger on your left hand —"

"And remember why you tied it there," I snarled. She just wouldn't shut up.

"Mom, what time is it?"

"You have five minutes left, Pat," said Deever. "You are surely taking a long time to make up your mind."

She got up and went into the kitchen. I could hear low voices and laughter. Then she came back, crunching on a celery stick.

She says I should take the red one. But she also knows I won't do it, because she is telling me to do it. But if I'm smart enough to figure that out, then I'll take the red one, and she'll be left with the green one.

Suppose she's figured out that I'll figure it out. Which one does she really want, then?

I was getting confused.

3:00

I looked at her. She was still chewing on the celery. Was she trying to say something to me with that green stick? She smiled at me, still chewing.

Maybe I ought to get back to thinking about which one I want, instead of which one she wants. The green one is pretty. Kind of a grass green. I've got to get that business about fly eggs out of my mind. That's just trickery.

Lots of nice-looking things are green. Lawns are green. Leaves are green. Olives. Emeralds. Watermelons.

Watermelons.

But the sweet part on the inside is red.

"Do you know anything about rotten garbage, Pat? It's ugly and slimy and probably full of fly eggs. Did I ever tell you that once I had a possum for a pet? Possums eat garbage. Did you know that? And they have funny green stuff growing all over their teeth."

I used to like brushing my teeth. Made them feel clean. And I like the taste of toothpaste. They put something in it that tickles your tongue. Sometimes when we run out of toothpaste, I brush with salt, and I even like the taste of that. But I wasn't looking forward to brushing my teeth ever again.

"What time do you think it is, Pat?" she asked.

"All right, Deever. Which one do you *really* want?"

"Oh, I don't have a real preference. I just thought the red one would be nice for you."

I balled my fist. I knew she wasn't going to tell me the truth.

"You're just saying that, right? I'll take the red one, and then you will get the green one, which is the one you really want. I know what you're trying to do, Deever."

She tilted her head, lifted her eyebrows, and kind of sniffed, like she was saying I had a right to my opinion even if I was wrong.

"Ma!" called E.J. from the bathroom. "There's a big green fly in here."

"See there!" said Deever. "I told you so."

Mom came to the rescue with a flyswatter clutched in her hand. I heard a single *whack!*, and she came walking out with a grin of victory on her face.

"Two minutes to go, Pat," she said as she passed.

"Mom, it's not fair to put all this pressure on me. I haven't had a single minute to think. Deever's been here jabbering away the whole time."

"I'll be back in two minutes," Mom said.

I whirled on Deever. I wanted to yell at her to go away, but she wasn't smiling like she was winning the war or anything. There was a kind of hurt look on her face.

"I thought I had been helping you, Pat," she said.

"Deever, a guy doesn't need help to pick the right color for a toothbrush."

"All right, then. I won't say another word." She sat back in her chair and looked at me. The hurt look stayed on her face. Now she was trying to make me feel guilty.

"One minute!" called Mom.

Which one? Red one? Green one? Ruby one? Emerald one? Somehow I knew she wanted the red one. I just knew it.

I could hear Mom stirring around in the kitchen. She was going to come marching out here any second.

"All right. I've decided," I said.

I stretched my hand out over the toothbrushes. I paused over the red one and looked at Deever's face, but I couldn't tell a thing. Then I moved my hand over the green one. Still nothing.

I scooped my hand down and grabbed the green one, watching her from the corner of my eye. Her face lit up like a Christmas tree.

"Good!" she said.

Now I knew. I dropped the green toothbrush and grabbed the red one. I pulled it close to me. This time I had won.

"Time's up!" yelled Mom.

I grinned at Deever and waited for her smile to fade. But it didn't happen.

She reached out in her dainty way. With two fingers she plucked the green toothbrush from the table.

"Wonderful!" she said. "Green is my favorite color."

Laughing is Good for You!

by Karen Burns

illustrated by Tim Haggerty

Imagine that you've had a really stressful day. You didn't do so hot on your history test. You forgot your gym clothes. And, to make matters worse, Dad packed liverwurst in your lunch!

How do you beat the stress and brighten up your day? Maybe a really great joke or a funny movie will do the trick. Doctors have been studying what happens inside our bodies when we laugh. They believe that getting the giggles can help us beat stress and stay healthy. Here's why:

When you first start to laugh, your heart beats very quickly. But after a few seconds, your heartbeat slows down a lot. That makes you feel very relaxed. Some doctors also think that when you laugh, your brain makes chemicals

called endorphins (en-DOOR-fins). These chemicals may help kill pain and make you feel happy. A good belly laugh is also good exercise for your heart. Experts say that laughing about 100 times a day gives your heart the same workout as rowing a boat for ten minutes!

For hospitals and nursing homes, this is news to smile about. Many of these places are starting to use clowns and carts full of comedy tapes, funny games, and joke books to help their patients get better. Kids know the power of humor, too. Fourth graders in Oceanside, New York, recently wrote a book full of comics, limericks, and jokes for patients in a local nursing home.

So remember, a few laughs a day can keep the doctor away.

THINK ABOUT READING

Answer the questions in the story map.

SETTING
1. Where does the story take place?

CHARACTERS
2. Who are the main characters in the story?

GOAL
3. What does Pat, the narrator in the story, want?

PROBLEM
4. What makes it hard for Pat to accomplish his goal?

COMPLICATIONS
5. How does Deever make Pat's decision difficult?

6. Why does Deever keep looking at her wristwatch?

7. Why does Deever tell Pat not to take the green toothbrush?

8. Why does Pat drop the green toothbrush and take the red one instead?

SOLUTION
9. In the end, does Pat choose the toothbrush that he wants? How do you know?

WRITE A TV ADVERTISEMENT

Which toothbrush would you rather have—
the red one or the green one? Write an ad
that will sell this color of toothbrush to
TV viewers. Figure out a way to persuade
people to buy it, and describe its best
features. Make this toothbrush sound more
appealing than any other kind.

LITERATURE CIRCLE

According to Karen Burns's article, laughing
is good for you. Talk about what made you
laugh in "Fifteen Minutes," and discuss how
you felt after finishing the story. Do you
agree with Karen Burns's ideas about
laughter? Why or why not? Then list
other kinds of humor that you
have read, heard, or seen.
Why are they funny?
How do they
compare with
"Fifteen Minutes"?

AUTHOR
LARRY CALLEN

Larry Callen always liked to
write short stories. When his
children were about to enter
school, he took a children's
literature class and wrote his
first story for young people.
It was a success! That was the
beginning of his career as an
author. Callen's first book,
Pinch, was written on a bus as
he traveled to and from work.
His goal is to write stories
that entertain adults as well
as young readers.

MORE FUNNY BOOKS

- *Henry Higgins*
  by Beverly Cleary
- *Pigs Might Fly*
  by Dick King-Smith
- *Calvin & Hobbes*
  by Bill Watterson

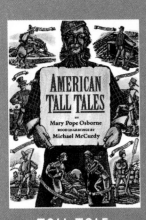

from

American Tall Tales

Sally Ann Thunder Ann Whirlwind

by Mary Pope Osborne

Wood Engravings by Michael McCurdy

SALLY ANN THUNDER ANN WHIRLWIND

DAVY CROCKETT

NOTES ON THE STORY

THE BACKWOODS WOMEN of Tennessee and Kentucky endured the same hardships as the men as they tried to carve a life out of the wilderness. They helped build cabins and clear land for planting. They hauled water from springs, grew cotton for clothes, and hunted wild animals. Though no early tall tales celebrate an abiding heroine, the Davy Crockett Almanacks do present rugged frontier women in a number of vignettes, such as "Sal Fink, the Mississippi Screamer," "Nance Bowers Taming a Bear," "Katy Goodgrit and the Wolves," and "Sappina Wing and the Crocodile." In these stories the Davy Crockett character tells about comically outrageous women who display amazing boldness and ingenuity.

In the following tale I have chosen to combine these various female characters into a single heroine—and have called her Sally Ann Thunder Ann Whirlwind, the name of Davy's fictional wife, who is briefly mentioned in the Davy Crockett Almanacks.

One early spring day, when the leaves of the white oaks were about as big as a mouse's ear, Davy Crockett set out alone through the forest to do some bear hunting. Suddenly it started raining real hard, and he felt obliged to stop for shelter under a tree. As he shook the rain out of his coonskin cap, he got sleepy, so he laid back into the crotch of the tree, and pretty soon he was snoring.

Davy slept so hard, he didn't wake up until nearly sundown. And when he did, he discovered that somehow or another in all that sleeping his head had gotten stuck in the crotch of the tree, and he couldn't get it out.

Well, Davy roared loud enough to make the tree lose all its little mouse-ear leaves. He twisted and turned and carried on for over an hour, but still that tree wouldn't let go. Just as he was about to give himself up for a goner, he heard a girl say, "What's the matter, stranger?"

Even from his awkward position, he could see that she was extraordinary—tall as a hickory sapling, with arms as big as a keelboat tiller's.

"My head's stuck, sweetie," he said. "And if you help me get it free, I'll give you a pretty little comb."

"Don't call me sweetie," she said. "And don't worry about giving me no pretty little comb, neither. I'll free your old coconut, but just because I want to."

Then this extraordinary girl did something that made Davy's hair stand on end. She reached in a bag and took out a bunch of rattlesnakes. She tied all the wriggly critters together to make a long rope, and as she tied, she kept talking. "I'm not a shy little colt," she said. "And I'm not a little singing nightingale, neither. I can tote a steamboat on my back, outscream a panther, and jump over my own shadow. I can double up crocodiles any day, and I like to wear a hornets' nest for my Sunday bonnet."

As the girl looped the ends of her snake rope to the top of the branch that was trapping Davy, she kept bragging: "I'm a streak of lightning set up edgeways and buttered with quicksilver. I can outgrin, outsnort, outrun, outlift, outsneeze, outsleep, outlie any varmint from Maine to Louisiana. Furthermore, *sweetie*, I can blow out the moonlight and sing a wolf to sleep." Then she pulled on the other end of the snake rope so hard, it seemed as if she might tear the world apart.

The right-hand fork of that big tree bent just about double. Then Davy slid his head out as easy as you please. For a minute he was so dizzy, he couldn't tell up from down. But when he got everything going straight again, he took a good look at that girl. "What's your name, ma'am?"

"Sally Ann Thunder Ann Whirlwind," she said. "But if you mind your manners, you can call me Sally."

From then on Davy Crockett was crazy in love with Sally Ann Thunder Ann Whirlwind. He asked everyone he knew about her, and everything he heard caused another one of Cupid's arrows to jab him in the gizzard.

"Oh, I know Sally!" the preacher said. "She can dance a rock to pieces and ride a panther bareback!"

"Sally's a good ole friend of mine," the blacksmith said. "Once I seen her crack a walnut with her front teeth."

"Sally's so very special," said the schoolmarm. "She likes to whip across the Salt River, using her apron for a sail and her left leg for a rudder!"

Sally Ann Thunder Ann Whirlwind had a reputation for being funny, too. Her best friend, Lucy, told Davy, "Sally can laugh the bark off a pine tree. She likes to whistle out one side of her mouth while she eats with the other side and grins with the middle!"

According to her friends, Sally could tame about anything in the world, too. They all told Davy about the time she was churning butter and heard something scratching outside. Suddenly the door swung open, and in walked the Great King Bear of the Mud Forest. He'd come to steal one of her smoked hams. Well, before the King Bear could say boo, Sally grabbed a warm dumpling from the pot and stuffed it in his mouth.

The dumpling tasted so good, the King Bear's eyes winked with tears. But then he started to think that Sally might taste pretty good, too. So opening and closing his big old mouth, he backed her right into a corner.

Sally was plenty scared, with her knees a-knocking and her heart a-hammering. But just as the King Bear blew his hot breath in her face, she gathered the courage to say, "Would you like to dance?"

As everybody knows, no bear can resist an invitation to a square dance, so of course the old fellow forgot all about eating Sally and said, "Love to."

Then he bowed real pretty, and the two got to kicking and whooping and swinging each other through the air, as Sally sang:

> *We are on our way to Baltimore,*
> *With two behind, and two before:*
> *Around, around, around we go,*
> *Where oats, peas, beans, and barley grow!*

And while she was singing, Sally tied a string from the bear's ankle to her butter churn, so that all the time the old feller was kicking up his legs and dancing around the room, he was also churning her butter!

And folks loved to tell the story about Sally's encounter with another stinky varmint—only this one was a *human* varmint. It seems that Mike Fink, the riverboat man, decided to scare the toenails off Sally because he was sick and tired of hearing Davy Crockett talk about how great she was.

One evening Mike crept into an old alligator skin and met Sally just as she was taking off to forage in the woods for berries. He spread open his gigantic mouth and made such a howl that he nearly scared himself to death. But Sally paid no more attention to that fool than she would have to a barking puppy dog.

However, when Mike put out his claws to embrace her, her anger rose higher than a Mississippi flood. She threw a flash of eye lightning at him, turning the dark to daylight. Then she pulled out a little toothpick and with a single swing sent the alligator head flying fifty feet! And then to finish him off good, she rolled up her sleeves and knocked Mike Fink clear across the woods and into a muddy swamp.

When the fool came to, Davy Crockett was standing over him. "What in the world happened to you, Mikey?" he asked.

"Well, I—I think I must-a been hit by some kind of wild alligator!" Mike stammered, rubbing his sore head.

Davy smiled, knowing full well it was Sally Ann Thunder Ann Whirlwind just finished giving Mike Fink the only punishment he'd ever known.

That incident caused Cupid's final arrow to jab Davy's gizzard. "Sally's the whole steamboat," he said, meaning she was something great. The next day he put on his best raccoon hat and sallied forth to see her.

When he got within three miles of her cabin, he began to holler her name. His voice was so loud, it whirled through the woods like a hurricane.

Sally looked out and saw the wind a-blowing and the trees a-bending. She heard her name a-thundering through the woods, and her heart began to thump. By now she'd begun to feel that Davy Crockett was the whole steamboat, too. So she put on her best hat—an eagle's nest with a wildcat's tail for a feather—and ran outside.

Just as she stepped out the door, Davy Crockett burst from the woods and jumped onto her porch as fast as a frog. "Sally, darlin'!" he cried. "I think my heart is bustin'! Want to be my wife?"

"Oh, my stars and possum dogs, why not?" she said.

From that day on, Davy Crockett had a hard time acting tough around Sally Ann Thunder Ann Whirlwind. His fightin' and hollerin' had no more effect on her than dropping feathers on a barn floor. At least that's what *she'd* tell you. *He* might say something else.

T★H★E
ZEBRA-RIDING COWBOY

A FOLK SONG FROM THE OLD WEST

Collected by Angela Shelf Medearis
Illustrated by María Cristina Brusca

AWARD WINNER

The Zebra-Riding Cowboy

ARRANGED BY
HOWARD SHELF

Come listen to my story, come listen to my song,
About a handsome stranger and a horse called Zebra Dun.

We were camped on the plains at the head of the Cimarron,
When along came a stranger who stopped to argue some.

He looked so very foolish, we began to look around;
We thought he was a greenhorn just escaped from town.

Such an educated fellow, his thoughts just came in herds;
He astonished all the cowboys with jaw-breaking words.

He just kept on talking till he made all the cowboys sick,
And they began to think to see how they could play a trick.

He said he'd lost his job out on the Santa Fe,
Was bound across the plains to strike the Seven D.

We asked him how it happened; he said, "Trouble with the boss,"
And asked if he could borrow a fat saddle horse.

This tickled all the boys to death, they laughed up their sleeves:
"We'll lend you a fine horse, as fat as you please."

Shorty grabbed a lariat and roped the Zebra Dun.
We gave him to the stranger and waited for the fun.

Old Dunny was an outlaw; he'd grown so awfully wild
That he could paw the moon down and jump for a mile.

But Dunny stood there still, just as if he didn't know,
Until we had him saddled, all ready to go.

When the stranger hit the saddle, old Dunny quit the earth
And traveled right straight upward for all that he was worth,
Pitching, squealing, screaming, and throwing wall-eyed fits,
His hind feet perpendicular, his front feet in the bits.

We could see the tops of mountains under Dunny's every jump,
But the stranger seemed to grow there, just like a camel's hump.

The stranger sat upon him and curled his black mustache
Like a summer boarder waiting for the hash.

He thumped him on the shoulders, and he spurred him when he whirled;
He showed all those cowboys who was top man in the world.

And when he had dismounted and stood there on the ground,
We knew he was a cowboy and not a gent from town.

The boss was standing close by, watching all the show;
He walked up to the stranger and said he needn't go:
"If you can use a lasso like you rode the Zebra Dun,
You're the man I've been looking for since the year One."

He spent the season with us, and the cowboys all agreed
There was nothing that he couldn't do, save stopping a stampede.

So there's one thing and a sure thing I've learned since I've been born,
Every educated fellow's not a plumb greenhorn.

THINK ABOUT READING

Answer the questions in the story map.

SETTING

1. Where does the story take place?

CHARACTERS

2. Who are the main characters in the story?

BEGINNING

3. How does Sally Ann Thunder Ann Whirlwind help Davy Crockett?

4. How does Davy Crockett feel about Sally after his rescue?

MIDDLE

5. What does Davy learn about Sally from the blacksmith, the preacher, and the schoolmarm?

6. What story does Lucy tell Davy Crockett about Sally and King Bear?

7. What does Mike Fink try to do, and how does Sally react?

ENDING

8. What does Davy Crockett do after he finds out what happened to Mike Fink?

9. How does Sally Ann respond?

WRITE AN INTRODUCTION

Sally Ann Thunder Ann Whirlwind is coming to your school to talk about life in the backwoods, and you are introducing her. Write an introduction for Sally. Be sure to tell a little bit about her, why she's important, and include some of her "best" qualities.

LITERATURE CIRCLE

In the American backwoods and wild west, people were admired for strength, courage, and determination. How do the main characters in "Sally Ann Thunder Ann Whirlwind" and "The Zebra-Riding Cowboy" display these qualities? What other tall tale heroes do you know? Discuss their characters traits and the amazing things they did. Record your ideas on a character web.

AUTHOR
MARY POPE OSBORNE

Mary Pope Osborne has traveled around the world and is interested in just about everything. Her writing shows it. She has written over forty books—including biographies; picture books; retellings of fairy tales, myths, and legends; historical fiction; and even fantasy chapter books for young readers. Osborne says, "I've been very lucky in that I've been able to channel so many different interests into books for children and young people."

MORE BOOKS BY
MARY POPE OSBORNE

- *Standing in the Light: The Captive Diary of Catherine Carey Logan (Dear America series)*
- *Favorite Greek Myths*
- *Favorite Medieval Tales*

How to
Create a Comic Strip

With a pen and a joke, you can make your own comic strip.

What's the funniest part of the newspaper? Many people would answer, the comics. A comic strip is a story told with words and pictures. Some comic strips can be about serious subjects, even when they are funny. The words and pictures are in frames, and the last frame is the punch line—the thing that makes us laugh. Often the pictures make us laugh before we even get to the punch line.

1 Brainstorm Ideas

Come up with a list of funny ideas for your comic strip. Include jokes, stories, and funny things that have happened to you. Check your source materials for ideas. When you've finished your list, choose one idea to use for your comic strip. What makes your idea funny? Why does it make you laugh? Can you make a joke out of it? What kind of characters will you use to tell the joke?

TOOLS

- paper, pencil, and ruler
- colored pencils, markers
- joke books, magazines, comic strips

2 Plan Your Comic Strip

After you've picked an idea from your list, think about how to arrange your comic strip. Here are the steps.

Write the Dialogue: Write out the joke. Decide which character will say which lines. Then rewrite the joke using the fewest words possible.

Set Up Your Strip: Before you draw the final version of your strip, sketch out the words and pictures in a diagram like the one shown here. Write the words. Then sketch the characters into the frames. Next, draw speech balloons around the words. Be sure the reader can tell which character is speaking.

How Am I Doing?

Before you create your comic strip, take a few minutes to ask yourself these questions.

- Did I pick a funny joke or idea?
- Did I think about dialogue and pictures for my strip?
- What kind of characters will I draw?

PANEL 1 — The characters

PANEL 2 — Set up the joke.

PANEL 3 — Add to the joke.

PANEL 4 — Give the punch line.

Add Finishing Touches

Jazz up the joke. Next you're ready to create the final version of your comic strip. Look over the sketches and words on your strip. Do you think the joke is funny? Do the expressions on your characters' faces match their words? If you need to make changes, now is a good time.

Pictures make the joke seem funnier. Turn your sketches into finished art. Use your art supplies and your imagination. Try making practice sketches with colored pencils and then with markers, to see which you prefer.

Create a background for your characters. Do your characters live in the woods? Are they standing on a city street? Think about what kind of background will help make your words even funnier.

Tips
- Use words like *zap* and *pow* to indicate sound effects.
- If you don't want to draw your characters, think about cutting out figures from magazines and newspapers.
- Use lots of bright colors.

4 Publish Your Comic Strip

When everyone's finished, put all the strips together to create giant newspaper "funny pages." Or you can bind the strips together to make a book. You can also submit your comic strip to the school newspaper.

CRASH

If You Are Using a Computer ...

Make a comic strip using your Card format. Begin your strip on the front, have one or two panels on the inside, and use the back for your punch line. Use the clip art, drawing tools, and speech balloons to make your strip look great.

CONGRATULATIONS

You've learned many ways that humor is used to make people laugh. Remember, a laugh a day is good for everyone.

Robb Armstrong
Cartoonist ▶

NATURE GUIDES

Enhydra lutris

SEA OTTER

NATURE GUIDES

THEME
Gathering and using information help us understand and describe the natural world.

UNIT 5

Welcome to

LITERACY PLACE

National Park

Gathering and using
information help us
understand and describe
the natural world.

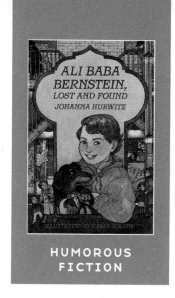

from
Ali Baba Bernstein, Lost and Found

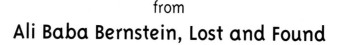

Ali Baba
Hunts for a Bear

by Johanna Hurwitz
illustrated by Michele Noiset

The summer after Ali Baba's tenth birthday, he and his parents went on a trip to Wyoming. When Mr. Bernstein first announced to his son that they were going to vacation in a couple of parks, Ali Baba thought he was making a joke.

The Bernsteins' apartment in New York City was near two parks—Riverside Park and Central Park. Both were nice places. When he was little, Ali Baba had played in the sandbox or on the swings and slides in the parks. It was good to have trees and grass in the middle of the city. But how could you take a vacation in the park?

"These parks are different," Mr. Bernstein explained to his son. "National parks are huge, and people come from all over the country to visit them."

"People come from all over the world," Ali Baba's mother added.

Ali Baba was sure they were exaggerating.

On the day that Ali Baba Bernstein was ten years, two months, and seven days old, they arrived in Grand Teton National Park in Wyoming. Then he saw that his parents had not been exaggerating at all. The park was huge. In fact, it looked bigger than Riverside Park and Central Park and a hundred other parks combined. And just as his parents had said, it was filled with thousands and thousands of tourists.

Some were Americans like Ali Baba. He began noticing the license plates on the cars. In the first hour in the park, he spotted plates from Illinois, Colorado, California, and Wyoming. The car that Mr. Bernstein had rented had license plates from Minnesota. When they stopped for lunch, a man came over to them.

"Whereabouts in Minnesota do you live?" he asked.

"We live in New York," said Mr. Bernstein, explaining about the rented car.

"I was born in St. Paul, Minnesota," said the man. "I thought you might come from there, too."

Ali Baba and his parents were staying in a little log cabin. In the parking lot near the cabins, there were three huge buses. The men and women coming out of the buses looked just like Americans, but Ali Baba couldn't understand a single word they said.

"What are they saying?" he asked his parents.

"I don't know," said Mrs. Bernstein. "They are speaking German." Because she didn't know the language, she could only guess what the people were talking about.

What most people seemed to be talking about were the animals. The park was filled with them. At home, the only animals Ali Baba ever saw in the park were squirrels and dogs. The dogs were supposed to be kept on leashes, but they often ran loose.

Here, there were herds of buffalo and antelope and deer. Sometimes you could see them very close to the road. Other times they were off in the distance.

Mr. Bernstein had brought a pair of binoculars, and Ali Baba kept busy searching for animals. He thought he would ask his father if he could borrow the binoculars when he got home. They seemed like very useful equipment for a would-be detective.

"I saw a bear," a girl told Ali Baba proudly as he was adjusting the binoculars at a lookout point the first morning.

"Where?" asked Ali Baba. He wondered if the girl was telling the truth. He hadn't seen any bears.

"Not here," said the girl. "When we were driving in Yellowstone National Park."

"Was it big?" asked Ali Baba.

"Huge," said the girl.

It seemed as if everything in the park was huge.

"Maybe I'll see a bear, too," said Ali Baba, putting the binoculars to his eyes.

"You probably won't," said the girl. "It's very hard to see them nowadays. My father said that when he came here twenty years ago, there were lots of bears."

"If you saw one, then I'll see one," said Ali Baba with certainty. He was determined to see a bear before he went back to New York City.

After that, Ali Baba spent all his time searching for a bear.

Mr. Bernstein took loads of pictures. He made Ali Baba smile into the camera at least a dozen times a day. Ali Baba found that very boring. It was embarrassing, too, if there were other people around. Most of the time, however, the other people were so busy posing and taking their own pictures that they didn't even notice.

"I see a bear!" Ali Baba shouted that afternoon.

"Where? Where?" asked his mother, looking around.

Mr. Bernstein grabbed his camera, ready to focus it at the elusive animal.

"Ha-ha! I made you look!" Ali Baba laughed. He had really fooled his parents.

"Do you remember the story of the boy who called wolf?" asked Mr. Bernstein. "If you try and trick us now, no one will believe you if you ever do see a real bear."

So Ali Baba kept watch for a bear. And he began to keep score of the animals he did see:

moose	17	marmot	1
buffalo	39	antelope	8
beavers	3	deer	12
gophers	61	coyote	1

He didn't bother to count mosquitoes. They had mosquitoes at home.

There were many things to do in the park. One morning, they got up extra early and took a ride on a rubber raft on the Snake River. Everyone, even Ali Baba who had passed his intermediate swimming test the summer before, had to wear bright orange life vests. It was very quiet out on the water. The splashing of the oars made the only sound. The guide told them to listen carefully. Soon they could hear the sounds of birds calling and animals grazing near the water.

"I see a bear!" Ali Baba called out. The hair stood up on his arms, and his heart began beating rapidly. It was an exciting moment, but it lasted only a second.

What Ali Baba saw wasn't a bear at all. It was a large tree stump. "I really thought it was a bear," Ali Baba

protested. He hadn't been trying to fool anyone this time. He felt silly making a mistake like that. The other people on the raft all laughed.

"It's pretty hard to find a bear around here these days," said the guide. "That stump is just the color of a bear. No wonder you got confused." Ali Baba knew he was saying that to make him feel better, but he didn't. He hadn't seen a bear, and he had been careless enough to mistake a tree stump for an animal. A good detective wouldn't do that.

"Is that a bear?" asked Mr. Bernstein a little later. Everyone on the raft turned to look. But it was the back end of a moose half hidden by a bush. Ali Baba smiled at his father. It was nice to see that other people made mistakes.

That afternoon, the family went horseback riding. Mr. Bernstein was the only one in the family who had ever ridden a horse before. Mrs. Bernstein was very nervous. Ali Baba felt a little scared himself, but he would never admit it. He wondered what would happen if a bear approached. Would it frighten his horse? Would he fall off?

"Are there any bears around here?" he asked the man in charge of the horses.

"If there were, the horses would smell them long before we could spot them," said the man. "The bears like to be left alone. They don't come where there are so many people and other animals."

So Ali Baba spent the next hour concentrating on riding and not on bears. It was a lot of fun, and he couldn't wait to go home and brag to Roger about his newest accomplishment. Still, even though he was having such a good time, Ali Baba wished he would see a bear before he went home. Perhaps he would have better luck at Yellowstone National Park, he thought as they drove to the second park.

Just as before, whenever they were driving along and they saw a group of parked cars, Mr. Bernstein would pull off along the side of the road, too. Parked cars usually meant that someone had spotted animals in the area. Ali Baba kept watching for a bear.

"Is there a bear?" Ali Baba always wanted to know.

"I saw a bear yesterday," said a boy who appeared to be a year or two older than Ali Baba.

"So did I," said Ali Baba. He was about to add that the bear he had seen turned out to be only a stump of an old tree. However, the older boy interrupted him.

"Hey, that's neat," the boy said, smiling at Ali Baba.

"It's getting really hard to see a bear around here these days. There're just a few of us who have done it. You must have good eyes, like me."

Ali Baba felt trapped. There was no way he could change his statement now.

"Aaaah, yeah," he mumbled.

"Where do you come from?" the boy asked.

"St. Paul, Minnesota," said Ali Baba. The words just flew out of his mouth even though they weren't true.

"I'm from Worthington, Ohio," the boy said. "My name's Greg. What's yours?"

Having already told two lies, even if one was not intentional, there was no way Ali Baba was going to identify himself. He couldn't even say his name was David, which was vague enough, as there were so many Davids in the United States.

"Larry," he said. The name just popped into his head. Ali Baba didn't know anyone named Larry, and he didn't know why he picked that name.

Luckily, at that moment, Greg's parents called him to get back into their car. They were ready to drive on.

"See you around," said Greg.

"Yeah," said Ali Baba, hoping that they would never meet again.

That evening at supper, there was a family with two small boys sitting at the next table in the park cafeteria.

"You know what?" one of them said to Ali Baba.

"What?"

"There's a kid around here named Barry, and he saw a bear."

"Really?" asked Ali Baba. He didn't feel he had
to impress these two boys. And besides, he still felt
uncomfortable about the story he made up to tell Greg.

"Yeah. He comes from St. Charles. That's in Missouri
near where we live."

That made two guys who had seen bears, Greg and
Barry. Ali Baba wished he had been that lucky.

The next day, Ali Baba sat eating an ice-cream cone
when he was approached by a little girl of about five or six.

"Did you see any bears?" asked the girl.

"No," said Ali Baba. "Did you?"

"No. But there must be one around, 'cause some boy
named Harry saw two of them."

"Really? How do you know?" asked Ali Baba.

"Some kids told me. Harry came here from St. Matthews.
That's in Kentucky where I live."

Ali Baba licked his ice-cream cone thoughtfully. Either
there were a lot more bears around than he had thought, or
else there were no bears at all. It was a curious coincidence
that Harry and Barry both came from cities that started with
the word *Saint*. In fact, when he thought of it, so did Larry,
the fellow he had invented. Larry came from St. Paul. Ali
Baba was sure he was onto something now.

Ali Baba walked over to his father. Mr. Bernstein was
comparing cameras with another man. A young girl stood
beside the man, and she looked at Ali Baba. "Have you seen
any bears?" he asked her.

The girl shook her head. "No," she said. "But I heard
about another girl named Mary, just like me, and she
saw a bear."

"I bet she lives in St. Paul or St. Matthews or somewhere like that," guessed Ali Baba.

"I don't know where she lives," said the Mary who stood along side of him.

Ali Baba started counting on his fingers: Larry, Barry, Harry, Mary. . . . He wondered how many other names there were that rhymed: Jerry, Carrie, Gary, Terry. He bet there were dozens of cities that sounded alike, too.

So when Ali Baba was ten years, two months, and seventeen days old, he returned home from a trip to Wyoming without having seen a single bear. However, he had solved a mystery that no one but he even knew existed. He had seen how a single accidental lapse from the truth had grown into a group of kids and a bunch of bears.

It was something to bear in mind for the future.

MENTOR

Veronica Gonzales-Vest

Park Ranger

Park rangers see some wild things!

Park ranger Veronica Gonzales-Vest works at the Sequoia National Park in California, which is famous for its giant trees. Sequoia trees are the largest living things in the world. Gonzales-Vest loves her job. She spends her days outdoors, patrolling the park and taking visitors on nature hikes.

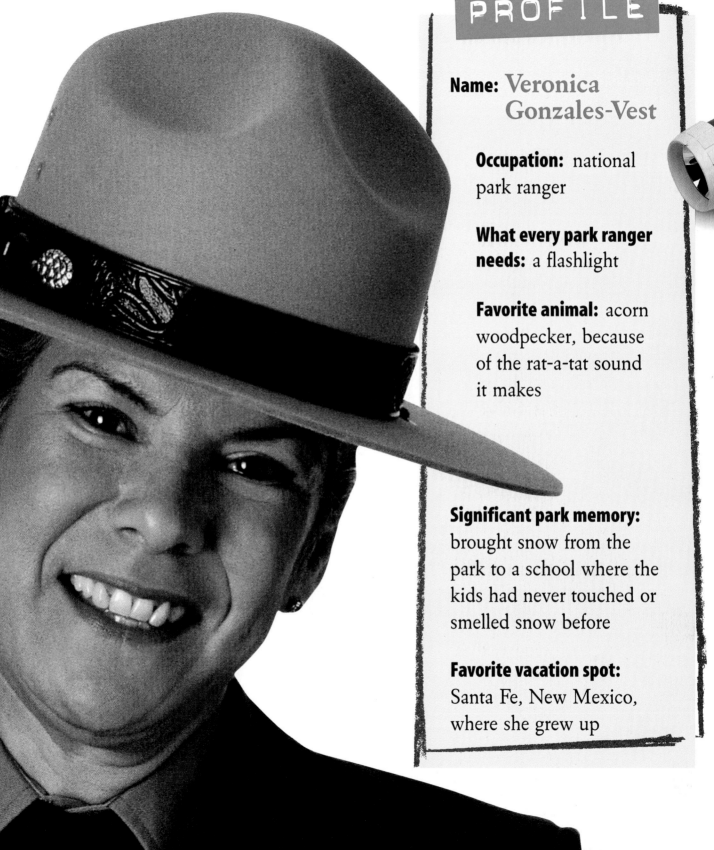

Name: Veronica Gonzales-Vest

Occupation: national park ranger

What every park ranger needs: a flashlight

Favorite animal: acorn woodpecker, because of the rat-a-tat sound it makes

Significant park memory: brought snow from the park to a school where the kids had never touched or smelled snow before

Favorite vacation spot: Santa Fe, New Mexico, where she grew up

QUESTIONS

for Veronica Gonzales-Vest

Here's how one park ranger manages information about nature.

Q How did you learn all the information about nature that you share with park visitors?

A I learned by observing the wildlife in the park, and talking to other park rangers. I also read lots of reference books. That's why, when I take people on nature hikes, I can tell them about the plants and animals they'll see. And I warn them not to wander off. It's not part of the park experience to become lunch for a bear!

Q Do you use special tools to observe nature?

A The tools I use are my eyes, ears, nose, hands, and brain. I use my senses—listening for birds, smelling wildflowers, and so on.

Q How do park rangers tell how old a sequoia tree is?

A Park rangers are skilled at "reading the rings." They take a core sample from the tree and then count the rings from the center out. One light-colored ring plus one dark ring equals one year's growth. Sequoias can live to be 3,200 years old!

Pocket Guide to Songbirds

A Field Guide to Butterflies

North American WILD FLOWERS

Q **What are some popular sites at Sequoia National Park?**

A The Tunnel Log is a popular attraction. It was made from the trunk of a sequoia and is wide enough to drive a car through. After a visit to the tunnel, people can say they've driven through a tree. Another favorite site is the General Sherman tree. This tree is probably over 2,000 years old. (Imagine a cake with that many candles!) It's also *very* large. One of its branches is over 140 feet long!

Q **Why do you think your job as a park ranger is important?**

A There isn't anywhere else like Sequoia National Park. I love telling people about the park. I see kids' eyes light up when they learn new nature facts. Some of them may decide to become park rangers!

Veronica Gonzales-Vest's Tips
for Young Naturalists

1 Use all your senses when observing nature.

2 Move quietly to avoid scaring the animals. You'll see more.

3 Be prepared. Carry a notebook and binoculars on your nature walks.

Think About Reading

Write your answers.

1. What is Ali Baba determined to see on his vacation?

2. Why is Ali Baba surprised when he realizes how huge the national parks are?

3. Which events on Ali Baba's trip would you like to experience? Why?

4. What point do you think the author is trying to make about telling the truth?

5. What tips might park ranger Veronica Gonzales-Vest give Ali Baba about observing wildlife in a national park?

Write a Postcard

What might Ali Baba write on a postcard to a friend back home? Choose one of the parks he visited. Write a postcard message about what he saw and did. Use action verbs and colorful adjectives to make the message exciting and interesting.

Literature Circle

What would happen if Ali Baba really saw a bear? Discuss how this event would change the ending of the story. What would Ali Baba do? How would the other characters react? Consider how the rest of the story might change to fit the new event and new ending. Make a story flow chart to show what happens in the story with the new ending.

AUTHOR

Johanna Hurwitz

Like Ali Baba Bernstein, author Johanna Hurwitz grew up in New York City and has visited national parks hoping to spot a bear. She never spied a bear on any of her trips, but she did have some luck in her own backyard. Once she saw a bear right outside her home in Vermont! Hurwitz says, "One of the wonderful things about being a writer is that you can use things from your own life, but you can make your characters react to situations perfectly."

MORE BOOKS BY

Johanna Hurwitz

- *Faraway Summer*
- *The Down & Up Fall*
- *Ali Baba Bernstein, Lost and Found*

Thirteen Moons on Turtle's Back
A NATIVE AMERICAN YEAR OF MOONS

JOSEPH BRUCHAC and
JONATHAN LONDON

Illustrated by
THOMAS LOCKER

NATIVE AMERICAN
LEGENDS

from Thirteen Moons on Turtle's Back

A NATIVE AMERICAN YEAR OF MOONS

by Joseph Bruchac and Jonathan London
illustrated by Thomas Locker

Grandfather leaned over the long spruce log. The small boy stood close, waiting for the old man to notice him.

Grandfather looked up, a small smile on his face.

"*Kway*, Sozap," he said, "you do well at watching. Come closer. See now what I have done."

Sozap reached up to touch the carved shape of Turtle.

"How many scales are on Old Turtle's back?" Grandfather said. "*Kina* look."

Sozap counted with care.

"Thirteen," he answered.

"*Unh-hunh!*" Grandfather said, "There are always thirteen on Old Turtle's back and there are always thirteen moons in each year. Many people do not know this. They do not know, as we Abenaki know, that each moon has its own name and every moon has its own stories. I learned those stories from my grandfather. Someday, Grandson, if your memory is as sharp as your eyes, you will be able to tell them to your grandchildren."

"Grandfather," Sozap said, "do other Native people have moons, too?"

The old man nodded. "Yes, Grandson."

Moon
of Popping Trees

Outside the lodge,
the night air is bitter cold.
Now the Frost Giant walks
with his club in his hand.
When he strikes the trunks
of the cottonwood trees
we hear them crack
beneath the blow.
The people hide inside
when they hear that sound.

But Coyote, the wise one,
learned the giant's
magic song,
and when Coyote sang it,
the Frost Giant slept.

Now when the cottonwoods
crack with frost again
our children know, unless
they hear Coyote's song,
they must stay inside,
where the fire is bright
and buffalo robes
keep us warm.

FIRST MOON
Northern Cheyenne

Budding Moon

One year Old Man Winter
refused to leave our land,
and so our people asked for help
from our great friend, Ju-ske-ha,
known to some as the Sun.
He knocked on the door
of Winter's lodge
then entered and sat
by Winter's cold fire.

"Leave here or you will freeze,"
Winter said,
but Ju-ske-ha breathed
and Winter grew smaller.
Ju-ske-ha waved his hand
and a white owl flew down
to carry Winter
back to the deep snow
of the north.

The lodge melted away
and the trees turned green
with new buds
as the birds began to sing.
And where the cold fire
of winter had been
was a circle of white May flowers.
So it happens each spring
when the Budding Moon comes.
All the animals wake
and we follow them
across our wide, beautiful land.

FIFTH MOON
Huron

458

Strawberry Moon

In late spring
a small boy
whose parents had died
went hunting game
down by the river
where the Jo-ge-oh,
the Little People who care
for the plants, live.

He shared what he caught
with those Little People.
In return they took him
in a magic canoe
up into the cliffs,
taught him many things
and gave him strawberries.

He was gone just four days,
but when he returned
years had passed
and he was a tall man.
He shared with his people
what he was taught and
gave them the sweetness
of the red strawberries.
So, each year, the Senecas
sing songs of praise
to the Little People,
thanking them again
for this moon's gift.

SIXTH MOON
Seneca

461

Moon
of Falling Leaves

Long ago, the trees were told
they must stay awake
seven days and nights,
but only the cedar,
the pine and the spruce
stayed awake until
that seventh night.
The reward they were given
was to always be green,
while all the other trees
must shed their leaves.

So, each autumn, the leaves
of the sleeping trees fall.
They cover the floor
of our woodlands with colors
as bright as the flowers
that come with the spring.
The leaves return the strength
of one more year's growth
to the earth.

This journey
the leaves are taking
is part of that great circle
which holds us all close to the earth.

TENTH MOON
Cherokee

Turtle's Calendar

Thirteen Moons

1) **Moon of Popping Trees**

2) **Baby Bear Moon**

3) **Maple Sugar Moon**

4) **Frog Moon**

5) **Budding Moon**

6) **Strawberry Moon**

7) **Moon When Acorns Appear**

8) **Moon of Wild Rice**

9) **Moose-Calling Moon**

10) **Moon of Falling Leaves**

11) **Moon When Deer Drop Their Horns**

12) **Moon When Wolves Run Together**

13) **Big Moon**

Authors' Note

The native people of North America have always depended upon the natural world for their survival. Watching the changes going on in the natural world with each season, they also look up into the sky and see it changing. In many parts of North America, the native people relate the cycles for the moon (called Grandmother Moon by many Native Americans) to those seasons. In every year, there are thirteen of those moon cycles, each with twenty-eight days from one new moon to the next.

Many Native American people look at Turtle's back as a sort of calendar, with its pattern of thirteen large scales standing for the thirteen moons in each year. As Grandfather says to Sozap and as an Abenaki elder said to me long ago, it reminds us that all things are connected and we must try to live in balance.

Joseph Bruchac and Jonathan London

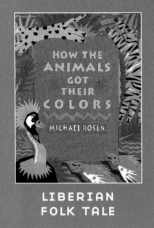

LIBERIAN FOLK TALE

FROM
HOW THE ANIMALS GOT THEIR COLORS

Retold by **MICHAEL ROSEN**
Illustrated by **JOHN CLEMENTSON**

AWARD WINNER

LEOPARD

See Leopard. He can leap so quick he's out of sight before you've blinked. Watch him.

See Nyomo. His eyes are so good, he can stand at the bottom of a tree and see a fly on the topmost leaf. Watch him.

You've heard of Lion? Wait for him. He comes later.

One day Leopard says to Nyomo, "Let's go, you and me, and find wild honey."

They walk, Leopard's paws pad on the ground. *Foop, foop, foop.* Nyomo's feet glide beside Leopard. *Shoo, shoo, shoo.*

"Look there!" says Leopard. "A bees' nest. I am the first to see a nest full of honey!"

They look inside. "No honey," says Nyomo. "Walk on."

They walk. *Foop, foop, foop* go Leopard's paws. *Shoo, shoo, shoo* go Nyomo's feet.

"Look there!" says Nyomo. "A bees' nest. I am the first to see a nest full of honey!"

They look inside. "Honey!" says Nyomo. "Let's eat."

They eat honey until their bellies are full and their eyes go wild. "Leopard," says Nyomo, "give yourself a name. What name do you want to call yourself?"

"Strongman," says Leopard. "And you?"

"I'm Ironman," says Nyomo. "And Ironman is a better name than Strongman."

Leopard growls, Leopard snarls, Leopard rages at that. He grabs Nyomo, ties a rope around his middle, and drags him through the forest. They meet Barking-deer.

"Say, Leopard, don't you know better than to go dragging Lion's brother along like that?" asks Barking-deer.

"I know what I know," says Leopard. "You just mind your own business, Barking-deer."

"Say, Nyomo," says Barking-deer, "will you tell me what's going on?"

"I said Ironman was a better name than Strongman, and Ironman is the name I'm going to have."

Barking-deer laughs. He laughs and laughs until it hurts. "You? Nyomo? Ironman? Little Nyomo who can't lift a log, can't bite a bone, can't even fight a fly—you call yourself Ironman in front of Leopard? You deserve everything you get."

Leopard is thinking: *Nyomo is Lion's brother. So I'll take him to Lion, and he'll tell Nyomo who's who around here.* Leopard drags Nyomo to Lion. When Lion sees his brother tied up, he is furious. Lion tells Leopard right there what to do.

"Set Nyomo free," says Lion. Leopard sets Nyomo free.

"Fetch water," says Lion. Leopard fetches water.

"Fill the bath," says Lion. Leopard fills the bath.

"Nyomo, my brother, bathe yourself in the clear, cool water." Nyomo climbs into the bath.

"Leopard, get under the bath. Stay there." Leopard gets under the bath.

Nyomo's hot, dry, dusty skin softens and shines in the bath, but the dirty water dribbles over Leopard. Leopard growls. "*Rrrr, rrrr, rrrr.*"

Now Nyomo rests. Lion and his wife bring food and sit and eat with Nyomo. They eat and eat and eat until all that's left is bits of bones, peels, and husks.

"Nyomo, dear brother," says Lion, pointing to the scraps. "Why not take these delicious little tidbits to Leopard?"

Nyomo takes bits of bones, peels, and husks to Leopard. This drives Leopard into a roaring rage.

"Lion," roars Leopard, "I'll tear you into so many pieces, it'll take ten years to count the bits."

Lion doesn't move.

"Lion, I'll throw you so high, you won't come down until next year."

Lion doesn't move.

"Lion, I'll squash you so flat, you'll blow away on the wind like a leaf."

Lion moves. Lion rises. Lion pounces on Leopard; Leopard fights back. Biting, clawing, raging. Every piece Leopard bites out of Lion, he swallows. Every piece Lion bites out of Leopard he drops on the ground.

Then, see who's coming—Old Mother. She comes near. She sees Lion and Leopard locked together, fighting in the hot dust. She sees Lion tearing at Leopard. "Run Leopard!" she cries, "Run Leopard, before Lion kills you!"

So Leopard runs. He runs and runs until he finds a pool of cool mud. With his paws, he picks up clumps of mud, and, *fap, fap, fap,* he pats them into the holes Lion made. *Fap, fap, fap,* he closes them over until there are no holes left. Then Leopard lies down to get better.

Everything's fine for Leopard now, but his skin stays spotty forever.

Think About Reading

Write your answers.

1. What does Grandfather tell Sozap about the thirteen moons on Old Turtle's back?

2. At what time of year does the Moon of Popping Trees appear? How do you know?

3. Which of the seasons—or moons—in *Thirteen Moons on Turtle's Back* do you like best? Why?

4. Why do you think the authors used poetry to describe the moons in a Native American year?

5. Both "Budding Moon" and "Leopard" tell how something came about. In what ways are the two tales different?

Write a Description

Each of the poems from *Thirteen Moons on Turtle's Back* tells about a particular season. Choose one of these poems and write a description about that time of the year. Paint a picture with your own words. Focus on colorful details and use adjectives and verbs that appeal to the senses. See if you can communicate a mood in your writing.

Literature Circle

Many cultures have stories that tell why things happen in the natural world. Talk about which events in nature are explained in *Thirteen Moons on Turtle's Back* and "Leopard." Discuss why different cultures may have made up these kinds of stories. Then think of other natural events that might be explained by a story and make a list of them.

AUTHOR
Joseph Bruchac

When Joseph Bruchac was a small boy, his Abenaki grandfather taught him how to walk quietly in the woods and how to fish. His grandmother encouraged his love of reading. Bruchac says, "It wasn't until I was grown, and had children of my own, that I turned to telling traditional Native American stories. I wanted to share those stories with my sons, so I started to write them down." His advice to beginning writers is, "Do it a page at a time, and keep doing it. You take one step to climb a mountain."

MORE BOOKS BY
Joseph Bruchac

- *First Strawberries: A Cherokee Story*
- *The Story of the Milky Way*
- *Eagle Song*

471

WORKSHOP

How to
Draw a Wildlife Diagram

The title
identifies the
subject.

The use of color
gives a more
accurate picture
of the subject.

A picture of a plant or animal provides a certain amount of information. A wildlife diagram gives even more details. That's why wildlife diagrams are often used to illustrate field guides and reference books.

What is a wildlife diagram? A wildlife diagram is a detailed drawing of a plant or an animal. As in all diagrams, each part of the picture is identified with a label. A wildlife diagram may include interesting facts about the plant or animal. Looking at a wildlife diagram is a quick way to get a lot of information!

Horse Chestnut Twig

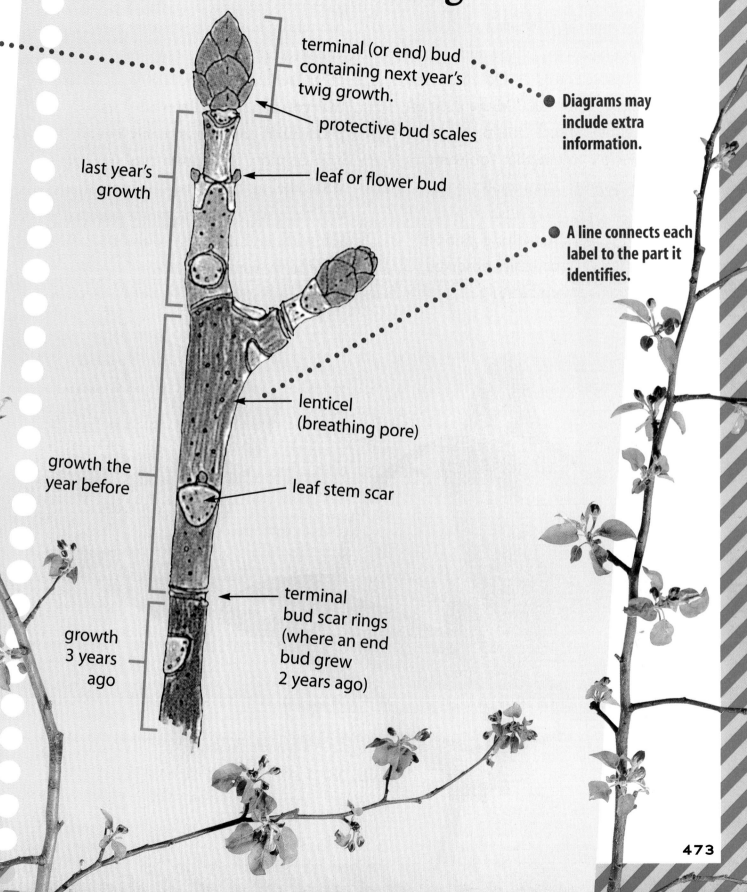

terminal (or end) bud containing next year's twig growth.

protective bud scales

last year's growth

leaf or flower bud

growth the year before

lenticel (breathing pore)

leaf stem scar

growth 3 years ago

terminal bud scar rings (where an end bud grew 2 years ago)

● **Diagrams may include extra information.**

● **A line connects each label to the part it identifies.**

473

1 Choose an Animal or a Plant

Think about the animals and plants you've seen. Is there a specific kind of bird or insect you like? Do you have a favorite kind of tree? Make a list of your favorite animals and plants. Then decide on one that you want to learn about. You may wish to pick something that can be easily observed up close.

TOOLS

- pencil
- ruler
- construction paper
- field guide or encyclopedia
- colored markers

2 Make a Diagram

Carefully observe the plant or animal you've selected, and draw a picture of it. You can also find a picture of it that you can trace. Then label its parts. Look through an encyclopedia, a field guide, or a nature book for help with labeling the parts. Use more than one resource to get information. Have fun with your diagram. Make it colorful by using markers.

Tips
- Trace a magazine photo if you are having trouble making an accurate sketch.
- Check an encyclopedia or a field guide for examples of diagrams.

3 Investigate Further

During your research you'll probably learn some interesting facts about the animal or plant you've chosen. How long does it live? What kinds of food does it need? Does it have any enemies? Decide on three "fascinating facts" to add to your diagram. Write them on the bottom of the page.

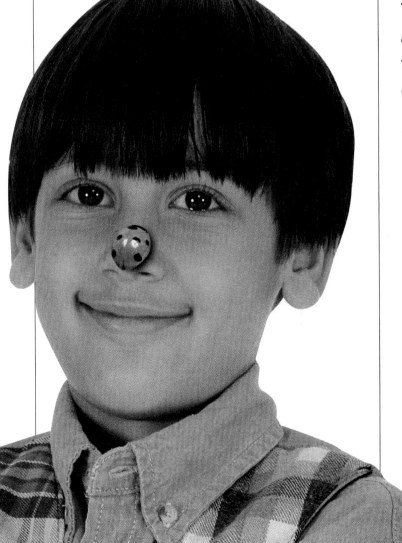

4 Classify the Diagrams

When everyone has finished, put all the diagrams together. Categorize the diagrams into two groups: animals and plants. For example, a diagram of a ladybug would be put in the same category as a diagram of a turtle. Then make a classroom reference book of your diagrams.

If You Are Using a Computer ...

Type and print out the title of your diagram and labels, using different fonts. Add clip art to illustrate the facts on the bottom of your diagram.

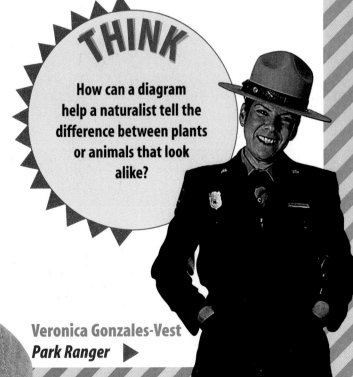

THINK

How can a diagram help a naturalist tell the difference between plants or animals that look alike?

Veronica Gonzales-Vest
Park Ranger ▶

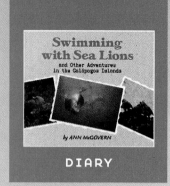

DIARY

from

Swimming
with SEA LIONS
and Other Adventures in the Galápagos Islands

by Ann McGovern

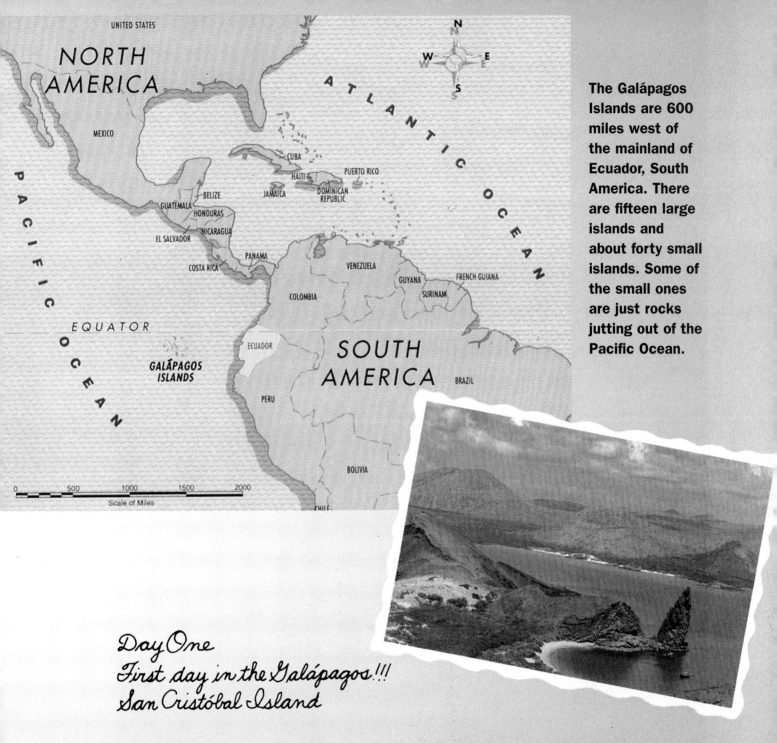

The Galápagos Islands are 600 miles west of the mainland of Ecuador, South America. There are fifteen large islands and about forty small islands. Some of the small ones are just rocks jutting out of the Pacific Ocean.

Day One
First day in the Galápagos!!!
San Cristóbal Island

Dear Diary,

I can't believe that Grandma and I have already spent almost a whole day in the Galápagos Islands. Everything is like a strange dream.

Today I walked right up to birds and they didn't fly away! Grandma talked to sea lions—and they talked back with funny barks and burps. I've never seen such tame wild creatures in my whole life!

Living on a boat is strange, too. Our boat is called the *Mistral*. Grandma and I share a small cabin. There's a tiny bathroom in our cabin.

477

It's funny to think of sleeping and eating and going to the bathroom on a boat for two weeks.

The Galápagos has been a dream trip of Grandma's for years. I'm so lucky she asked me to come along.

I think I'll start from the beginning. There was snow on the ground when Grandma and I left New York. After three different plane rides, we came to these hot islands on the equator, in the Pacific Ocean!

When we landed at the little airport, we were met by Andy, our guide. I found out that every boat that travels around the Galápagos Islands has a licensed guide who knows everything about these islands and the creatures who fly, crawl, and swim here.

Grandma is keeping a diary of Andy's facts for me to add to *my* diary. I'm going to put her pages at the end. This is the symbol I'll use to show that there's more information in Grandma's diary.

The *Mistral*—my home for two weeks. There were eight other passengers and four crew members.

Andy says we'll spend most of our days on shore walking around the islands, looking at the creatures—mostly birds and reptiles. I asked him about swimming, my favorite sport. He said sometimes we'll swim from a beach, and sometimes we'll jump off the boat into the water.

A few people plan to scuba dive, including Grandma! She says she wants to dive with fish that are found only here. And she wants to look at hammerhead sharks, huge manta rays, and sea turtles.

I was on the ship for only an hour when I saw my first flying fish skimming just above the water.

Still Day One Later

Dear Diary,

We are anchored close to land. Dozens of sea lions doze and sun on the shore. Others play in the water.

I jumped off the boat and got a big surprise. Even though it's broiling hot in the middle of the day, the waters of the Galápagos Islands feel real cold.

Grandma snorkeled with me. We peered down into the sea through our clear face masks. We use snorkel tubes for breathing, and the fins on our feet make it easy to swim.

I saw yellow-tailed surgeonfish beneath me—there must have been a hundred of them!

Suddenly a big body—then another—bolted past us. Grandma and I were quickly surrounded by *ten* adorable young sea lions!

It was a circus in the sea! Sea lion pups dived beneath us, blowing silvery bubbles through their noses. They somersaulted and flipped themselves into pretzel shapes. They chased and nipped each other. They are like big kittens. They seemed to be showing off just for us. They never scared me.

But the big male sea lion on shore did scare me with his bellowing roar! The other sea lions answered the bull with barks and coughing and burping sounds. It sounded like they were going to throw up.

Andy told us that the bull sea lions try to keep other males away. They also keep watch for sharks.

Sea lions live on almost every island so I will be seeing a lot of them. I'm glad because so far they are my most favorite creatures.

I took this shot of a playful sea lion pup with an underwater camera. Isn't she adorable?

Andy didn't mind when this finch flew up and pulled out a strand of his hair. I never saw anything like that before! Andy said the bird just wanted the hair for its nest.

Still later

Tonight I saw my first Galápagos sunset. The sky was glowing, and the sun was setting over a big rock that rose out of the sea.

Day Two
Santa Cruz

Dear Diary,

This morning we anchored in Academy Bay off Santa Cruz, one of the four islands in the Galápagos where people live.

I'm so excited! After lunch I'm going to see giant Galápagos tortoises—the largest land tortoises in the world! At the Charles Darwin Research Station I'll get to see them up really close. Grandma says the station was named for Charles Darwin, who sailed to the Galápagos in 1835 on the ship the *Beagle* and later became a famous scientist.

I just found out that *galápagos* means tortoise in old Spanish.

This tortoise is hiding in its shell. Maybe I scared it. (I didn't mean to.)

Later

Dear Diary,

I am so mad I could cry!

I read up on giant tortoises before lunch. Once there were hundreds of thousands of these huge tortoises on the Galápagos Islands.

Long ago, explorers, pirates, and seal and whale hunters came here. They stayed at sea for many months, and sometimes years. The fresh meat of the giant tortoises kept them from starving to death. The sailors knew that tortoises can stay alive for a year without food or water, so they stacked them by the hundreds in the damp, dark holds of their ships, one on top of another. Oh, those poor creatures.

Rats are no friends of tortoises, either. There were never rats here until the ships brought them. The rats swam to shore and began to destroy tortoise eggs and young tortoises. Rats are still around today. No wonder there are so few giant tortoises left.

The good news is that today there's hope for the tortoises. Andy told me that thanks to the Charles Darwin Research Station and the National Park Service, a lot of giant tortoises are being saved.

Before bedtime

Dear Diary,

I saw them! I couldn't believe my eyes! I had read that giant tortoises can weigh over 500 pounds so I wasn't expecting a little box turtle. But I never dreamed there could be such big tortoises. And they looked so old with their great wrinkled necks and teary eyes.

At the Research Station the bigger tortoises are kept outdoors in large fenced areas, and the younger ones are in indoor pens.

My favorite tortoise is Lonesome George. Once he lived on Pinta Island with thousands of other tortoises. Hunters came to Pinta and took all the tortoises they could find. But somehow they missed one tortoise.

In 1973, workers from the Darwin Station came to Pinta Island to get rid of the wild goats that were destroying so much of the plants. The workers discovered the one tortoise that was left behind. Since he was the only one of his species left, they named him Lonesome George and brought him back to the station.

Grandma and Marty, one of the passengers, are surrounded by giant tortoises on Santa Cruz Island.

Spooky *scalesia* trees grow only in the Galápagos.

In the middle of the night

Dear Diary,

I can't stop worrying about tortoises. They're still in danger. Besides the goats that eat the plants and the grasses that are the tortoises' food, there are cats, dogs, pigs, rats, and donkeys that roam the islands and destroy tortoise eggs and baby tortoise hatchlings.

When I grow up, I want to work at the Charles Darwin Research Station and help save the baby tortoises.

Day Three
Santa Cruz

Dear Diary,

What a day! I talked Grandma into letting me go with Andy and a few others to look for giant tortoises in the highlands.

Andy told me to wear a scarf around my neck, but it was such a hot day that I stuck it in my pocket.

We got on a rickety old bus and started our climb into the highlands. Pretty soon we were in an evergreen forest. We got out and hiked the rest of the way. The woods smelled good, like spices, but it was spooky. Strange moss hung from the branches of twisted trees.

And talk about mud! Sometimes I was almost up to my knees in muddy goo. We seemed to walk for hours—then I saw my first tortoise in the wild! I was so excited I began to shout.

I guess I shouted too loud because right away its head and feet disappeared into its shell, or *carapace* as Andy calls it. And that carapace was all any of us saw of any tortoise the whole day!

On the way back, I was feeling bad about scaring the tortoise when suddenly I felt a stinging bite on my neck. Then another, and another, till my neck felt like it was on fire!

I began to dance around like crazy. Andy ran over to me and rubbed some cooling lotion on my neck.

He told me I was being bitten by fire ants that drop from trees. If I had worn my scarf around my neck like he had told me to, they wouldn't have been able to attack me.

I squeezed my eyes shut to keep from crying. First, I scared the only tortoise we saw. Second, it was my own stupid fault that I got bitten by fire ants. And third, Andy is mad at me.

Dear Diary, you know what? I'm sorry I ever came to the Galápagos.

A giant tortoise like this can live for over 100 years.

Later

Dear Diary,

Andy's not mad at me after all! He came up on deck of the *Mistral* where I was watching the sunset. Together we watched the sky glow and quickly turn night-black. He told me a story about a special expedition he had gone on to see the giant tortoises on Isabela Island.

With a group of people, he had hiked up to the top of the volcano where everything grows lush green and where the fog swirls so thick and wet that it drips water. The thousands of tortoises that live there aren't shy, like the Santa Cruz tortoises. They didn't even seem to care that people were around. They just kept on munching plants.

When the tents were set up, the tortoises plodded up to inspect them. They sniffed the gear, too, and stepped on it and began to chew on it! The people had to build a fence of logs to keep the curious tortoises out of camp.

Then, Andy said, it started to pour. Dozens of tortoises came to drink the rainwater that collected in pools. Andy said it was magical.

The way he talked, I could picture the whole expedition.

I love Galápagos tortoises more than anything.

A Galápagos sky just as the sun is setting—a sight I will never forget.

More About the Galápagos

**Here are a lot more facts that Grandma
kept for me in her diary.**

Day One
More About Sea Lions, page 480

Sea lions live in groups. One big male bull takes charge of a family of about forty females and their young. Andy says these sea lions are closely related to the California sea lions.

Day Two, Santa Cruz
More About Charles Darwin, page 481

Charles Darwin was a young British naturalist whose job on a round-the-world voyage on the *Beagle* was to collect and study plants and animals.

Charles Darwin Research Station, page 482

In 1959, the Charles Darwin Foundation was formed to protect the unusual life on the Galápagos. Scientists from all over the world come to study the plants and animals.

The Charles Darwin Research Station sends workers to different islands to collect tortoise eggs. They bring the eggs back to the station where they are protected until they hatch. Thousands of hatchlings have been raised at the station. The little tortoises are cared for until they are five years old, old enough to have a good chance of surviving in the wild. Then the tortoises are returned to their own islands where eventually they mate and produce young tortoises.

The creatures of the Galápagos are protected by rules made by the Charles Darwin Research Station and the Galápagos National Park Service.

All the guides make sure the rules are followed. Touching or feeding any of the creatures, wandering off the marked trails, or taking anything—even a broken shell or a piece of lava—is against the rules.

WILD THINGS

illustrated by Steve Jenkins

THE CATERPILLAR

Brown and furry
Caterpillar in a hurry;
Take your walk
To the shady leaf or stalk.

May no toad spy you,
May the little birds pass by you;
Spin and die,
To live again a butterfly.

—Christina G. Rossetti

THE HIPPOPOTAMUS

Behold the hippopotamus!
We laugh at how he looks to us,
And yet in moments dank and grim
I wonder how we look to him.
Peace, peace, thou hippopotamus!
We really look all right to us,
As you no doubt delight the eye
Of other hippopotami.

—Ogden Nash

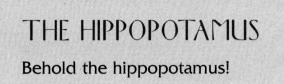

THE BAT

By day the bat is cousin to the mouse.
He likes the attic of an aging house.

His fingers make a hat about his head.
His pulse beat is so slow we think him dead.

He loops in crazy figures half the night
Among the trees that face the corner light.

But when he brushes up against a screen,
We are afraid of what our eyes have seen:

For something is amiss or out of place
When mice with wings can wear a human face.

—Theodore Roethke

THE WILD GEESE RETURNING

The wild geese returning
Through the misty sky—
Behold they look like
A letter written
In faded ink!

– Tsumori Kunimoto

JOYFUL JABBER

Every morning the jays swoop
into junipers and piñons, bloom
blue on the branches, broadcast
the news that seeds and water
wait on the warm, flat boulder
behind our house.
More than twenty jays gather
at the table, jabber joyful.

I think of my friend far away and wish
we were feasting together,
soaking up this desert light until we too would soar
over cottonwood and aspen tossing
their gold, over cinnamon hills
and the secrets of canyons,
her hand safe in my hand.

                                        —Pat Mora

493.

Think About Reading

Write your answers.

1. How is the diary writer able to see the sea lions under the water?

2. Why is she worried about the Galápagos tortoises?

3. If you were with the girl in the Galápagos Islands, which activities would you most enjoy? Explain your answers.

4. Why do you think the author used a fictional diary to present facts about the Galápagos Islands?

5. What do the diary entries and the poems have in common?

Write an E-Mail Message

Imagine that you are the diary writer in *Swimming with Sea Lions*. Write an E-mail message to a friend or family member back home about one of your adventures in the Galápagos Islands. Describe the event. Tell what was exciting about it and how you felt. Be sure to follow the E-mail format. At the beginning of the message, write the name of the person who will receive the message and a short phrase telling what the message is about.

Literature Circle

Author Ann McGovern presents facts and information about wildlife in the Galápagos Islands in a fictional diary format. Discuss other nonfiction books about wildlife. How are these books similar to or different from *Swimming with Sea Lions*? What kinds of graphic aids are used? How is the written information presented? Record your findings on a chart. Then talk about which format you like the best.

AUTHOR
Ann McGovern

Author and world traveler Ann McGovern has had lots of adventures in many different places. She keeps a diary of her real-life experiences and uses them when she begins to write a book about a nonfiction topic. Because she loves to scuba dive, many of her books are about the sea. McGovern stresses that feelings and curiosity are as important to a writer as adventures. She encourages young authors with these words, "Keep a journal. Turn off the TV, and pick up a good book."

MORE BOOKS BY
Ann McGovern

- *Playing with Penguins & Other Adventures in Antarctica*
- *Shark Lady*
- *If You Lived in Colonial Times*

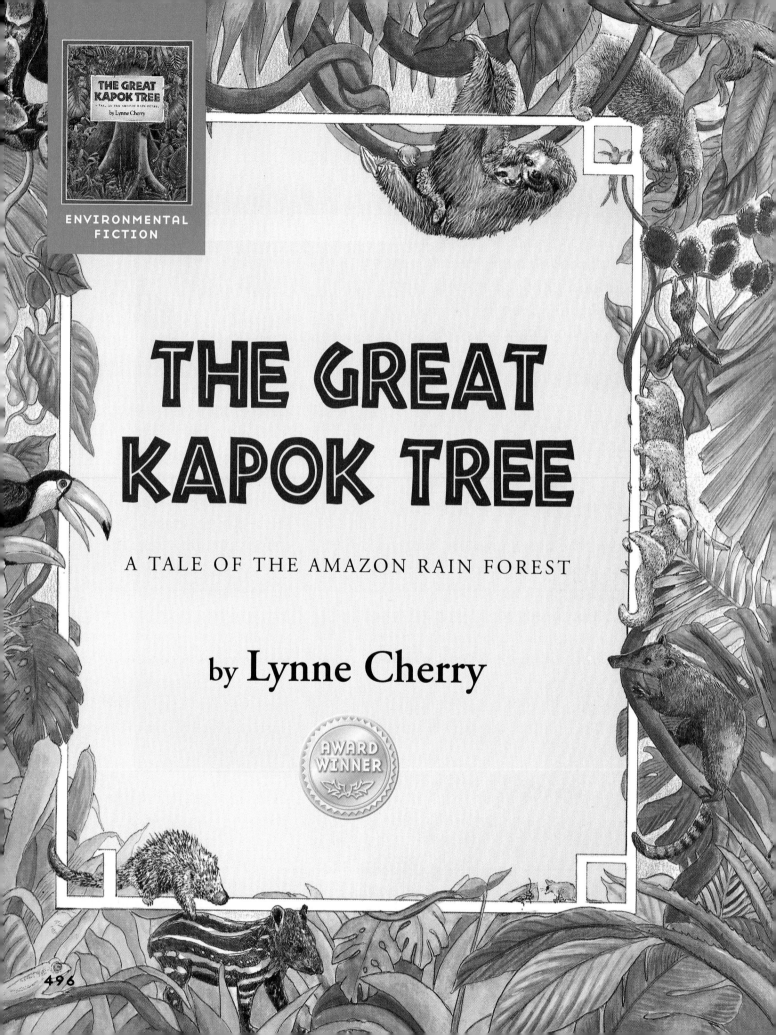

THE GREAT KAPOK TREE

A TALE OF THE AMAZON RAIN FOREST

by Lynne Cherry

AWARD WINNER

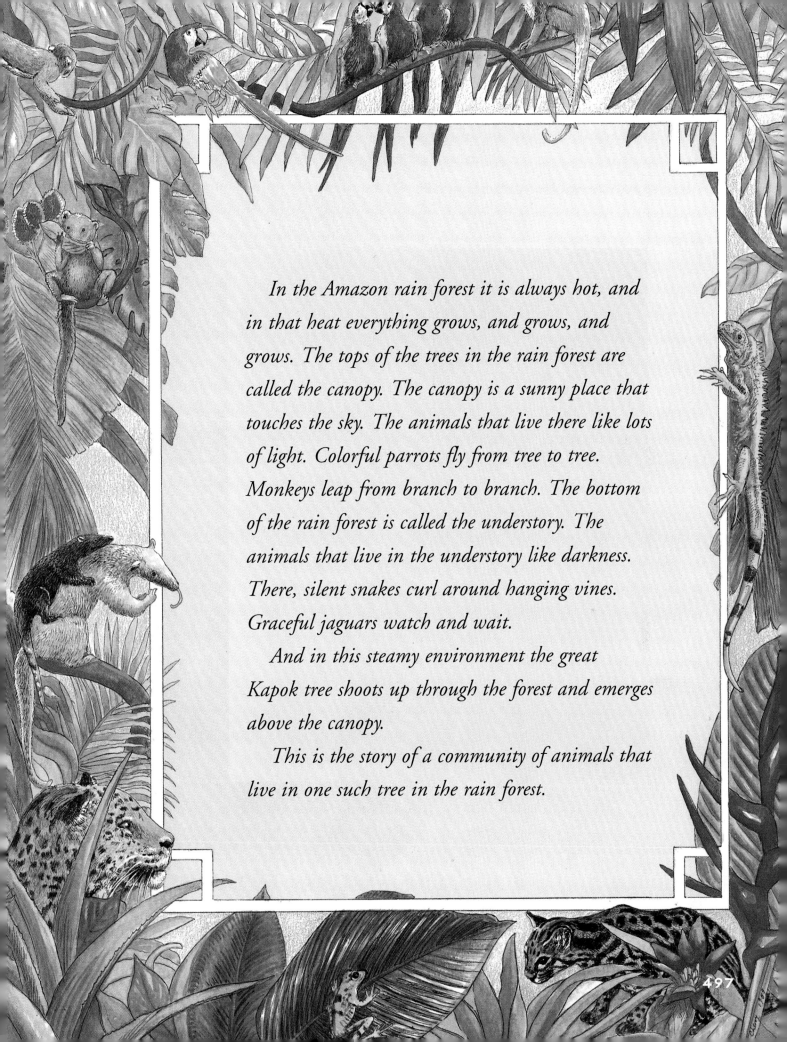

In the Amazon rain forest it is always hot, and in that heat everything grows, and grows, and grows. The tops of the trees in the rain forest are called the canopy. The canopy is a sunny place that touches the sky. The animals that live there like lots of light. Colorful parrots fly from tree to tree. Monkeys leap from branch to branch. The bottom of the rain forest is called the understory. The animals that live in the understory like darkness. There, silent snakes curl around hanging vines. Graceful jaguars watch and wait.

And in this steamy environment the great Kapok tree shoots up through the forest and emerges above the canopy.

This is the story of a community of animals that live in one such tree in the rain forest.

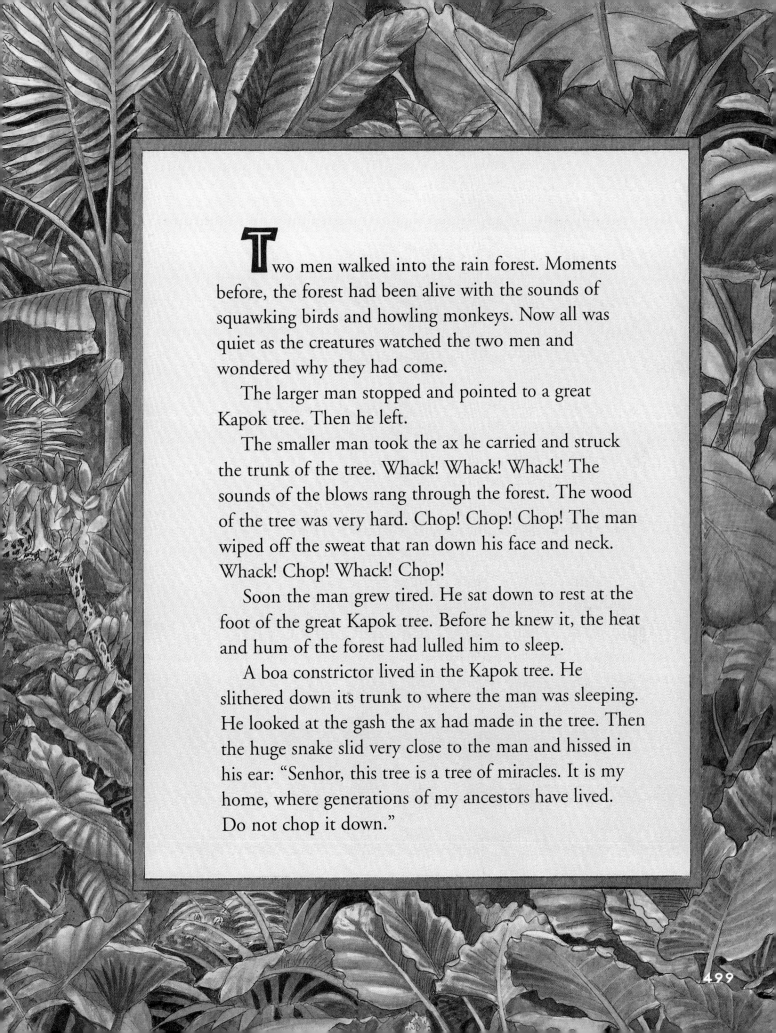

wo men walked into the rain forest. Moments before, the forest had been alive with the sounds of squawking birds and howling monkeys. Now all was quiet as the creatures watched the two men and wondered why they had come.

The larger man stopped and pointed to a great Kapok tree. Then he left.

The smaller man took the ax he carried and struck the trunk of the tree. Whack! Whack! Whack! The sounds of the blows rang through the forest. The wood of the tree was very hard. Chop! Chop! Chop! The man wiped off the sweat that ran down his face and neck. Whack! Chop! Whack! Chop!

Soon the man grew tired. He sat down to rest at the foot of the great Kapok tree. Before he knew it, the heat and hum of the forest had lulled him to sleep.

A boa constrictor lived in the Kapok tree. He slithered down its trunk to where the man was sleeping. He looked at the gash the ax had made in the tree. Then the huge snake slid very close to the man and hissed in his ear: "Senhor, this tree is a tree of miracles. It is my home, where generations of my ancestors have lived. Do not chop it down."

A bee buzzed in the sleeping man's ear: "Senhor, my hive is in this Kapok tree, and I fly from tree to tree and flower to flower collecting pollen. In this way I pollinate the trees and flowers throughout the rain forest. You see, all living things depend on one another."

A troupe of monkeys scampered down from the canopy of the Kapok tree. They chattered to the sleeping man: "Senhor, we have seen the ways of man. You chop down one tree, then come back for another and another. The roots of these great trees will wither and die, and there will be nothing left to hold the earth in place. When the heavy rains come, the soil will be washed away and the forest will become a desert."

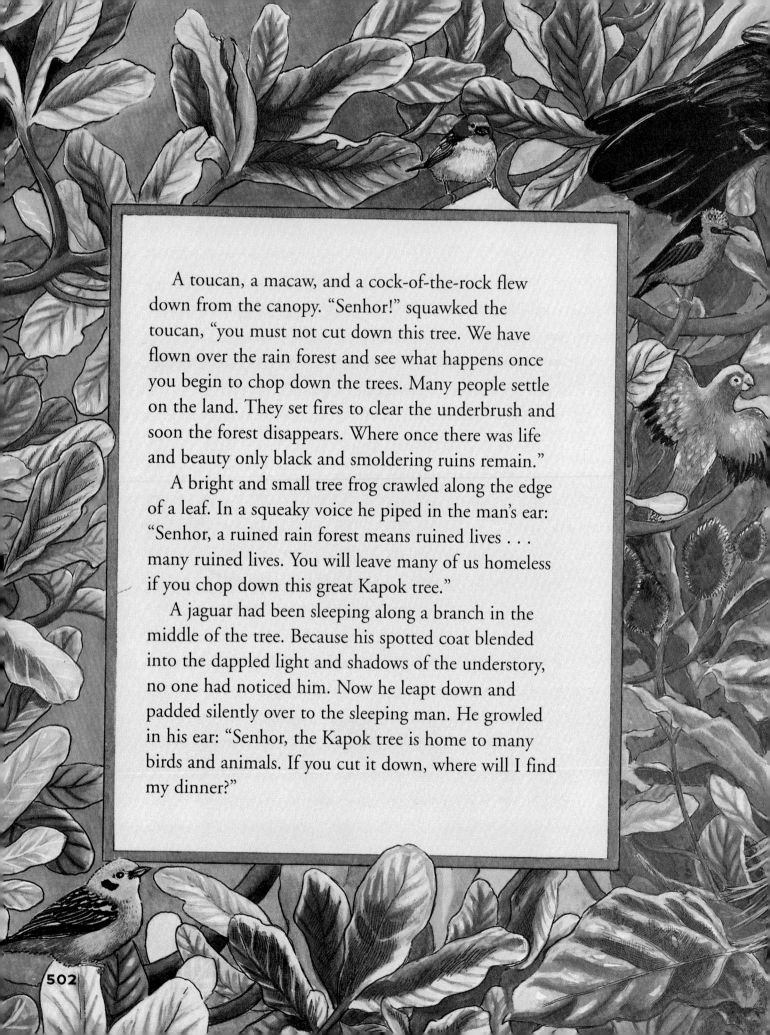

A toucan, a macaw, and a cock-of-the-rock flew down from the canopy. "Senhor!" squawked the toucan, "you must not cut down this tree. We have flown over the rain forest and see what happens once you begin to chop down the trees. Many people settle on the land. They set fires to clear the underbrush and soon the forest disappears. Where once there was life and beauty only black and smoldering ruins remain."

A bright and small tree frog crawled along the edge of a leaf. In a squeaky voice he piped in the man's ear: "Senhor, a ruined rain forest means ruined lives . . . many ruined lives. You will leave many of us homeless if you chop down this great Kapok tree."

A jaguar had been sleeping along a branch in the middle of the tree. Because his spotted coat blended into the dappled light and shadows of the understory, no one had noticed him. Now he leapt down and padded silently over to the sleeping man. He growled in his ear: "Senhor, the Kapok tree is home to many birds and animals. If you cut it down, where will I find my dinner?"

Four tree porcupines swung down from branch to branch and whispered to the man: "Senhor, do you know what we animals and humans need in order to live? Oxygen. And, Senhor, do you know what trees produce? Oxygen! If you cut down the forests you will destroy that which gives us all life."

Several anteaters climbed down the Kapok tree with their young clinging to their backs. The unstriped anteater said to the sleeping man: "Senhor, you are chopping down this tree with no thought for the future. And surely you know that what happens tomorrow depends upon what you do today. The big man tells you to chop down a beautiful tree. He does not think of his own children, who tomorrow must live in a world without trees."

A three-toed sloth had begun climbing down from the canopy when the men first appeared. Only now did she reach the ground. Plodding ever so slowly over to the sleeping man, she spoke in her deep and lazy voice: "Senhor, how much is beauty worth? Can you live without it? If you destroy the beauty of the rain forest, on what would you feast your eyes?"

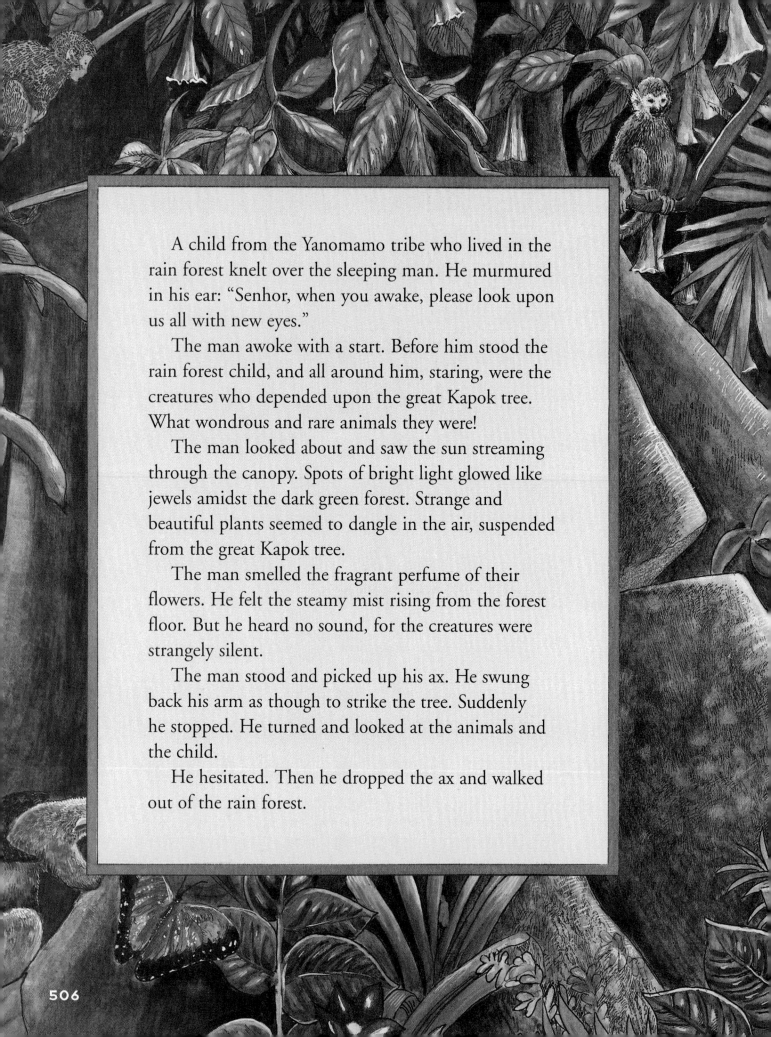

A child from the Yanomamo tribe who lived in the rain forest knelt over the sleeping man. He murmured in his ear: "Senhor, when you awake, please look upon us all with new eyes."

The man awoke with a start. Before him stood the rain forest child, and all around him, staring, were the creatures who depended upon the great Kapok tree. What wondrous and rare animals they were!

The man looked about and saw the sun streaming through the canopy. Spots of bright light glowed like jewels amidst the dark green forest. Strange and beautiful plants seemed to dangle in the air, suspended from the great Kapok tree.

The man smelled the fragrant perfume of their flowers. He felt the steamy mist rising from the forest floor. But he heard no sound, for the creatures were strangely silent.

The man stood and picked up his ax. He swung back his arm as though to strike the tree. Suddenly he stopped. He turned and looked at the animals and the child.

He hesitated. Then he dropped the ax and walked out of the rain forest.

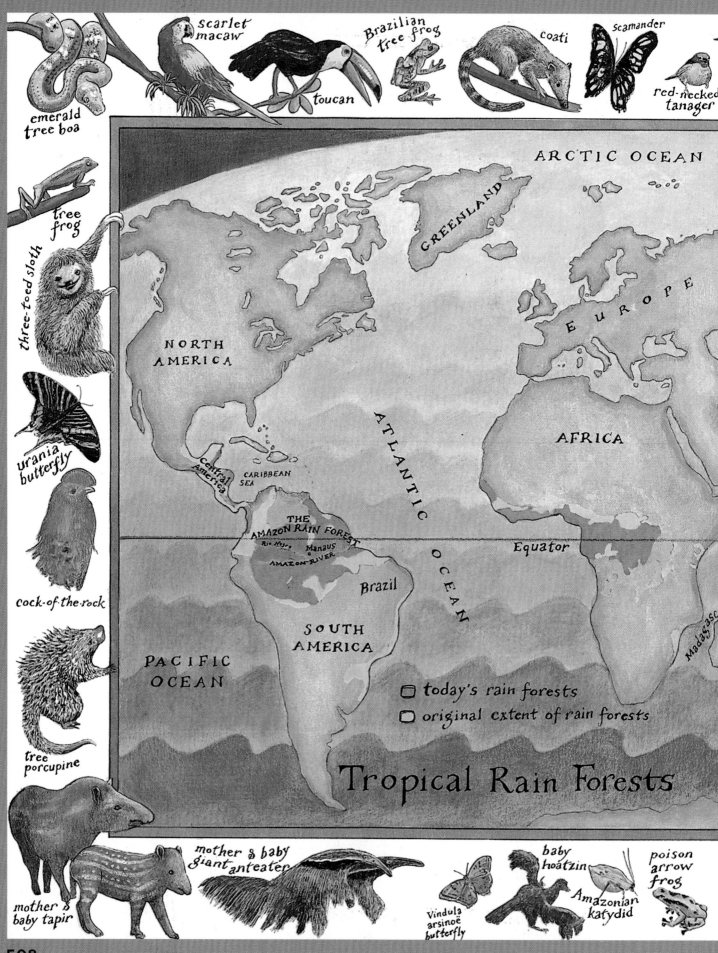

emerald
tree boa

scarlet
macaw

toucan

Brazilian
tree frog

coati

Scamander

red-necked
tanager

tree
frog

three-toed sloth

urania
butterfly

cock-of-the-rock

tree
porcupine

mother &
baby tapir

mother & baby
giant anteater

Vindula
arsinoë
butterfly

baby
hoatzin

Amazonian
katydid

poison
arrow
frog

ARCTIC OCEAN

GREENLAND

EUROPE

NORTH
AMERICA

AFRICA

ATLANTIC

Central
America

CARIBBEAN
SEA

THE
AMAZON RAIN FOREST

Rio Nure   Manaus
AMAZON RIVER

Brazil

Equator

OCEAN

Madagascar

SOUTH
AMERICA

PACIFIC
OCEAN

☐ today's rain forests
☐ original extent of rain forests

Tropical Rain Forests

508

golden anager · parrot · Squirrel monkey · jaguar · Anteos menippe butterfly · tamandua -or- anteater · boa constrictor

silky anteater

moustached tamarin

ASIA

Japan

PACIFIC OCEAN

India · Indochina · Philippines · Malaysia

Indonesia · New Guinea

INDIAN OCEAN

AUSTRALIA

of the World

ANTARCTICA

EMERGENTS

Emergents

Canopy

CANOPY

Middle Layer

UNDERSTORY

Shrub Layer

Herb Layer

woolly monkey

iguana

passion-flower butterfly

Siproeta stelenes butterfly

kinkajou

violet-tailed sylph

chestnut-capped puffbird · parakeet · blue morpho butterfly · ocelot · Hamadryas arinome butterfly · red-legged honey creeper · Papilio androgeus butterfly

from **NATIONAL AUDUBON SOCIETY** FIRST FIELD GUIDE: INSECTS
written by **Christina Wilsdon**

MONARCH
Danaus plexippus

M onarchs are amazing fliers and navigators. Every autumn, millions of them migrate from eastern and central North America south to Mexico and begin the journey back north in the spring: a round trip of thousands of miles! In spring, females lay eggs on their way back north, and their newly hatched offspring complete the trip for them.

LOOK FOR: Large, brown-orange wings with black veins and thick black outlines, which are dotted with white. Caterpillar feeds on milkweed, causing adult butterfly to taste bad to most birds.

WINGSPAN: 3 1/2 – 4".

HABITAT: Fields, roadsides, and other areas where milkweed grows.

RANGE: Widespread except far north.

SIMILAR SPECIES

VICEROY
Limenitis archippus

LOOK FOR: Wings similar to the Monarch, but somewhat smaller and darker with a crosswise black line on each wing. **WINGSPAN:** 3". **HABITAT:** Meadows, fields, wetlands. **RANGE:** Widespread.

RED ADMIRAL
Vanessa atalanta

LOOK FOR: Dark brown fore wings with white spots and wide orange bands. **WINGSPAN:** 1 3/4 – 2 3/8". **HABITAT:** Woods, meadows, gardens. **RANGE:** Widespread except far north.

MOURNING CLOAK
Nymphalis antiopa

LOOK FOR: Purplish-brown wings; black band with blue spots is edged with yellow. **WINGSPAN:** 3 3/8". **HABITAT:** Woods, streamsides, gardens. **RANGE:** Widespread except far north; rare in Deep South.

THINK ABOUT READING

Answer the questions in the story map.

SETTING

1. Where does the story take place?

CHARACTERS

2. Who is the main human character in the story?

3. Who appears while the man is sleeping?

PROBLEM

4. What is the smaller man's job in the rain forest?

EVENTS

5. While the man with the ax is sleeping, what do the animals whisper to him?

6. What does the Yanomamo child ask the man to do?

SOLUTION

7. What happens when the man awakes?

WRITE A STORY CONTINUATION

What happens next in *The Great Kapok Tree*? Write a continuation of the story. Decide which characters you want to use. Figure out what they will do and say. Perhaps the animals will take action, or maybe the smaller man will describe his "dream" to the larger man. Include dialogue between the characters in your continuation. Be sure to use correct punctuation in the dialogue.

LITERATURE CIRCLE

Authors of fiction and nonfiction usually have a purpose for writing a book. What purpose did Lynne Cherry have when she wrote *The Great Kapok Tree*? Discuss whether or not you think she was successful and explain why. Then talk about Christina Wilsdon's purpose for writing about the Monarch butterfly. Compare the writing of these two authors and record your ideas on a Venn diagram.

AUTHOR AND ILLUSTRATOR
LYNNE CHERRY

Imagine sitting by a jungle stream, watching a group of monkeys swing through the trees! Lynne Cherry did just that when she was getting ready to write *The Great Kapok Tree*. She wanted to see the rain forest for herself, so she traveled to South America to get information for the book. Ms. Cherry says she has a great desire to make the world a better place, and she hopes that her books will help readers understand how important it is to take care of the environment.

MORE BOOKS BY
LYNNE CHERRY

- *Flute's Journey: The Life of a Wood Thrush*
- *A River Ran Wild*
- *The Armadillo from Amarillo*

How to
Make a
Field Guide

**Create a field guide for
a close-up look at nature.**

A field guide is a great way to present different kinds of information. It can be a book or a pamphlet that tells about the plant and animal life in an environment. Most guides contain a collection of facts, diagrams, and pictures. They put lots of information right at your fingertips. Create your own field guide for an outdoor place.

My Field Guide

Terns on the beach.

Sea lions getting a suntan

dried seaweed

The Pacific Ocean

The design looks like a starfish.

Scallop Shell

The sand dollar's mouth

Sand from Seal Beach

The sand dollar is a kind of sea urchin. When it's alive it has lots of short spines all over its body. These spines help it to burrow into the sand.

Go Exploring

Visit an outdoor environment that you want to describe in a field guide. Maybe it's a city park, your own backyard, the beach, or a nearby lake. Be sure to wear protective clothing. When you arrive, spend a few minutes quietly observing the plants and animals in the surrounding area. Which ones are most plentiful? What is unusual about them?

Poison oak

Poison ivy

TOOLS

- notebook and pencil

- field guides, reference books, nature magazines

- paper, colored pencils, and markers

- magnifying glass

- protective clothing— long pants, long-sleeved shirt, socks, gloves

- camera (optional)

Tips
- Be still so you don't scare the animals.
- Concentrate on one small area at a time.
- Use encyclopedias and field guides to identify plants and animals in your environment.
- If you have a camera, take some photos of the things you are observing.

2 Record What You Found

Get out your notebook and list the interesting plants and animals that you see. When you're done with your list, check off at least eight items that you want to include in your field guide. Write a description of each item, using lots of details. Make sketches and diagrams to help you remember what each plant and animal looks like.

How Am I Doing?

Before you put your field guide together, take a minute to ask yourself these questions:

- Did I write clear notes that will help me remember everything in the environment?

- Did I label my sketches?

- Have I identified the plants and animals I selected?

3 Make Your Guide

Now it's time to put your field guide together. Here are some ideas.

- Assembling the Pages: Attach several sheets of paper together to make a book.

- The Cover: Create a title for your guide and add some art to make it come alive. Be sure to include your name as the author.

- Pictures: Paste your sketches and diagrams onto the pages of your field guide. Having trouble drawing? Use reference books to identify the plants and animals you observed, and then trace the pictures from the books. You can also use pictures from magazines.

- Nature Facts: Write facts about each plant or animal on the page where it appears.

4 **Present Your Guide**

- Share your field guides with another class.

- Trade field guides with a friend. Visit the place some-one else explored in his or her guide and see what you can learn!

If You Are Using a Computer ...

- **Print out fun captions to add to your guide.**
- **Make a cover with the title-page maker.**

CONGRATULATIONS

You've learned several ways to record and organize information about nature. Now you are an informed nature watcher!

Veronica Gonzales-Vest
Park Ranger ▶

IT TAKES A LEADER

IT TAKES A LEADER

THEME

In every community there are people who inspire others to take action.

UNIT 6

Welcome to

LITERACY PLACE

Newspaper Office

In every community
there are people
who inspire others
to take action.

Dinner at Aunt

by Faith Ringgold

My aunt Connie is a great artist. She and Uncle Bates live in a big beautiful house on the beach in Sag Harbor, Long Island. Every summer they invite our whole family to come for a delicious dinner and a special showing of Aunt Connie's artwork. I could hardly wait for this year's dinner—not only for the food but also for the art, which was to be a big surprise.

Connie's House

Another surprise was Lonnie, my aunt and uncle's adopted son. I fell in love with him the first time I saw him. Have you ever seen a little black boy with red hair and green eyes? Neither had I before Lonnie. While the rest of the family relaxed on the beach before dinner, Lonnie and I went in the house and played hide-and-seek.

I heard some noises up in the attic and climbed the stairs to see if Lonnie was up there.

"Come out, come out, wherever you are," I sang out.

"Come in, Melody," a strange voice answered. "We would like to talk to you."

"Lonnie, stop trying to scare me with that strange voice," I said.

"I am Fannie Lou Hamer, born in 1917 in Mississippi. I was a civil rights activist and public speaker. I worked with Martin Luther King for voters' rights in the South. I helped thousands of people register to vote."

"My dream was education. I am Mary McLeod Bethune, born in 1875 in South Carolina. I founded Bethune-Cookman College. I was a special adviser to Presidents Franklin D. Roosevelt and Harry S. Truman and founded the National Council of Negro Women, an organization that has more than one million members."

"I was a sculptor. My name is Augusta Savage, and I was born in 1892 in Florida. I founded The Savage Studio of Arts and Crafts in Harlem. I taught many artists to paint, draw, and sculpt. Maybe you've heard of one of my students, the famous painter Jacob Lawrence?"

"My name is Dorothy Dandridge. Born in 1922 in Ohio, I was the first African-American actress to become a Hollywood star. I was nominated for an Academy Award in 1954 for Best Actress for the film *Carmen Jones*. I starred in other films with famous actors such as James Mason and Joan Fontaine."

"I am Zora Neale Hurston, born in 1901 in Florida."

"I know who you are," I said. "You're a famous writer."

"Yes, Melody. In the 1930s I was the most prolific African-American writer. My books—*Their Eyes Were Watching God, Moses, Man of the Mountain*, and *Mules and Men*—are considered among the best examples of American writing."

"I was born way back in 1803 in Connecticut. My name is Maria W. Stewart. Back then, women could not be public speakers, yet I spoke out for the human rights of oppressed blacks. I was also the first African American to lecture in defense of women's rights."

"I am Bessie Smith, empress of blues. I was born in 1894 in Tennessee. I was once the highest paid African-American artist in the world. The great jazz trumpeter Louis Armstrong was one of my accompanists. I inspired many singers with my soul and spirit."

"People called me Moses. I am Harriet Tubman, born in 1820 in Maryland. I brought more than three hundred slaves to freedom in the North in nineteen trips on the Underground Railroad— and never lost a passenger. Among them were my aged mother and father and my ten brothers and sisters."

"I am Sojourner Truth, born in 1797 in New York State. I was an itinerant preacher and an abolitionist with Frederick Douglass and William Lloyd Garrison. I spoke out for women's rights during slavery, when no American woman had the right to vote. I met and spoke with President Abraham Lincoln."

"I am Marian Anderson, born in 1902 in Pennsylvania. Arturo Toscanini, the great conductor, said a voice such as mine is heard only once in a hundred years. I was denied the right to sing at Constitution Hall by the Daughters of the American Revolution in Washington, D.C. In protest, I sang on the steps of the Lincoln Memorial to a crowd of 75,000. I was known as the world's greatest living contralto and was the first African American to perform with the Metropolitan Opera Company."

"Someday I want to be an opera singer, too," Lonnie said.

"My name is Madame C.J. Walker. I was born in 1867 in Louisiana. I was the first self-made American woman millionaire. I employed more than three thousand people in my cosmetics company. My invention, the hair-straightening comb, changed the appearance of millions of people."

"What do you think of us, children?" the paintings asked.

"I am very proud to be an African-American woman," I said.

"You are only a nine year old, Melody, not a woman," Lonnie said.

"And who do you think you are, Lonnie, with your red hair and green eyes? Not many African Americans look like you!"

"My hair is red and my eyes are green, but I am black, ten years old, and just as proud as you to be African American!"

Just then Uncle Bates appeared at the attic door.

"Since you two have already discovered Aunt Connie's surprise, you can help me take the paintings down to hang in the dining room."

Lonnie and I helped Uncle Bates hang the paintings on the dining room walls, then Aunt Connie called the family to dinner to see the big surprise.

Grandpa Bates was our family's toastmaster. Last year he toasted my sister Dee Dee and her fiancé, Carl's, engagement. Today he toasted Lonnie, who was Aunt Connie and Uncle Bates's son from now on. Then Lonnie read an African proverb in Swahili: *"Mti mzuri huota kwenye miiba,"* "A good tree grows among thorns." Aunt Connie's smile told us she knew we had been talking to the paintings.

Lonnie and I winked back at her, keeping the secret.

Aunt Connie's dinners are the best. We had roast turkey, duck, cranberry sauce, corn bread, stuffing, macaroni and cheese, candied sweet potatoes, and fresh greens. Seated around the table were the usual people: Aunt Connie and Uncle Bates, my mother and father, Grandma and Grandpa Bates, my sister Dee Dee and her new husband, Carl, and Mr. and Mrs. Tucker. But only Lonnie and I knew that today's dinner was extra special. It was magical. As we ate, Aunt Connie spoke about each of the women in her portraits.

Aunt Connie's paintings were no longer hanging on the dining room walls but sitting in the chairs around the table as our dinner guests. Aunt Connie's voice faded into the background, and our

family disappeared as Sojourner Truth spoke in support of the women's vote:

"Look at me . . . . I have plowed and planted and gathered into barns and no man could head me . . . I have borne thirteen children and seen most all sold into slavery, and when I cried out a mother's grief, none but Jesus heard me. And ain't I a woman?"

Harriet Tubman spoke about slavery: "There was one of two things I had a right to, liberty or death; if I could not have one, I would have the other, for no man should take me alive."

Maria Stewart spoke next, about a woman's right to speak in public. "Men of eminence have mostly risen from obscurity; nor will I, although female of a darker hue and far more obscure than they, bend my head or hang my harp upon willows, for though poor I will virtuous prove."

"Connie, your art is a great inspiration to us all," said Uncle Bates.

"Their lives speak more powerfully than any paintings could," Aunt Connie said. "Don't you think so children?" She winked her eye at Lonnie and me.

"When I grow up, I want to sing in opera houses all over the world. I know it will be hard, but not as hard for me as it was for Marian Anderson," said Lonnie.

"I want to be the president of the United States when I grow up," I said, "so I can change some of the things that make people's lives so sad. I know I can do it because of these women."

"Amen! Amen!" everybody chimed.

"I never thought my wife and the mother of our children would be the president of the United States," Lonnie whispered in my ear.

"And I never thought I would marry an African-American opera singer with red hair and green eyes," I whispered back.

"But what will our children think of Aunt Connie's secret, Melody?"

"Our children will love the secret. We will have delicious family dinners, and they will be magical just like Aunt Connie's, and our children, Lonnie, will be just like us."

MENTOR

Suki Cheong

Editor

This editor knows what the scoop is!

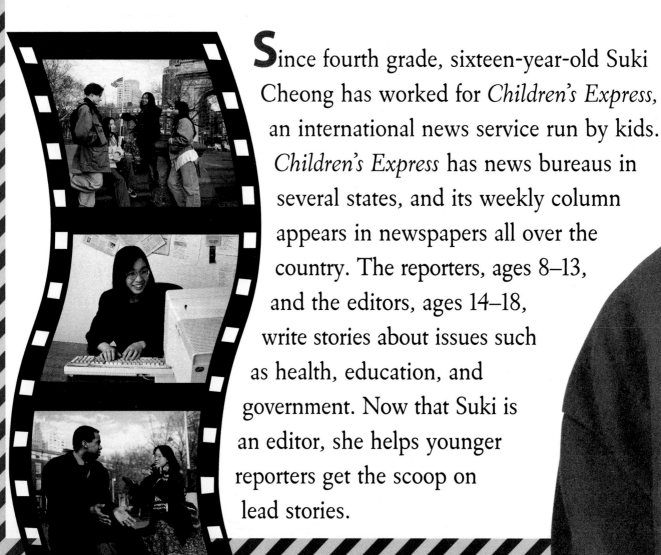

Since fourth grade, sixteen-year-old Suki Cheong has worked for *Children's Express*, an international news service run by kids. *Children's Express* has news bureaus in several states, and its weekly column appears in newspapers all over the country. The reporters, ages 8–13, and the editors, ages 14–18, write stories about issues such as health, education, and government. Now that Suki is an editor, she helps younger reporters get the scoop on lead stories.

PROFILE

Name: Suki Cheong

Job: student, Senior Editor/*Children's Express*

Education: Stuyvesant High School, New York City

Awards: Both a Peabody and an Emmy award for Presidential election coverage

Role Model: Hillary Rodham Clinton

Favorite Newspaper Section: The Op-Ed pages

QUESTIONS

for Suki Cheong

Discover how Suki Cheong writes about issues from a kid's point of view.

Q What was your first job at *Children's Express?*

A I started out as a reporter at *Children's Express*. Right away, I was responsible for preparing questions and doing interviews.

Q What's your job now that you are an editor?

A It's not like a typical news editor's job. I don't just edit the story—my job is to guide the reporter. I research the subject that we're doing an article on, and gather together statistics and facts we might need. If it's an interview, I set up a time and place for the interview, then brief the reporter. After an interview, I help write the actual article. I also help organize projects, conferences, and roundtable discussions.

Q Who chooses the stories that go into *Children's Express?*

A Every month we have a meeting with all the kids in the bureau. We brainstorm and then vote on our ideas. Then the reporters decide which ones they want to work on.

Q What issues do you think are important to write about?

A Any issues that affect children are important, such as violence in schools and on the streets, education, and health. The most interesting interview I ever did was with Miguel, a sixteen-year-old who lives in a violent neighborhood. I felt it was important for people to hear his story.

Q Do you think that *Children's Express* can have an effect on your community and others?

A The purpose of *Children's Express* is to make sure that kids have a voice in their community. Maybe our stories don't always make an immediate difference. But they will make people think about an issue in a new way—from a kid's point of view.

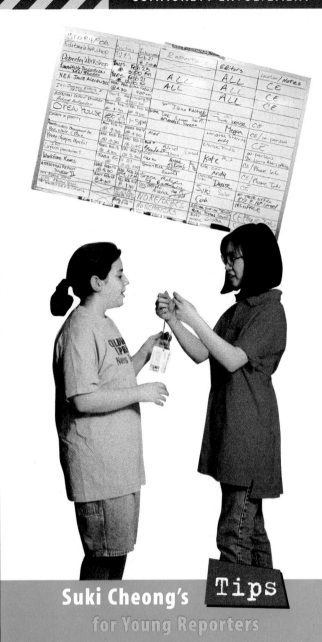

Suki Cheong's Tips
for Young Reporters

1 Research the subject of your story or interview.

2 If it's an interview, prepare your questions ahead of time. Ask permission if you want to tape the interview.

3 Before you start writing, decide how you want to organize your story.

CHILDREN'S EXPRESS News Team

THINK ABOUT READING

Write your answers.

1. Why have Melody and her family come to Aunt Connie's house?

2. What do the portraits in the attic have in common?

3. Which of the women in the paintings do you admire most? Give reasons for your answer.

4. Why do you think the author chose to let the paintings "talk" and tell about themselves?

5. In what way is Suki Cheong like the famous women in Faith Ringgold's paintings? Explain your answer.

WRITE A THANK-YOU NOTE

You are one of the lucky people who attended Aunt Connie's dinner party. Write her a thank-you note telling her what a great time you had. Mention one or two things that you especially enjoyed about your visit. Be sure to thank the rest of her family, too. You may wish to ask Aunt Connie's family to have dinner with you, too. In your thank-you note, be sure to include the date, a greeting, and a friendly closing.

LITERATURE CIRCLE

Dinner at Aunt Connie's House presents factual details in a fictional story. What do you think Faith Ringgold's purpose was in writing this book? Discuss why she might have decided to use fiction and nonfiction in the same story. Tell whether or not you think the book achieves the author's purpose, and give reasons to support your opinions. Record your ideas on a concept web.

AUTHOR / ILLUSTRATOR
FAITH RINGGOLD

Faith Ringgold grew up in Harlem, New York, in the 1930s. She says, "My childhood was the most wonderful period of my life—till now." As a child, she visited art museums, listened to stories told by her family and friends, and learned to sew. As an adult, Ringgold combined her knowledge of sewing with her love of storytelling and began to create story quilts—an art form that *she* created. It was one of these story quilts that inspired Faith Ringgold to write her award-winning picture book, *Tar Beach*.

MORE BOOKS BY
FAITH RINGGOLD

- *Aunt Harriet's Underground Railroad in the Sky*
- *Bonjour, Lonnie*
- *Tar Beach*

MAYAN TALE

RAIN

STORY AND PICTURES BY
DAVID WISNIEWSKI

The city lay in darkness, yet the *Ah Kin Mai* had been awake for hours. Trembling, the old priest consulted his charts and calendars once again. "*Kintunyaabil*," they declared. "A year of terrible drought."

The sky reddened and the blazing face of Lord Sun appeared. Without rain, his dreadful heat would soon devour the corn. And without corn, the people would perish.

The *Ah Kin Mai* blew a long clear note on his conch shell. The people had to know their fate. Perhaps Chac, the god of rain, would also hear and have mercy.

On the ball court, Pik played *pok-a-tok* with his friends. Like his father, who competed before the supreme ruler in full costume, Pik had great skill. He blocked a pass with his shoulder and sent the ball flying through the stone ring above his head. "Game!" he cried.

"Hush!" warned the others. "Listen!"

The call of the *Ah Kin Mai* floated in the dusty air. The boys ran to hear what fate the new year would bring.

Pik listened impatiently to the prophecy. "Do the gods have nothing better to do than torment us?" he whispered to his companions. "Things would be different if I were the Ah Kin Mai. I would just tell Chac to get to work!"

The boys' laughter was cut short by a chorus of croaking. The little frogs of the forest, the *uo*, filled the trees about them. Knowing *uo* to be the heralds of Chac, the boys fled. But before Pik could take a step, he was whisked into the swirling clouds above.

The voice of Chac rumbled like thunder. "Is it right for such a small creature to bear such a large tongue?"

Pik bowed before the rain god. "O Mighty Chac, I misspoke," he said politely. "I beg your forgiveness."

"Forgiveness must be earned," Chac replied.

Pik thought quickly. "May I earn it playing *pok-a-tok*? That is what I do best!"

"You wish to challenge *me*?" boomed Chac.

Pik nodded nervously.

"Very well!" Chac agreed. "Two days hence, we shall play. Bring a team if you can find one. Two games of three shall decide your fate."

"What if I win?" Pik asked.

"You will earn my forgiveness and rain for your people," Chac replied.

"And if I lose?"

Chac laughed and the air smelled like lightning. "You will become a frog and croak my name forever."

"But I don't want to be a frog!" wailed Pik.

"You should have thought of that before insulting Chac," said his father sternly. "Challenging a god to *pok-a-tok*! No wonder your friends refuse to join your team."

"Won't you?" Pik asked hopefully.

"No, I will not," his father replied. "Much more than skill is required." He emptied the contents of a leather pouch onto a table. "At your *hetzmek*, these things were placed in your baby hands: a planting stick, to make the hole for the corn seed, and a ball—"

558

"To make me a great player!" Pik interrupted. "It has done so!"

"But there is more," his father chided. "Here is a jaguar tooth, that you might share Jaguar's fierce strength. And here is a quetzal feather, that you might receive Quetzal's silent speed. And, most precious of all, the water of the sacred *cenote*, that you might make its deep wisdom your own. Seek their counsel. Perhaps they will know how to help you."

Rising early, Pik came upon Jaguar by first light. "*Otzilen*," he said respectfully. "I have need."

"Indeed," replied Jaguar, inspecting his claws. "All the forest knows of your plight. Fate is against you, but a victory over Chac would give us rain, and that is something we sorely need. I will help you if I can."

"But how?"

"Doesn't your father wear a jaguar cloak when he plays
before royalty? Tomorrow, I will be your cloak. More than that,
I do not know."

At noon, Pik searched the trees for sign of Quetzal. "*Otzilen!*" he cried. "I have need!"

Quetzal lit upon a branch and regarded him kindly. "I have heard of your challenge to Chac," she said. "Fate is harder than stone, yet it must be broken for the rains to come. I will help you if I can."

"How?" asked Pik.

"Doesn't your father wear a fancy headdress when he plays before royalty? My beautiful feathers will be your crown. More than that, I do not know."

As the sun set, Pik lowered himself into the darkness of the sacred *cenote*. Far below, dark water swirled through the great caves it had carved below the earth. "*Otzilen*," Pik whispered, and his plea echoed in the vastness.

With the faintest breath of air, the words of the *cenote* entered his ear. "I know your step," the *cenote* sighed, "for I flow beneath

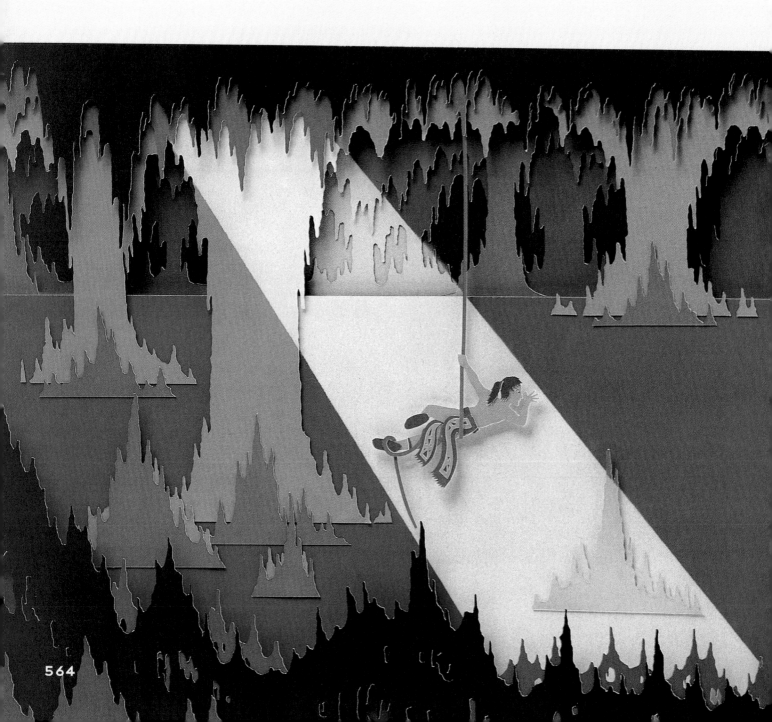

the ball court. Though fate says otherwise, Chac's rains must continue, for they are my constancy and strength. Go now. Tomorrow, I will be with you."

"But how?" asked Pik.

"Tomorrow," came the echo, and all was still.

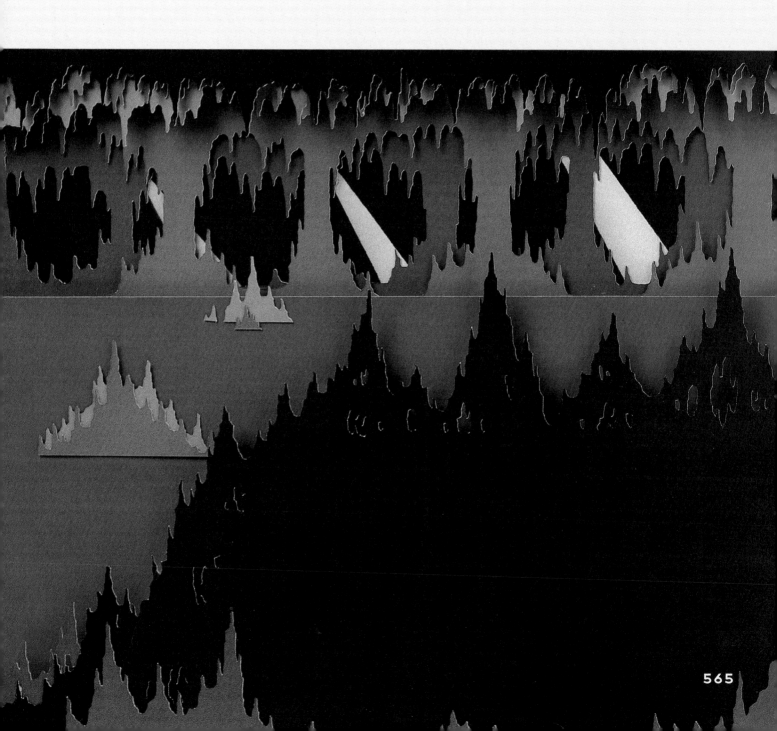

The next day, all marveled as Pik strode toward the ball court. A magnificent jaguar cloak hung from his shoulders, and brilliant quetzal feathers streamed from his headdress. Then the people grew silent as the *uo* announced the arrival of Chac in the sky above.

The rain god nodded his readiness to the *Ah Kin Mai*. With shaking hands, the priest held the ball aloft. "Begin!" he cried, and cast it into the court.

A great gust of wind stole the ball from Pik, and a twisting column of cloud blasted it down the court. Chac had sent a whirlwind to play for him!

Instantly, Jaguar leaped from Pik's shoulders. Seizing the ball in his powerful jaws, he sped to the other side and soared through the ring.

"One!" shouted Pik.

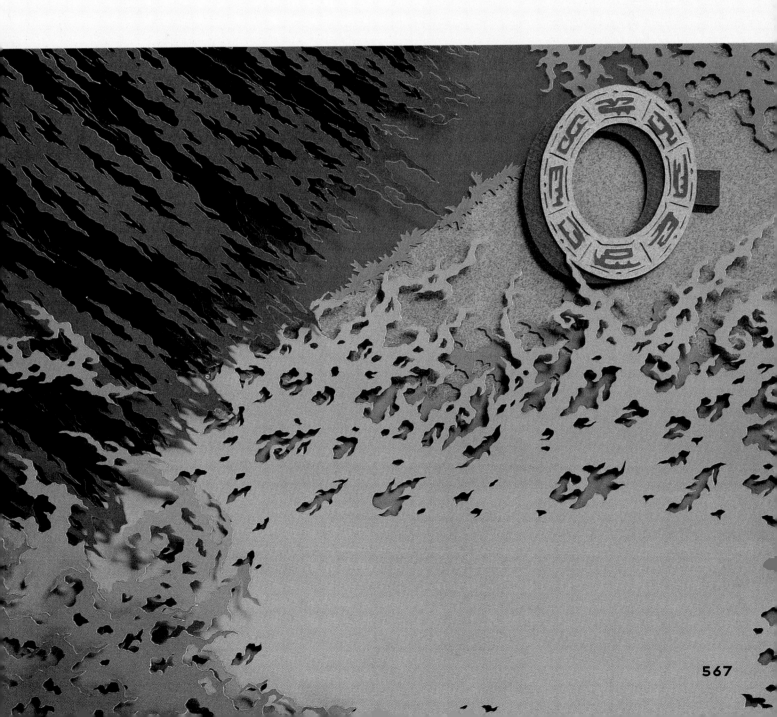

Again the old priest tossed the ball into play. At that moment, Chac loosed a score of lightning bolts. They fell with blinding fury, tearing the earth and spinning the ball toward the goal.

Quetzal flew from Pik's head and snatched the ball with her talons. Yet the lightning was stronger than she. Still clutching the ball, Quetzal was driven through the ring.

"One for me!" thundered Chac. He came down from the clouds, and his colossal form dwarfed the tallest temples. "Now I will break this tie!"

The ball fell to the court again. Pik scrambled backward as Chac lifted his huge foot. Then, with a terrific crack, the ground gave way, and Chac plunged into the *cenote* below.

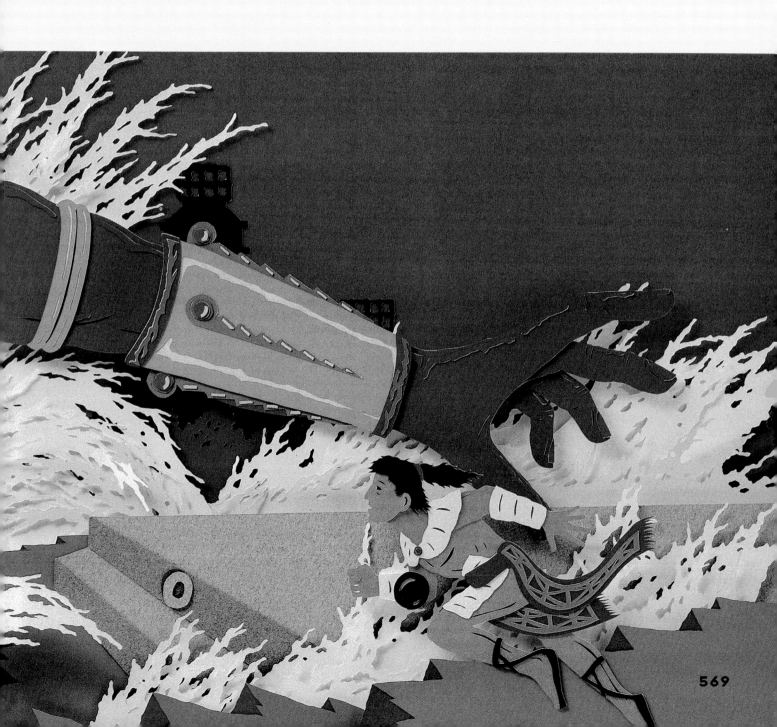

Racing skillfully over the broken ground, Pik sent the final goal flying through the center of the ring. "Mine!" he whooped.

Chac lifted himself out of the hole in silence. Without a word, he took Pik in his great hand and soared into the heavens. "You have won, little man," Chac muttered, "and I cannot say that I am pleased. But we had an agreement."

He placed Pik by the enormous gourd that hung from his belt. "Gently now," Chac warned, "Don't flood the world."

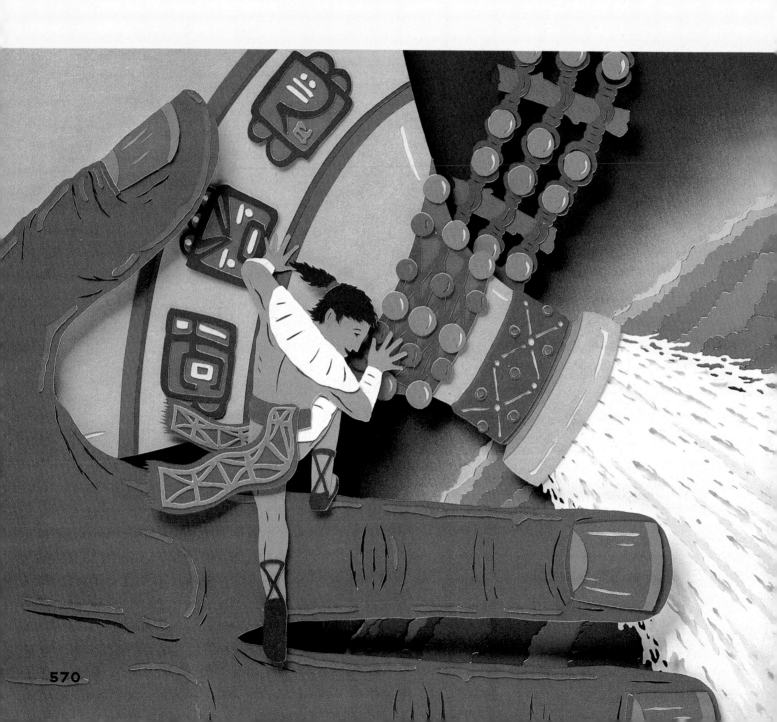

Using both hands, Pik tilted the gourd. A great rain gushed from it and fell to the thirsty earth below.

Chac kept his word to Pik that season and for many seasons thereafter.

In time, the fine young ball player with the strength of a jaguar and the speed of a quetzal gained great renown. He became known as Rain Player, for distant thunder greeted his entrance on the court, and gentle showers followed each victory.

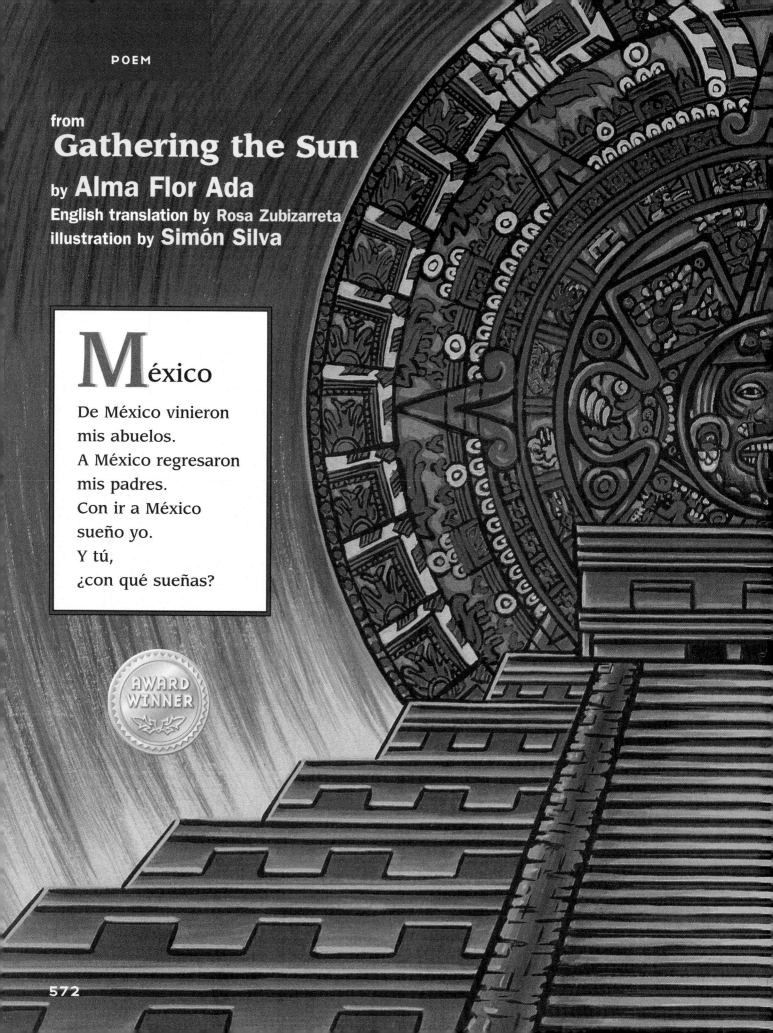

POEM

from
Gathering the Sun
by **Alma Flor Ada**
English translation by Rosa Zubizarreta
illustration by Simón Silva

México

De México vinieron
mis abuelos.
A México regresaron
mis padres.
Con ir a México
sueño yo.
Y tú,
¿con qué sueñas?

Mexico

My grandparents
came from Mexico.
My parents
returned to Mexico.
My dream is
to visit Mexico.
And you,
what is your dream?

THINK ABOUT READING

Answer the questions in the story map.

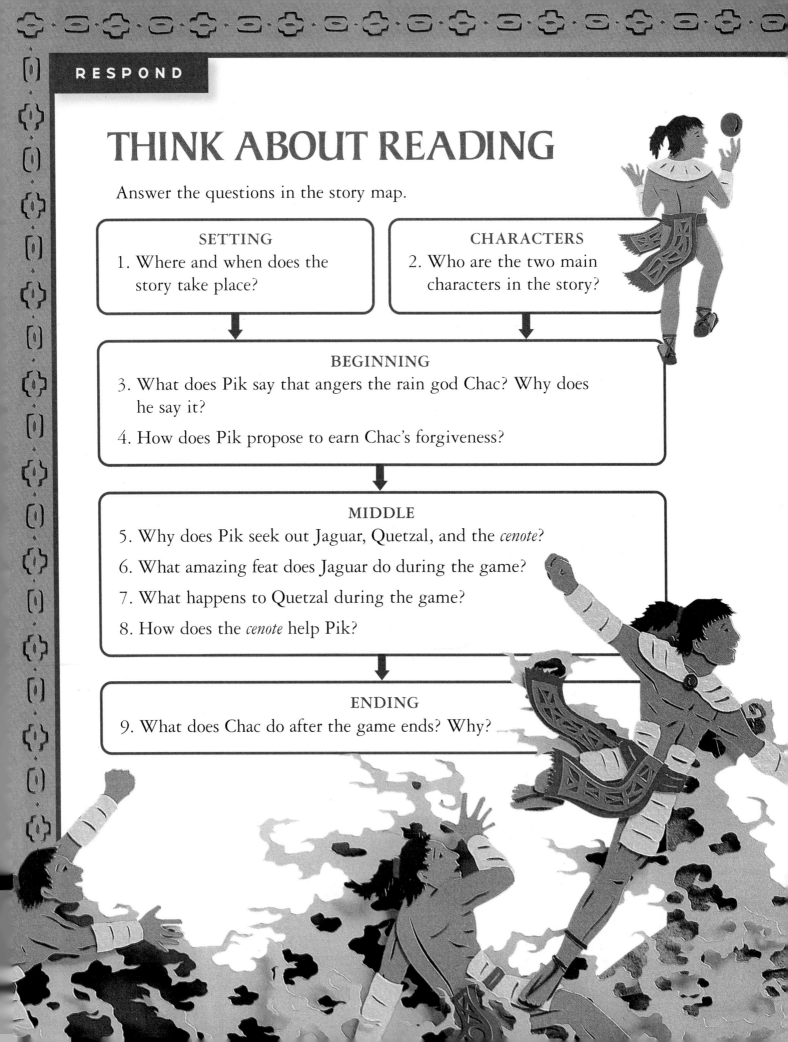

SETTING	CHARACTERS
1. Where and when does the story take place?	2. Who are the two main characters in the story?

BEGINNING

3. What does Pik say that angers the rain god Chac? Why does he say it?

4. How does Pik propose to earn Chac's forgiveness?

MIDDLE

5. Why does Pik seek out Jaguar, Quetzal, and the *cenote*?

6. What amazing feat does Jaguar do during the game?

7. What happens to Quetzal during the game?

8. How does the *cenote* help Pik?

ENDING

9. What does Chac do after the game ends? Why?

WRITE AN ART REVIEW

Imagine that the illustrations for *Rain Player* and the poem "México" are on display in your school. Choose one of the illustrators and write a review of his artwork for your school newspaper. Describe the medium that the illustrator used. Tell what is unique or unusual about the artwork, and consider how well the illustrations go with the story or poem. Finally, tell whether you like the illustrations and explain why. End your review with a recommendation.

LITERATURE CIRCLE

Author David Wisniewski creates an unusual world in *Rain Player*. Discuss how he makes the setting, the events, and the characters in the story believable. Talk about the importance of the illustrations in the story. Record your ideas on a concept web. Then discuss what you like best about the story.

AUTHOR/ILLUSTRATOR
DAVID WISNIEWSKI

David Wisniewski's first job was clowning around—in the circus. There he used his artistic abilities to create his own colorful costumes and props. Later, Wisniewski and his wife started a shadow puppet theater, where he made intricate shadow puppets from paper and wrote plays for them. All these experiences helped when he began to write picture books and illustrate them with elaborate cut-paper art. Wisniewski often writes original folk tales about cultures around the world. He says, "Though demanding, making words and pictures fit and flow...is enormously satisfying."

MORE BOOKS BY
DAVID WISNIEWSKI

- *Sundiata: Lion King of Mali*
- *The Warrior and the Wise Man*
- *The Wave of the Sea-Wolf*

How to
Make a Public-Service Announcement

How can you make information available to your community? One way is through a public-service announcement on radio or television.

What's a public-service announcement? Public-service announcements give information to the community. They are broadcast free of charge by radio and TV stations. Have you ever listened to the radio and heard that your school is closed because of bad weather? That's a public-service announcement! A public-service announcement may also tell about a community event, such as a book fair or a fund drive.

phone number or address for more information

AMERICAN RED CROSS ·

Radio: 30

Live Announcer Script

name of the group involved

body of message

Somewhere in the country…this very day…disaster struck. In fact, disaster strikes every single day. Which means every single night someone needs food, shelter, and a place to rest. You can make a difference. Please support the American Red Cross. Call 1-800-842-2200. Because every night is another night someone needs your help.

1 Choose a Topic

Brainstorm a list of real community issues or events for your public-service announcement. Perhaps a group in your town plans to raise money for a new park, or maybe your school is putting on a play. Make a list of events and issues. Then choose the one that means the most to you.

TOOLS

- pencil and paper
- local newspapers
- posterboard and colored markers
- tape recorder (optional)

2 Organize Your Facts

Do research to learn more about the issue or event you chose. You can read the local newspaper, watch the local TV news, or talk to people in your community. Take notes on what you learn. When you're finished, see whether you can answer the "5 Ws": *Who, What, When, Where,* and *Why.* If you can't, you'll need to do some more research.

Support THE In-line Skating Park

3 Write a Script

Here's how to write a script for your public-service announcement.

- Say that you are making a public-service announcement.

- Tell the name of the group that you represent.

- State the reason for the announcement.

- If you are announcing an event, give the time and place that it will be held.

- Explain to the audience members how they can get more information.

- Try to use words that will catch your audience's attention.

Tips
- State your message in the fewest words possible.
- Use action verbs to make your announcement more interesting.
- Listen to radio and TV announcers to see how they sound.
- Practice saying your announcement before you present it.

4 Present Your Public-Service Announcement

There are many ways to present your public-service announcement. You can read it "live" to the class, or read it into a tape recorder and play the tape for the class. You may want to add music and sound effects to make the announcement more dramatic.

If You Are Using a Computer...

Use the Record and Playback tools as you write your public-service announcement on the computer. You also may want to create a public-service announcement for a newspaper, using clip art and borders.

THINK

Why are public-service announcements an important service for the community?

Suki Cheong
Editor ▶

The Rag Coat

Lauren Mills

AWARD WINNER

The Rag Coat

by Lauren Mills

In winter, Papa carried me to church in a burlap feed sack because I didn't have a coat. Mama, Papa, Clemmie, and me—we'd all hitch a ride on Jeremy Miller's hay wagon and huddle under Mama's big quilt. I know Papa loved that quilt, because he said it had all the nice, bright colors of the day in it, and the day was something he hardly ever saw. He worked down in the black coal mines and didn't come up till the sun was gone.

I told Papa it was warmer under that quilt than if I *had* a coat. He always laughed when I said that, and told me, "Minna, you got the right way of thinking. People only need people, and nothing else. Don't you forget that."

Papa got sick with the miner's cough and couldn't work much, so Mama stitched day and night on her quilts to try to make some money.

When I was old enough to start school, I couldn't go. They needed me at home to help Mama. I would card all her quilt stuffing and keep Clemmie's dirty fingers out of all that cotton. I made a doll for myself by stitching up some of Mama's quilt scraps and stuffing cotton inside. I talked to her like she was my friend, because I didn't have any. Mama was too busy for much talk, and when Papa was home he mostly stared out the window.

The summer I was eight, Papa called me over to his rocking chair. I climbed up on his lap and he said, "You're getting big, Minna."

"Too big for laps?" I asked.

"Not too big for mine," he said softly, "but too big to still be at home. It's nearing time you went to school."

I could hardly hold back my smiling just thinking about all the friends I would have. But I didn't want to leave Mama without a helper. "Papa," I said, "I can't go to school. Mama needs me here."

Papa just looked at me real steady and said, "They have books at school, Minna. You can learn things from those books that you can't learn at home."

"But I don't have a coat, Papa," I quietly reminded him.

"Minna," he said, "don't you worry about a coat. I'll think of something." But he never got the chance. Papa died that summer.

Everyone came at once and brought us food. I couldn't figure out how so many people could squeeze into our little cabin, but somehow they managed it. They all said they knew my papa well.

I sat on a stool back by the woodstove with Clemmie on my lap, so no one would step on us.

I couldn't stand it! They all wore black, black like the coal mines that killed my papa. He didn't even like black. He liked all the bright colors of the day. So why were they wearing black, I wondered.

School started in September. Mama said I could go, but I decided not to. I still didn't have a coat to wear, and I knew it was no use starting something I'd have to quit when the weather turned cold.

Other mothers who had children in school came over to quilt with Mama. I called them the Quilting Mothers. That fall they were all working on a pattern called Joseph's Coat of Many Colors. I looked at it and said, "That Joseph sure was lucky to have such a coat. I wish I had one like that."

"Why do you say that, Minna?" Mrs. Miller asked me.

"Because then I could go to school," I said, a little embarrassed that I had mentioned it.

"Well now, Minna," said Mrs. Miller, "I don't know that any of us has a spare coat we could hand down to you, but I'm sure we have some scraps to spare. We could piece them together, and you'd have a coat like Joseph's after all." Mrs. Miller looked around the room, and the other mothers nodded.

Mama quickly protested. "You all need those rags for your own quilts. Don't go giving us things you need yourselves."

They paid no attention to Mama. Mrs. Hunter said, "And we could use feed bags for the inside of the coat."

My eyes filled with tears, but I wasn't embarrassed anymore. I said, "I have a feed sack Papa used to carry me in!" I ran and fetched it. "Will this do?"

Yes, it would do just fine, they told me. Then I thought of something important. "But you need to make quilts to *sell*. You can't take time out to quilt a coat."

"First things first," said Mrs. Miller, and they all repeated it. Mama smiled and shook her head, and I saw tears in her eyes, too.

The very next day I went to school, running most of the way to keep warm and thinking all the while of the coat I would soon have.

The schoolhouse was just one room filled with fourteen children. I had seen most of them at church but never got the chance to talk to them much.

I knew I would love school, even though I was put in the front row with the youngest ones, and Clyde Bradshaw whispered that it was because I was dumb. Then Shane Hunter pulled my braid, and Souci Miller said I asked the teacher too many questions. But our teacher, Miss Campbell, smiled at me and said, "Smart people are those who have asked a lot of questions."

My most favorite thing about school was Sharing Day. Each of us had our own day when we shared something special with the class.

Clyde Bradshaw brought in the watch his grandpa gave him. It still ticked, and he made sure we all heard it.

On her day Lottie showed us the porcelain doll her aunt from New York had sent her. We all thought it was the most beautiful thing ever and wanted to touch it, but Lottie wouldn't let anyone near it. She said, "Nope, it's mine," which made everybody mad.

I knew just what I would show when it was my Sharing Day, but I kept it a secret, and I knew the Quilting Mothers would keep it a secret, too.

Each day I hurried home to see my coat. It was looking like the colors of the fall days—the yellow-golds of the birch leaves, the silvery grays and purples of the sky, the deep greens and browns of the pines, and the rusty reds of the chimney bricks—all the colors Papa would have chosen. I decided to put a piece of his work jacket in there. It just seemed right.

The mothers worked as quickly as they could, but the cold weather was quicker. At recess Souci asked me why I didn't wear a coat. I told her I couldn't jump rope as well with one on. Jumping a lot kept me warm. I was fast becoming the best rope-jumper in the school.

Not last night but the night before
Twenty-four robbers came knocking at my door.

That was my favorite rope tune.

One night when Mama looked sad I told her things could be worse. We could have twenty-four robbers knocking at our door.

She said, "Now, what on earth would they want from *us*, Minna?"

"Oh, Mama, they would want the coat, first thing," I said. She laughed then, but I was most serious.

Finally my coat was done. It was so beautiful, and the Quilting Mothers had finished it in time for my Sharing Day!

That morning I walked to school looking down at all the different colored pieces of cloth in my coat. All the stories the Quilting Mothers had told me about the rags and who they belonged to, I knew by heart. I had ended up choosing the most worn pieces for my coat because the best stories went with them. I was still looking down and repeating each story to myself when I bumped into Clyde outside the schoolyard.

"Hey, Rag-Coat!" he said, and all the others laughed. Before I knew it, Souci, Lottie, and Clyde were dancing around me singing, "Rag-Coat! Rag-Coat!"

Lottie said, "Look, it's even dirty with soot!" and she poked her finger into my papa's cloth!

Then Souci said, "Hey, Minna, you were better off with *no* coat than with that old, ragged thing."

"Maybe you're right!" I yelled. "If I had *no* coat, then I never would have come to school!" I broke through their circle and ran away from them, far into the woods.

I found an old log and sat on it for a long time, too angry to cry. I just stared across the fields Papa used to gaze at.

"Oh, Papa, I wish you were here," I said, and then I couldn't help but cry. I cried for Papa, and I cried for the Quilting Mothers, who had wasted their time. I was crying so hard I rocked that old log.

Then all at once I stopped because I felt something warm and familiar. The feed bag inside my coat made me feel like Papa's arms were around me again. I could almost hear him say, "Minna, people only need people, and nothing else. Don't you forget that."

I jumped off the log, wiped the tears from my cheeks, and brushed the leaves off my coat. "I won't forget it, Papa," I said, and I headed back to school.

When I walked into the schoolroom, Miss Campbell looked up, surprised. "Why, Minna," she said, "I was told you ran home sick."

Souci jumped up, her face all red. "That's not true, Miss Campbell," she blurted out. "We lied to you. Minna left because we made fun of her old coat."

"I'll tell her, Souci," I said. "It's not an *old* coat. It's a *new* coat."

"But it's just a bunch of old rags," said Lottie.

"It is not just a bunch of old rags!" I said. "My coat is full of stories, stories about everybody here."

They all looked at me, real puzzled.

"Don't you see? These are all *your* rags!" They still seemed puzzled.

So I showed them. "Look, Shane, here is that blanket of yours that your mama's sister gave her the night you were born. The midwife said you wouldn't live but three days because you were so small. But your mama wrapped you up tight in that blanket and put you in a little box by the woodstove. And your papa kept the fire all night for three weeks. Of course, you lived, all right," I said, looking up at Shane. Shane was big. "And you hung on to that blanket for years, until it was nothing but shreds."

"My blanket," he whispered. "I thought I'd *never* see it again." He looked at his old rag like he wanted to touch it.

Then the others began discovering their old, favorite things and crowded around me. They each wanted their story told, and I remembered every one.

I even showed the piece of the woolen jacket Souci had let her calf wear when it was sick. Lottie's rag was a faded piece from the fancy dress her aunt from New York had sent for her seventh birthday. And Clyde had a scrap from the pants that he always wore when he went fishing with his grandpa.

Souci said, "Minna, I sure am sorry we ever said anything bad about your coat."

"Me, too," I heard the others murmur.

"I wouldn't blame you if you didn't let us touch it," Lottie said.

"I wouldn't blame you if you didn't want to be our friend at all!" said Clyde.

"Friends share," I said, and I let them each touch their rag. Then I showed them the feed sack inside my coat and told them how it made me feel my papa's arms again.

Shane put his hand on my shoulder and said, "Minna, I bet you got the warmest coat in school."

"Well, it took a *whole lot of people* to make it warm," I told him, and we all laughed.

from JZUR
ZuZu

AROUND THE WORLD

Eye on the PRIZE

NAL

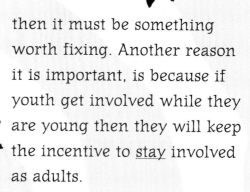

Hi, my name is Rhiannon Chavis-Legerton. I am from a small town in the southeastern part of North Carolina called Pembroke. I am a 13-year-old Lumbee Indian who has lived here all of my life. My family works in the community for justice, equality, and for correct treatment of the environment. Our organization is called the Center for Community Action.

I have been taught that youth should be involved with community work. Over time, I have grown to understand why this is so. The reason I think so is because youth have a strong say in the community. Many government officials will sometimes listen to youth more than they would adults. They figure that if the youth are strong enough to speak out

then it must be something worth fixing. Another reason it is important, is because if youth get involved while they are young then they will keep the incentive to <u>stay</u> involved as adults.

Before you can become fully involved, there will be many obstacles to overcome in the process. One of these is to ignore all of the remarks thrown at you by other people such as, "You won't win, why not just give up trying?" Over time, you will find that the only reason people say things like this is because they are really scared that you will win. Another obstacle is that if you have one teeny tiny bit of concern that you will have to work with people of other races, then get rid of it right away.

Eye on the Prize

This is because when you are fighting for something right, then it is most likely that people from other races are too. But over time, you will see that they have the same thoughts and ideas as you do.

I have done much work for change. Right now I will tell you about some of it. When I was about 5 years old, threats were made that an incinerator would be put near my home. My family and many other families worked and planned together to think of a way to stop it.

There was something for everyone to do, young and old. I have also been to Alabama to help the Choctaw stop a waste dump. I gave a speech there that was quoted on TV and in the newspaper. I am now in a multi-cultural play about a time in Robeson County when there was a lot of hatred and prejudice against people of color.

If anyone reading would like to get involved, here are some starting tips. Keep an update on the problems going on in your community. Always keep a cool head and don't blow your top every time something doesn't go your way. Go in expecting to win, and if you do, praise yourself, but don't get a big head because it might affect your attitude on the next issue. And the last tip I have is give all you can to the work and cooperate with others.

Since I have been fighting for people's rights, I have found it easier to do if you live by certain sayings.

The first one is to never give up, your luck will turn around one day.

🌹 The next one is to always look ahead, never dwell in the past or you will accomplish nothing.

🌹 The last thing that I live by is to keep your eyes on the prize, the light is never too bright.

"...Get Everyone involved, including children, because if they're not they might have bad dreams or thoughts because they hear _you_ talking about it. They don't understand what is happening So... just REMEMBER - if you have them, (KIDS) INVOLVE THEM!"
— excerpt from a speech by Rhiannon (when she was 11-yrs old!)

Think About Reading

Answer the questions in the story map.

> **CHARACTERS**
> 1. Who is the main character in the story?

> **SETTING**
> 2. When and where does the story take place?

> **PROBLEM**
> 3. Why doesn't Minna want to go to school at first?

EVENTS

> 4. What do the Quilting Mothers decide to do for Minna?
>
> 5. At school, why does Minna become the best rope-jumper?
>
> 6. What happens the first time that Minna wears her rag coat to school?
>
> 7. Why does Minna decide to go back to the school house?

> **SOLUTION**
> 8. What do Minna's classmates discover about the rag coat? How do they feel?

Write a Character Sketch

Minna is a memorable character. Write a character sketch that tells all about her. Include what she thinks is important, what she does well, and what her most admirable qualities are. You may wish to use a quote by Minna that shows what kind of person she is. Be sure to include a physical description of her, too. Choose active verbs and colorful adjectives to make your character sketch lively and interesting.

Literature Circle

Think about the way *The Rag Coat* is told. First identify who is telling the story and discuss why you think the author chose this character to be the narrator. Do you think this was a good choice? Why or why not? Talk about how the story might change if another character or an outside narrator related the events. Then look at "Eye on the Prize." The article is written in first person. Discuss how it would change if it were written in third person.

AUTHOR/ILLUSTRATOR
Lauren Mills

As a child, Lauren Mills learned quilting, weaving, and dollmaking from her mother, grandmother, and aunt. She even had a patchwork coat of her very own! These pleasant childhood memories and her fondness for the crafts made by the people of Appalachia inspired Mills to write and illustrate her award-winning book, *The Rag Coat*.

MORE BOOKS BY
Lauren Mills

- *Tatterhood and the Hobgoblins: A Norwegian Folktale*
- *The Dog Prince*

BIOGRAPHY

Teammates

Jackie Robinson

"Pee Wee" Reese

by **Peter Golenbock**
illustrated by **Paul Bacon**

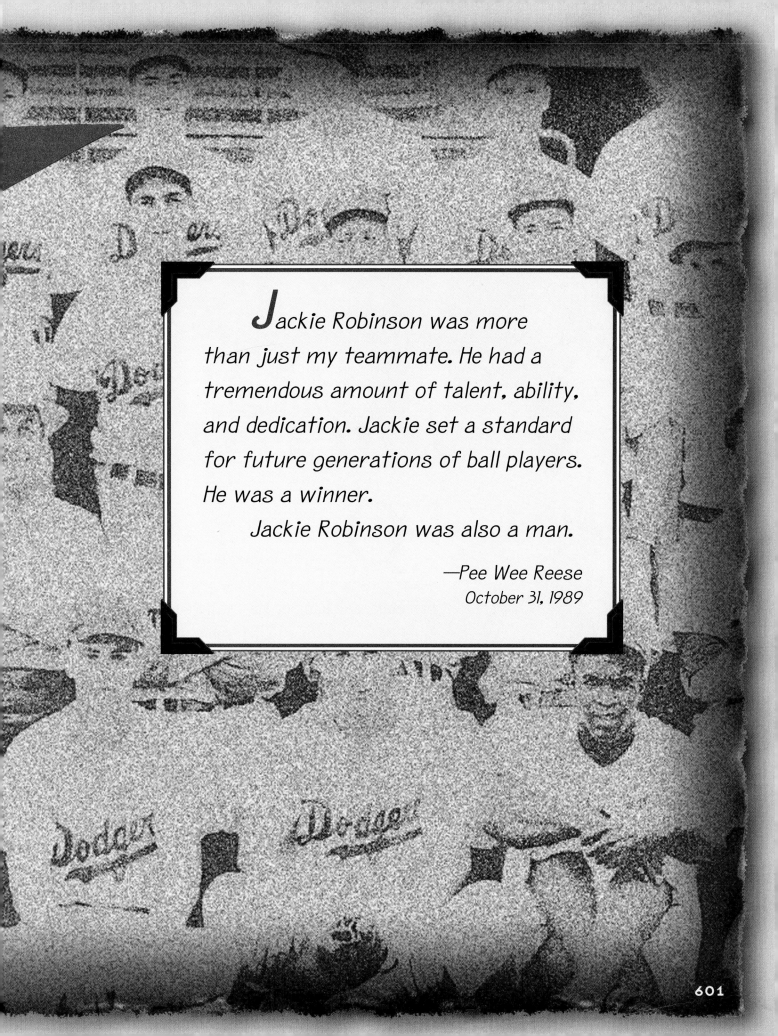

*J*ackie Robinson was more than just my teammate. He had a tremendous amount of talent, ability, and dedication. Jackie set a standard for future generations of ball players. He was a winner.

Jackie Robinson was also a man.

—Pee Wee Reese
October 31, 1989

SATCHEL PAIGE

Once upon a time in America, when automobiles were black and looked like tanks and laundry was white and hung on clotheslines to dry, there were two wonderful baseball leagues that no longer exist. They were called the Negro Leagues.

The Negro Leagues had extraordinary players, and adoring fans came to see them wherever they played. They were heroes, but players in the Negro Leagues didn't make much money and their lives on the road were hard.

Laws against segregation didn't exist in the 1940s. In many places in this country, black people were not allowed to go to the same schools and churches as white people. They couldn't sit in the front of a bus or trolley car. They couldn't drink from the same drinking fountains that white people drank from.

Back then, many hotels didn't rent rooms to black people, so the Negro League players slept in their cars. Many towns had no restaurants that would serve them, so they often had to eat meals that they could buy and carry with them.

Life was very different for the players in the Major Leagues. They were the leagues for white players. Compared to the Negro League players, white players were very well paid. They stayed in good hotels and ate in fine restaurants. Their pictures were put on baseball cards and the best players became famous all over the world.

Many Americans knew that racial prejudice was wrong, but few dared to challenge openly the way things were. And many people were apathetic about racial problems. Some feared that it could be dangerous to object. Vigilante groups, like the Ku Klux Klan, reacted violently against those who tried to change the way blacks were treated.

The general manager of the Brooklyn Dodgers baseball team was a man by the name of Branch Rickey. He was not afraid of change. He wanted to treat the Dodger fans to the best players he could find, regardless of the color of their skin. He thought segregation was

SPORT KINGS GUM

BABE RUTH

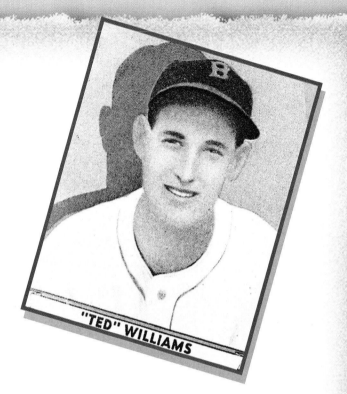

"TED" WILLIAMS

unfair and wanted to give everyone, regardless of race or creed, an opportunity to compete equally on ballfields across America.

To do this, the Dodgers needed one special man.

Branch Rickey launched a search for him. He was looking for a star player in the Negro Leagues who would be able to compete successfully despite threats on his life or attempts to injure him. He would have to possess the self-control not to fight back when opposing players tried to intimidate or hurt him. If this man disgraced himself on the field, Rickey knew, his opponents would use it as an excuse to keep blacks out of Major League baseball for many more years.

Rickey thought Jackie Robinson might be just the man.

Jackie rode the train to Brooklyn to meet Mr. Rickey. When Mr. Rickey told him, "I want a man with the courage not to fight back," Jackie Robinson replied, "If you take this gamble, I will do my best to perform." They shook hands. Branch Rickey and Jackie Robinson were starting on what would be known in history as "the great experiment."

At spring training with the Dodgers, Jackie was mobbed by blacks, young and old, as if he were a savior. He was the first black player to try out for a Major League team. If he succeeded, they knew, others would follow.

Initially, life with the Dodgers was for Jackie a series of humiliations. The players on his team who came from the South, men who had been taught to avoid black people since childhood, moved to another table whenever he sat down next to them. Many opposing players were cruel to him, calling him nasty names from their dugouts. A few tried to hurt him with their spiked shoes. Pitchers aimed at his head. And he received threats on his life, both from individuals and from organizations like the Ku Klux Klan.

Despite all the difficulties, Jackie Robinson didn't give up. He made the Brooklyn Dodgers team.

But making the Dodgers was only the beginning. Jackie had to face abuse and hostility throughout the season, from

April through September. His worst pain was inside. Often he felt very alone. On the road he had to live by himself, because only the white players were allowed in the hotels in towns where the team played.

The whole time Pee Wee Reese, the Dodger shortstop, was growing up in Louisville, Kentucky, he had rarely even seen a black person, unless it was in the back of a bus. Most of his friends and relatives hated the idea of his playing on the same field as a black man. In addition, Pee Wee Reese had more to lose than the other players when Jackie joined the team.

Jackie had been a shortstop, and everyone thought that Jackie would take Pee Wee's job. Lesser men might have felt anger toward Jackie, but Pee Wee was different. He told himself, "If he's good enough to take my job, he deserves it."

When his Southern teammates circulated a petition to throw Jackie off the team and asked him to sign it, Pee Wee responded, "I don't care if this man is black, blue, or striped"— and refused to sign. "He can play and he can help us win," he told the others. "That's what counts."

CROSLEY FIELD

Very early in the season, the Dodgers traveled west to Ohio to play the Cincinnati Reds. Cincinnati is near Pee Wee's hometown of Louisville.

The Reds played in a small ballpark where the fans sat close to the field. The players could almost feel the breath of the fans on the backs of their necks. Many who came that day screamed terrible, hateful things at Jackie when the Dodgers were on the field.

More than anything else, Pee Wee Reese believed in doing what was right. When he heard the fans yelling at Jackie, Pee Wee decided to take a stand.

With his head high, Pee Wee walked directly from his shortstop position to where Jackie was playing first base. The taunts and shouting of the fans were ringing in Pee Wee's ears. It saddened him, because he knew it could have been his friends and neighbors. Pee Wee's legs felt heavy, but he knew what he had to do.

As he walked toward Jackie wearing the gray Dodger uniform, he looked into his teammate's bold, pained eyes. The first baseman had done nothing to

provoke the hostility except that he sought to be treated as an equal. Jackie was grim with anger. Pee Wee smiled broadly as he reached Jackie. Jackie smiled back.

Stopping beside Jackie, Pee Wee put his arm around Jackie's shoulders. An audible gasp rose up from the crowd when they saw what Pee Wee had done. Then there was silence.

Outlined on a sea of green grass stood these two great athletes, one black, one white, both wearing the same team uniform.

"I am standing by him," Pee Wee Reese said to the world. "This man is my teammate."

CASEY AT THE BAT

Based on the classic American poem by
Ernest Lawrence Thayer

adapted by
Barbara Pitts

illustrated by
James Bennett

Characters

Announcer – excited old-timer—baseball is his LIFE!

Reporter – this is the most important game he's has ever reported!

Mudville's Coach – he's mostly worried about his own job!

Mudville Fans

Weeper – moans and cries

Screamer – angry and loud

Smiler – smiles and nods hopefully

Frowner – frowns and mopes

Know-it-all – wants to be the coach, the umpire, and the players!

Fans – everyone speaking together

This play is really a poem. The lines have been turned into speaking parts for actors. The poem was written to sound as if it were a serious and respectful description of an important battle, but it is actually meant to be funny. This kind of a poem is called a mock epic.

Announcer: The outlook wasn't brilliant for the Mudville nine that day;
The score stood four to two with but one inning more to play.
And then, when Cooney died at first, and Barrows did the same,
A sickly silence fell upon the patrons of the game.

Frowner: A straggling few got up to go in deep despair. The rest
Smiler: Clung to that hope which springs eternal in the human breast;
Weeper: They thought, if only Casey could but get a whack at that
Screamer: We'd put up even money now, with Casey at the bat.

Coach: But Flynn preceded Casey, as did also Jimmy Blake,
Know-it-all: And the former was a lulu and the latter was a cake;
Frowner: So upon that stricken multitude grim melancholy sat,
For there seemed but little chance of Casey's getting to the bat.

Smiler: But Flynn let drive a single, to the wonderment of all,
Screamer: And Blake, the much despised, tore the cover off the ball;
Reporter: And when the dust had lifted, and men saw what had occurred,
Smiler: There was Jimmy safe at second, and Flynn a-hugging third.

WEEPER   REPORTER   FROWNER
SMILER   SCREAMER   KNOW-IT-ALL

Fans: Then from five thousand throats and more there rose a lusty yell;
It rumbled through the valley, it rattled in the dell;
It knocked upon the mountain and recoiled upon the flat,

Announcer: For Casey, mighty Casey, was advancing to the bat.

Smiler: There was ease in Casey's manner as he stepped into his place;
There was pride in Casey's bearing and a smile on Casey's face.
And when, responding to the cheers, he lightly doffed his hat,

Know-it-all: No stranger in the crowd could doubt 'twas Casey at the bat.

Fans: Ten thousand eyes were on him as he rubbed his hands with dirt;
Five thousand tongues applauded when he wiped them on his shirt;

Coach: Then while the writhing pitcher ground the ball into his hip,

Reporter: Defiance gleamed from Casey's eye, a sneer curled Casey's lip.

Screamer: And now the leather-covered sphere came hurtling through the air,

Know-it-all: And Casey stood a-watching it in haughty grandeur there.

Reporter: Close by the sturdy batsman the ball unheeded sped;

Announcer: "That ain't my style," said Casey. "Strike one," the umpire said.

Fans:	From the benches, black with people, there went up a muffled roar,
	Like the beating of the storm waves on a stern and distant shore.
Screamer:	"Kill him! Kill the umpire!" shouted someone on the stand.
Weeper:	And it's likely they'd have killed him had not Casey raised his hand.
Reporter:	With a smile of Christian charity great Casey's visage shone;
	He stilled the rising tumult, he bade the game go on;
Coach:	He signaled to the pitcher, and once more the spheroid flew;
Frowner:	But Casey still ignored it, and the umpire said, "Strike two."
Know-it-all:	"Fraud!" cried the maddened thousands, and echo answered "Fraud!"
Reporter:	But one scornful look from Casey and the audience was awed;
	They saw his face grow stern and cold, they saw his muscles strain,
	And they knew that Casey wouldn't let that ball go by again.
Weeper:	The sneer is gone from Casey's lip, his teeth are clenched in hate,
Screamer:	He pounds with cruel violence his bat upon the plate;
Announcer:	And now the pitcher holds the ball, and now he lets it go,
Smiler:	And now the air is shattered by the force of Casey's blow.
Know-it-all:	Oh, somewhere in this favored land the sun is shining bright,
Frowner:	The band is playing somewhere, and somewhere hearts are light;
Coach:	And somewhere men are laughing, and somewhere children shout,
Weeper:	But there is no joy in Mudville—
Fans:	Mighty Casey
All:	Has struck out.

Think About Reading

Write your answers.

1. In what ways was life hard for players in the Negro Leagues?

2. What qualities did Branch Rickey hope to find in Jackie Robinson?

3. If you could meet one of the people in *Teammates*, who would you choose? Why?

4. What qualities did Pee Wee Reese have that allowed him to accept Jackie Robinson as a teammate?

5. How is the author's purpose in writing *Teammates* different from the poet's purpose in writing "Casey at the Bat"?

Write a Catalogue Description

Why is *Teammates* a great book? Your job is to tell the world. Write a short description of this nonfiction book that might appear in a publisher's catalogue. Be sure to include a brief summary of the events in the book and a description of the book's special features. Tell why young readers will want to read it. Remember, your goal is to promote the book.

Literature Circle

Teammates is a serious book about a historic time in baseball while "Casey at the Bat" is a humorous poem about the popular sport. There are hundreds more books, stories, films, and TV shows about baseball. List some that you know. Then discuss what kind of story each one is. You may want to talk about genres, themes, settings, and characters. Record your ideas on a chart. Then talk about which kinds of baseball stories you find most satisfying.

AUTHOR
Peter Golenbock

When he was thirteen, Peter Golenbock went to a World Series game between the Brooklyn Dodgers and the New York Yankees. After the game, he was introduced to Jackie Robinson. Robinson towered above him, and Golenbock's hand "disappeared" in the tall ballplayer's huge hand. Years later, when Golenbock heard the story of Jackie Robinson and Pee Wee Reese, he knew he had to write about these extraordinary men.

MORE BOOKS ABOUT
Baseball

- *The All-American Girls Professional Baseball League* by Trudy J. Hanmer

- *Black Diamond: The Story of the Negro Baseball Leagues* by Patricia C. and Fredrick L. McKissack

PROJECT

How to

Create an Op-Ed Page

State your opinion in a letter to the editor.

Many newspapers have an Op-Ed page. Editorials and letters to the editor appear on this page. Editorials are articles in which a newspaper's editors give their opinions. The letters are from readers who react to news articles they have read in the paper or discuss a local or national issue. Many different kinds of issues are discussed on the Op-Ed page.

Temple edges
Will meet UMass in Atlantic 10 c

The P

Concerns deepen about the dollar

The decline against other currencies continues.
"Everyone seems to want currencies other than th dollar," one observer s

By Andrew Casse
ISQUIRER STAFF WRI

All were being b
for the stomach-t
dollar, a plunge t
of inflation, recess
squeeze on America
ards.
The dollar fell to a recor
92.59 yen in late afternoon tradi
New York, down from Friday's
93.70. It also declined again
German mark, dropping
marks, th
level
than
and

OP-ED DEPT

The letter arrives at the Op-Ed Department.

INCOMING LETTERS

EDITOR

The letter is read by an editor.

Once approved, it goes to the fact checker who verifies the information in the letter.

FACT CHECKER

PROOF READER

The letter then goes back to the Op-Ed Department, where it is edited for publication.

Explore Your Options

Think about a list of topics for a letter to the editor. Focus on issues that are important in your school or community, and choose the one you care about the most. Research the topic by reading community newspapers, talking to people, and listening to the local news. Take notes as you do your research. Decide what your opinion is about the issue.

TOOLS

- paper and pen
- local newspapers
- envelope and stamp

Tips

- If you want, work with a classmate to gather information about an issue. You take one side of the issue, and your friend takes the other.
- Interview people and write down their opinions. Be sure to get their names.
- Call or write to community leaders and see how they feel about the issue.

2 Organize Your Information

Once you have researched the issue you want to write about, it's time to outline your letter. The first part of your letter will introduce the issue. The second part will give facts and maybe some quotes about the issue.

Your last paragraph will state your opinion on the issue and any suggestions you might have. Make notes about what you will include in each part of your letter.

How Am I Doing?

Before you write your letter to the editor, take a few minutes to ask yourself these questions.

- Did I choose an issue that's important to my community?

- Did I gather facts and examples to support my opinion?

- Did I make an outline to organize my material?

Write Your Letter to the Editor

On the right side of a piece of paper, write your address and the date. On the left side, write the newspaper's address. (You can find this information inside the newspaper.) Then write *Dear Editor:* and begin your letter. Use persuasive writing to get your point across, and support your opinions with facts and quotes. End with *Yours truly* or *Sincerely*. Sign your letter, and print your name underneath. Use this letter to create a class Op-Ed page. Mail a copy of your letter to the local newspaper, too. Be sure to put a stamp on the envelope!

Editor
Op-Ed Dept.
Newspaper Times
1112 Print Rd.
Typee, TN 40432

24 Seal Dr.
Oakridge, TN 43044
3/13/95

To Editor:
I am writing to express ...

Jane Smith
24 Seal Drive
Oakridge, TN 43044

Op-Ed Department
Newspaper Times
1112 Print Rd.
Typee, TN 40432

4 Assemble the Op-Ed Page

Gather all the letters in the class to create a big Op-Ed page. You may wish to use mural paper or a posterboard as the base. Work together to arrange the letters. Make up a name for your class newspaper, and then add the date. Display the Op-Ed page on a school bulletin board so that everyone can read it.

If You Are Using a Computer ...

Write your letter on the computer in the letter format. Choose a letterhead and create your own personal stationery. You also may want to create a headline banner for your Op-Ed page, using a large special font.

You have discovered how to bring about change. Remember to use the skills you've learned to help you take a stand on important issues.

Suki Cheong
Editor ▶

GLOS

You will find all your vocabulary words in alphabetical order in the Glossary. Look at the sample entry below to see how to use it.

This is the **entry word** you look up. It is divided into syllables.

This part tells you how to **pronounce** the entry word. It uses the marks in the **pronunciation key**.

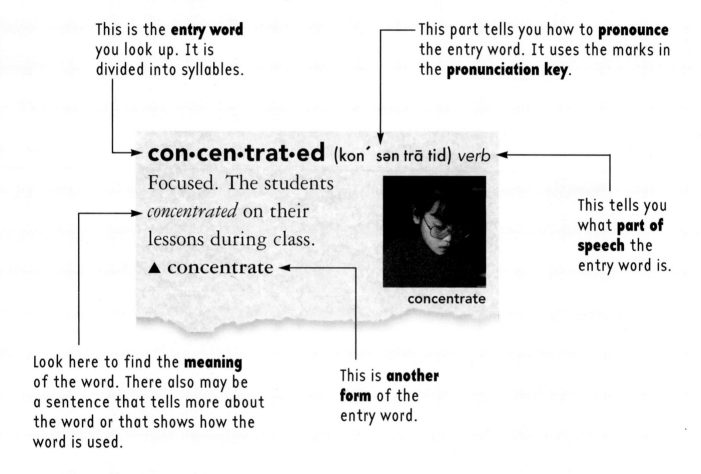

con·cen·trat·ed (kon´ sən trā tid) *verb*
Focused. The students *concentrated* on their lessons during class.
▲ concentrate

concentrate

This tells you what **part of speech** the entry word is.

Look here to find the **meaning** of the word. There also may be a sentence that tells more about the word or that shows how the word is used.

This is **another form** of the entry word.

a	add	o͞o	took	ə =	
ā	ace	ō͞o	pool	a in *above*	
â	care	u	up	e in *sicken*	
ä	palm	û	burn	i in *possible*	
e	end	yo͞o	fuse	o in *melon*	
ē	equal	oi	oil	u in *circus*	
i	it	ou	pout		
ī	ice	ng	ring		
o	odd	th	thin		
ō	open	th	this		
ô	order	zh	vision		

The **pronunciation key** will help you figure out how to pronounce the entry word.

a·bode

(ə bōd´) *noun*
A home. I went home to
my comfortable *abode*.

abode

ab·o·li·tion·ist

(ab ə lish´ ə nist) *noun*
A person who worked to
abolish slavery. Frederick
Douglass was a famous
abolitionist.

ac·tiv·ist

(ak´ tə vist) *noun*
A person who takes action
to help the community.

anx·ious

(angk´ shəs) *adjective*
Worried. She was *anxious*
about her lost dog.

ap·a·thet·ic

(ap´ ə thet´ ik) *adjective*
Having little interest;
indifferent. He is
apathetic about most
television programs.

ap·pe·tiz·ing

(ap´ ə tīz ing) *adjective*
Appealing to the appetite.
That potato salad looks
very *appetizing*.

as·tro·naut

(as´ trə nôt´) *noun*
A person who is trained
to fly in a spacecraft.

WORD HISTORY

The word **astronaut**
comes from two Greek
words: *astron*, which
means "star," and
nautes, which means
"sailor." An astronaut
is a sailor who travels
among the stars.

au·di·ence

(ô´ dē əns) *noun*
The people who read an
author's work. She is a
successful author because
she has a large *audience*.

au·to·mat·ic

(ô´ tə mat´ ik) *adjective*
Made to move and work
without the control of
a human being. He
bought an *automatic*
bread maker that mixes
and bakes fresh bread.

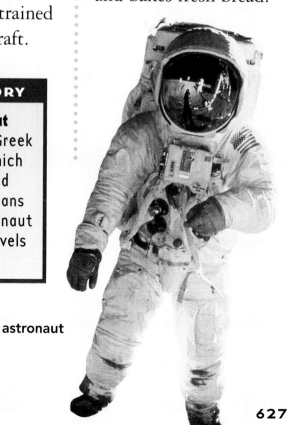

astronaut

be·seech·ing·ly
(bi sēch´ ing lē) *adverb*
In a way that asks or
pleads for something.
He looked at his father
beseechingly. ▲ **beseech**

bon·net (bon´ it) *noun*
A hat with a wide brim
and ribbons that tie
under the chin.

bonnet

boy·cott
(boi´ kot) *noun*
A planned refusal to
have anything to do
with a person, group,
or nation. They
organized a *boycott* of
unsafe products.

bur·lap (bûr´ lap)
noun A rough cloth
woven from jute or
hemp.

buz·zards
(buz´ ərdz) *noun*
Large birds with dark
feathers, broad wings,
and heads without
feathers. ▲ **buzzard**

buzzard

WORD HISTORY

The word **boycott**
comes from a person's
name. In 1897 an
English landlord named
Charles Boycott
refused to lower rents
on his property in
Ireland. The tenants
responded by paying
him no rent at all.

cal·lig·ra·pher
(kə lig´ rə fər) *noun*
A person who has
beautiful handwriting.
He asked a *calligrapher*
to write the invitations.

WORD HISTORY

The word **calligrapher**
comes from two Greek
words. The word *kallia*
means "beauty," and
the word *graphein*
means "to write."

calm (käm) *adjective*
Relaxed or peaceful.
Listening to soft music
makes me feel *calm*.

Thesaurus
calm
relaxed
serene
tranquil

can·o·py
(kan´ ə pē´) *noun*
The tops of the trees in
the rain forest.

chal·lenge
(chal´ inj) *verb*
To invite someone to
compete in a game.
I *challenge* you to a
tennis match.

char·ac·ter
(kar´ ik tər) *noun*
Any letter, symbol, or
figure that is used in
writing. The letter *A*
is a *character* in the
English alphabet.

chemist

chem·ist
(kem´ ist) *noun*
A scientist who is an
expert in studying the
chemical properties of
substances.

civ·il rights
(siv´ əl rīts´) *noun*
The rights of personal
liberty guaranteed to
U.S. citizens by the
Constitution and acts
of Congress.

clutched (klutcht)
verb Held onto
something tightly.
I *clutched* my bag so
I wouldn't lose it.
▲ clutch

co·los·sal
(kə los´ əl) *adjective*
Extremely large.

WORD HISTORY

The word **colossal**
comes from the Greek
word *kolossus*, which
means "statue."
About 2,000 years ago
the Colossus of Rhodes,
a 100-foot-tall bronze
statue, stood at the
harbor entrance on
the Greek island of
Rhodes. After that,
colossus took on the
meaning of "huge"
or "gigantic."

a	add	o͞o	took	ə =
ā	ace	o͞o	pool	a in *above*
â	care	u	up	e in *sicken*
ä	palm	û	burn	i in *possible*
e	end	yo͞o	fuse	o in *melon*
ē	equal	oi	oil	u in *circus*
i	it	ou	pout	
ī	ice	ng	ring	
o	odd	th	thin	
ō	open	th	this	
ô	order	zh	vision	

compass

coral reef

com·pass

(kum´ pəs) *noun*
An instrument that shows directions, such as north, south, east, and west. The hiker used a *compass* to find which way was north.

com·pet·ed

(kəm pēt´ id) *verb*
Tried hard to outdo others at a game or a task. Jesse *competed* in a bowling tournament.
▲ compete

com·rades

(kom´ radz) *noun*
Friends or companions. I went to the movies with my *comrades*.
▲ comrade

Thesaurus
comrades
companions
buddies
friends
pals

con·cen·trat·ed

(kon´ sən trā´ tid) *verb*
Focused one's thoughts and attention on something. The students *concentrated* on their lessons during class.
▲ concentrate

cor·al reefs

(kôr´ əl rēfs´) *noun*
Lines or strips of coral lying near the surface of the ocean. Many kinds of fish live among the *coral reefs*.
▲ coral reef

concentrate

cor·o·na·tion
(kôr´ ə nā´ shən) *noun*
The ceremony at which
a king or a queen is
crowned.

coun·sel (koun´ səl)
noun Guidance or
advice. I ask for my
parents' *counsel* before
I make big decisions.

> ### WORD STUDY
>
> **Counsel** sounds like
> another noun, *council*.
> A *council* is a group
> of people chosen to
> look after a town,
> country, or an
> organization.

cun·ning (kun´ ing)
adjective Crafty, clever,
or sly. The *cunning* fox
tricked the silly dogs.

deep-sea (dēp´ sē´)
adjective Having to do
with the deeper parts
of the ocean.

de·signed (di zīnd´)
verb Drew something
that could be built or
made. Dad *designed* a
tree house for our
backyard. ▲ **design**

des·ti·na·tion
(des´ tə nā´ shən) *noun*
The place where
someone is going to.
Our *destination* was
Austin, Texas.

de·vised (di vīzd´)
verb Thought up or
invented something.
They *devised* a way
to solve the problem.
▲ **devise**

dis·may (dis mā´) *noun*
Loss of heart,
confidence, or courage.
The beginning skier
looked at the steep
slope with *dismay*.

dis·tract·ed
(dis trakt´ id) *verb*
Weakened one's
concentration. The
loud music *distracted*
me and made studying
impossible.
▲ **distract**

ed·i·tor
(ed´ i tər) *noun*
A person who checks
and corrects a piece of
writing so that it is
ready for publication.

eld·er (el´ dər)
noun Someone who is
older and respected by
the community. The
mayor asked an *elder*
for advice.

a	add	o͝o	took	ə =
ā	ace	o͞o	pool	a in *above*
â	care	u	up	e in *sicken*
ä	palm	û	burn	i in *possible*
e	end	yo͞o	fuse	o in *melon*
ē	equal	oi	oil	u in *circus*
i	it	ou	pout	
ī	ice	ng	ring	
o	odd	th	thin	
ō	open	ŧh	this	
ô	order	zh	vision	

en·dur·ance
(en d͞oor´ əns) *noun*
The ability to put up with hardship or to last under continued effort. The settlers' *endurance* helped them survive the harsh winter.

WORD HISTORY

The word **endurance** comes from the Latin word *indurare*, which means "to harden." People with endurance harden or strengthen themselves so they can continue with a difficult task.

ep·i·sode
(ep´ ə sōd´) *noun*
One event in a series of events.

ex·ca·vate
(eks´ kə vāt´) *verb*
To dig a hole; to take apart. The scientists will carefully *excavate* the ancient ruins.

excavate

ex·pe·di·tion
(ek´ spi dish´ ən) *noun*
A long trip made for a specific purpose, such as exploration or research. They went on an *expedition* to the Antarctic to study penguins.

fic·tion·al
(fik´ shə nl)
adjective
Anything made-up or imagined. The *fictional* characters in the novel were very believable.

find·ings
(fin´ dingz) *noun*
Conclusions reached after observation and research. When the experiment was over, she analyzed her *findings*. ▲ **finding**

flax

flax (flaks) *noun*
A kind of plant that has blue flowers. The seeds are used to make linseed oil.

flickered
(flik´ ərd) *verb*
Moved unsteadily; fluttered. The candle flame *flickered* in the breeze. ▲ **flicker**

for·mu·la
(fôr′ myə lə) *noun*
An exact method for producing a particular medicine, food, or mixture.

fright·ened
(frīt′ ənd) *adjective*
Scared. The dog was *frightened* by the loud noise.

Thesaurus
frightened
scared
afraid
fearful
terrified

fron·tier
(frun tēr′ *or* fron tēr′)
noun The far edge of a country where few people live.

gadg·et
(gaj′ it) *noun*
A small device or tool.

grate·ful·ly
(grāt′ fəl lē) *adverb*
Thankfully. "Thanks for mowing the lawn," said Dad *gratefully*.

ham·mer·head
(ham′ ər hed) *noun*
A kind of shark that has a hammer-shaped head.

hammerhead

hard·ship
(härd′ ship) *noun*
Difficulty or suffering. The pioneers endured weeks of *hardship* as they crossed the steep mountains in covered wagons.

her·o·ine
(her′ ō in) *noun*
A girl or woman admired for her bravery and courage. In the movie, the *heroine* saved the town.

a	add	o͞o	took	ə =
ā	ace	o͞o	pool	a in *above*
â	care	u	up	e in *sicken*
ä	palm	û	burn	i in *possible*
e	end	yo͞o	fuse	o in *melon*
ē	equal	oi	oil	u in *circus*
i	it	ou	pout	
ī	ice	ng	ring	
o	odd	th	thin	
ō	open	th	this	
ô	order	zh	vision	

hom·age

(hom´ ij or om´ ij) *noun* Respect or honor. To pay *homage* to the queen, please bow.

hos·til·i·ty

(ho stil´ i tē) *noun* Resistance; conflict; ill will. There was much anger and *hostility* between the enemies.

hu·mil·i·a·tions

(hyōō mil´ ē ā´ shənz) *noun* Extreme embarrassments or feelings of great foolishness. The hero suffered many *humiliations* before he reached his goal. ▲ humiliation

---

WORD HISTORY

The word **humiliations** comes from the Latin word *humiliatus* which means "to humble."

---

hys·ter·i·cal·ly

(hi ster´ i klē) *adverb* In a way that seems out of control due to extreme emotion. The frightened child sobbed *hysterically*. ▲ hysterical

im·prove·ments

(im prōōv´ mənts) *noun* Changes or additions that make something better. New windows and doors were *improvements* to the house. ▲ improvement

in·ci·dent

(in´ si dənt) *noun* An event; something that happens. She described the funny *incident* to the class.

in·dig·nant·ly

(in dig´ nənt lē) *adverb* In a way that expresses anger or scorn because something is not fair. ▲ indignant

in·no·cent·ly

(in´ ə sənt lē) *adverb* In a way suggesting that a person has no guilt or knowledge of something. The child looked *innocently* at the broken toy. ▲ innocent

in·struct·ed

(in strukt´ id) *verb* Taught a subject or skill. ▲ instruct

in·vi·ta·tions

(in´ vi tā´ shənz) *noun* Written notes that invite people to events or parties. ▲ invitation

June 18

Dear Chris,

I'd like to invite you to a barbecue at my house on Saturday, July 10 at 1:00 p.m. We will play outdoor games, so wear comfortable clothes. I hope you can come.

Your friend,

Kim

R.S.V.P. 555-1234

invitation

jab·ber·ing

(jab´ ər ing) *verb*
Talking in a fast,
confused, or foolish
way that is hard to
understand. ▲ jabber

jag·uar (jag´ wär)

noun A large, powerful
cat with brownish-
yellow fur and black
spots, similar to a
leopard.

jaguar

ka·pok tree

(kā´ pok trē´) *noun*
A kind of silk-cotton
tree that grows in the
Amazon rain forest.

king·dom

(king´ dəm) *noun*
A country ruled by
a king or a queen.

la·bor-sav·ing

(lā´ bər sā´ ving)
adjective Designed to
decrease work. The
washing machine is a
labor-saving device.

lab·y·rinth

(lab´ ə rinth) *noun*
A set of winding
intricate passages
through which it is
hard to find one's way.
The word *maze* is a
synonym for *labyrinth*.

launch·es

(lônch´ iz) *noun* The
acts of sending off
space shuttles or rock-
ets into outer space.
She watched two space
shuttle *launches* on TV.
▲ launch

launch

a	add	o͝o	took	ə =
ā	ace	o͞o	pool	a in *above*
â	care	u	up	e in *sicken*
ä	palm	û	burn	i in *possible*
e	end	yo͞o	fuse	o in *melon*
ē	equal	oi	oil	u in *circus*
i	it	ou	pout	
ī	ice	ng	ring	
o	odd	th	thin	
ō	open	ŧh	this	
ô	order	zh	vision	

learned (lûrnd) *verb*
Gained knowledge through study, practice, or experience. ▲ **learn**

leg•end
(lej´ ənd) *noun*
A story handed down from earlier times. Legends are often based on fact, but they may not be entirely true.

li•censed
(lī´ sənst) *verb* Granted legal permission to do something. She was *licensed* to drive a bus. ▲ **license**

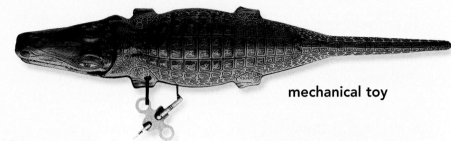

mechanical toy

lit•er•ate
(lit´ ər it) *adjective*
Able to read and write.

lodge
(loj) *noun* A type of Native American dwelling.

ma•rine
bi•ol•o•gist
(mə rēn´ bī ol´ ə jist) *noun* A scientist who studies living things that make their home in the sea.

mead•ow•lark
(med´ ō lärk´) *noun*
A songbird with a yellow breast marked with a black "V."

me•chan•i•cal
(mə kan´ i kəl) *adjective*
Of, or related to, machines. I wound up the *mechanical* dog to make it walk.

meadowlark

mem•o•ry (mem´ ə rē)
noun The ability to remember things.

mold•ed (mōl´ did)
verb Made or formed into a shape. ▲ mold

mon•arch
(mon´ ərk *or* mon´ ärk)
noun A ruler, such as a king or a queen, who inherits a position. The princess became the new queen and *monarch* when her father died.

mor•sels (môr´ səlz)
noun Small pieces of food. I put out *morsels* of bread for the birds.
▲ morsel

morsel

na•tion•al park
(nash´ ə nl park´) *noun* An area of land set aside and preserved by the federal government for the public to visit.

monarch

nat•u•ral•ist
(nach´ ər ə list *or*
nach´ rə list) *noun*
A person who studies plants and animals.

a	add	o͞o	took	ə =
ā	ace	o͞o	pool	a in *above*
â	care	u	up	e in *sicken*
ä	palm	û	burn	i in *possible*
e	end	yo͞o	fuse	o in *melon*
ē	equal	oi	oil	u in *circus*
i	it	ou	pout	
ī	ice	ng	ring	
o	odd	th	thin	
ō	open	ŧh	this	
ô	order	zh	vision	

nov·els
(nov´ əlz) *noun*
Long fictional stories.
She read three *novels*
by the same author.
▲ novel

op·pos·ing
(ə pō´ zing) *verb*
Being against
something; resisting.
The town was *opposing*
the construction of
a new highway.
▲ oppose

op·pressed
(ə prest´) *verb*
Treated in an unjust
and harsh way. The
characters in the story
were *oppressed* by their
ruler. ▲ oppress

paddock

pad·dock
(pad´ ək) *noun*
A fenced area where
horses exercise or graze.

park rang·er
(park´ rān´ jər) *noun*
A person whose job it
is to take care of a park
or forest.

pat·ent·ed
(pat´ ən tid) *verb*
Obtained a document
from the government
that gives a person the
right to be the only
one who can make and
sell an invention. The
inventor *patented* her
invention. ▲ patent

FACT FILE

- The first United
States invention was
patented in 1790.

- There are about 27
million patents on
file at the United
States Patent
Office.

- Fewer than five
percent of all
patents are ever
used or sold.

park ranger

pat·tern
(pat´ ərn) *noun*
The way in which shapes and colors are placed to form a design.

pet·ti·coat
(pet´ ē kōt´) *noun*
A kind of slip worn under a skirt or dress.

plea (plē) *noun* An
extremely emotional request. The lawyer made a *plea* for mercy to the jury.

Thesaurus
plea
request
appeal
entreaty

pattern

plight (plīt) *noun*
A situation of great danger or hardship. Everyone is saddened by the *plight* of the flood victims.

prai·rie (prâr´ ē)
noun A large area of flat or slightly rolling grasslands.

prep·a·ra·tions
(prep´ə rā´ shenz)
noun The actions taken to get ready for something. ▲ preparation

pub·lished
(pub´ lisht) *verb*
Printed and offered for sale. Her book was *published* last summer.
▲ publish

a	add	o͞o	took	ə =
ā	ace	o͞o	pool	a in *above*
â	care	u	up	e in *sicken*
ä	palm	û	burn	i in *possible*
e	end	yo͞o	fuse	o in *melon*
ē	equal	oi	oil	u in *circus*
i	it	ou	pout	
ī	ice	ng	ring	
o	odd	th	thin	
ō	open	ᵺ	this	
ô	order	zh	vision	

prairie

rain forest

rain for·est

(rān´ fôr´ ist) *noun*
A dense tropical forest,
in an area that has a
high annual rainfall.

FACT FILE

- The temperature in a
  tropical **rain forest**
  stays at about 80°F
  all year long.

- An average of 100 to
  200 inches of rain
  falls throughout the
  year.

- The ground or floor
  of the rain forest is
  almost continually in
  shade.

---

realm

(relm) *noun*
A kingdom. The good
king was respected
throughout his *realm*.

reign (rān) *noun*

The period during
which a king or a
queen rules a country.
The queen's *reign* lasted
for twenty years.

WORD STUDY

The word **reign** has
two homophones. The
first, *rain*, refers to
water that falls from
clouds. The second,
rein, refers to a strap
attached to a bridle
that allows a rider to
guide a horse.

---

re·lief (ri lēf´) *noun*

A feeling of freedom
from pain or worry.
It was a *relief* to hear
that our cousins
arrived safely.

rep·u·ta·tion

(rep yə tā´ shən) *noun*
Someone's worth or
character as judged by
others. He has a
reputation for being
a good teacher.

re·search

(ri sûrch´ or rē´ sûrch)
noun Close and careful
study of a subject.

sched·ule

(skej´ ool or skej´əl) *noun*
A list of times when
certain things are done
or take place. He had
an exercise *schedule* that
he followed faithfully.

scraps (skraps) *noun*
Small bits and pieces that are left over from something larger. ▲ scrap

> **T h e s a u r u s**
> **scraps**
> remnants
> odds and ends
> bits and pieces

seg•re•ga•tion
(seg´ ri gā´ shən) *noun*
The act or practice of keeping people or groups apart.

se•quoi•a
(si kwoi´ ə) *noun*
A giant evergreen tree that can reach a height of over 300 feet. Sequoias grow mostly in California.

sequoia

scuba dive

site (sīt) *noun*
The place where something is located. The White House is a famous historical *site*.

scu•ba dive
(skoo´ bə dīv´) *verb*
To swim underwater wearing scuba gear.

a	add	o͝o	took	ə =
ā	ace	o͞o	pool	a in *above*
â	care	u	up	e in *sicken*
ä	palm	û	burn	i in *possible*
e	end	yo͞o	fuse	o in *melon*
ē	equal	oi	oil	u in *circus*
i	it	ou	pout	
ī	ice	ng	ring	
o	odd	th	thin	
ō	open	ŧh	this	
ô	order	zh	vision	

sloth

sloth (slôth *or* slōth) *noun* A slow-moving, tree-dwelling mammal with claws like hooks that inhabits the tropical forests of Central and South America.

FACT FILE

- The **sloth** moves so slowly on the ground that it only covers about 6.5 feet every minute.

- In the trees, the sloth moves a little faster, sometimes covering as much as 10 feet in a minute.

snarled (snärl) *verb* Spoke in a sharp, angry manner. ▲ snarl

sniffed (snift) *verb* Breathed in strongly through the nose. ▲ sniff

snor·keled (snôr´ kəld) *verb* Swam underwater wearing a mask with a tube for breathing. The kids *snorkeled* along the reef in the bay. ▲ snorkel

space mis·sion (spās´ mish´ ən) *noun* A project that a group of specialists is sent into space to do.

space shut·tle (spās´ shut´ l) *noun* An airplane-like spacecraft designed to transport people and cargo between Earth and space.

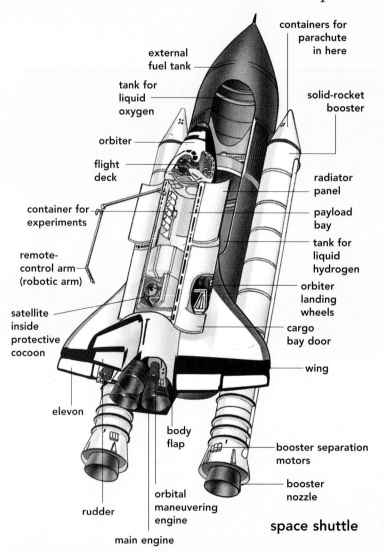

containers for parachute in here

external fuel tank

tank for liquid oxygen

orbiter

flight deck

container for experiments

remote-control arm (robotic arm)

satellite inside protective cocoon

elevon

rudder

main engine

orbital maneuvering engine

body flap

solid-rocket booster

radiator panel

payload bay

tank for liquid hydrogen

orbiter landing wheels

cargo bay door

wing

booster separation motors

booster nozzle

space shuttle

space suit

(spās´ sōot´) *noun*
A pressurized suit worn by astronauts that controls temperature and supplies them with oxygen.

space·ship

(spās´ ship´) *noun*
A vehicle used for space travel.

stand (stand) *noun*
A firm opinion about an issue. He took a *stand* against slavery.

WORD STUDY

The word **stand** can also mean:

- to be on your feet; not sitting
- to occupy a place or location
- the place where a witness sits to testify in court
- a small, open-air place where things are sold

submersible

stitched

(sticht) *verb*
Sewed together. She *stitched* the quilt together from scraps. ▲ stitch

stu·pen·dous

(stōo pen´ dəs or styōo pen´ dəs)
Amazing or awesome. That dancer does the most *stupendous* jumps I've ever seen.

sub·mers·i·ble

(səb mûr´ sə bəl) *noun*
A vessel built to operate under water; usually a submarine.

sub·stance

(sub´ stəns) *noun*
The material that makes up something. The *substance* in the glass was water.

a	add	ōo	took	ə =		
ā	ace	ōo	pool	a in *above*		
â	care	u	up	e in *sicken*		
ä	palm	û	burn	i in *possible*		
e	end	yōo	fuse	o in *melon*		
ē	equal	oi	oil	u in *circus*		
i	it	ou	pout			
ī	ice	ng	ring			
o	odd	th	thin			
ō	open	ŧh	this			
ô	order	zh	vision			

sus·pen·sion bridge

(sə spen´ shun brij´)

noun A bridge that is hung by cables anchored to towers.

suspension bridge

syl·la·bar·y

(sil´ ə ber´ ē) *noun*
A writing system in which each syllable of a spoken language is expressed by a different character or letter.

tech·nique

(tek nēk´) *noun*
A certain way of doing things; a special method. She had her own special *technique* for painting chairs.

Thesaurus

technique

ability
style
approach
system

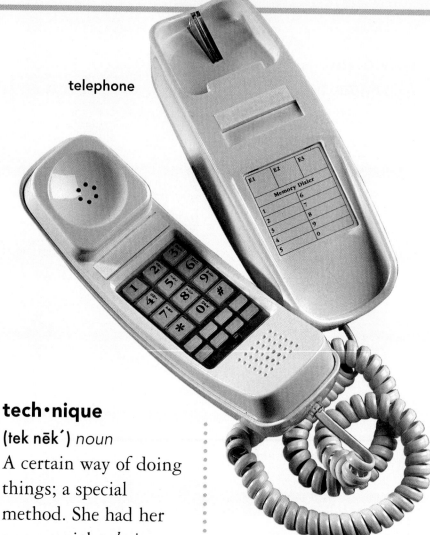

telephone

tel·e·phone

(tel´ ə fōn´) *noun*
An instrument for talking to people over distances that converts sounds into electrical impulses that travel through wires.

ther·mom·e·ter
(thər mom´ i tər) *noun*
An instrument used to
measure temperature.

thermometer

tile·fish (tīl´ fish´) *noun*
A large fish with yellow
spots on its body found
in the deep waters of
the Atlantic.

tin·kered (ting´ kərd)
verb Made minor
repairs and adjustments
to something. The
repair person *tinkered*
with the computer.
▲ tinker

Thesaurus
tinkered
repaired
mended
fiddled with

tou·can
(tōō´ kan *or* tōō´ kän)
noun A brightly
colored tropical bird
with a large beak.

trans·fixed
(trans fikst´) *verb*
Made motionless by
wonder or amazement.
The little boy was
transfixed as he watched
his first snowfall.
▲ transfix

trans·late
(trans´ lāt) *verb*
To put into the words
of a different language.
She was able to
translate French into
English.

toucan

a	add	o͞o	took	ə =
ā	ace	o͞o	pool	a in *above*
â	care	u	up	e in *sicken*
ä	palm	û	burn	i in *possible*
e	end	yo͞o	fuse	o in *melon*
ē	equal	oi	oil	u in *circus*
i	it	ou	pout	
ī	ice	ng	ring	
o	odd	th	thin	
ō	open	ᵺ	this	
ô	order	zh	vision	

tilefish

treach·er·ous

(trech´ ər əs) *adjective*
Dangerous. Heavy fog
is *treacherous* for drivers.

Thesaurus
treacherous
dangerous
hazardous
perilous

trem·ble

(trem´ bəl) *verb*
To shake from fear,
cold, or excitement.
My hands sometimes
tremble when I'm afraid.

Thesaurus
tremble
shake
quake
quiver

tumbleweed

tum·ble·weeds

(tum´ bəl wēds´) *noun*
Plants that break away
from their roots in the
autumn and are blown
by the wind.
▲ tumbleweed

Un·der·ground Rail·road

(un´ dər ground´
rāl´ rōd´) *noun*
The name of the escape
system used by slaves
in the South to travel
north to freedom.

un·der·sto·ry

(un´ dər stôr´ ē) *noun*
A layer of shrubs and
trees that only grow
from 10 to 50 feet
above the floor of a
rain forest.

FACT FILE

• From the 1840s to
the 1860s, the
Underground Railroad
helped 60,000 slaves
escape to freedom.

• Harriet Tubman,
a well-known
"conductor," helped
over 300 slaves
escape to freedom.

vac•cine (vak sēn´)
noun A preparation of weakened germs that is used to inoculate a person against disease. There is a *vaccine* for measles.

var´mint (vär´ mənt)
noun A person or animal that is considered troublesome. That squirrel is a pesky *varmint*.

vir•tu•al re•al•i•ty
(vûr´ choo əl rē al´ i tē)
noun Imaginary three-dimensional environments that are created by computer technology.

voy•age (voi´ ij) *noun*
A long journey, such as one made on a ship.

wildlife

vul•can•ized
(vul´ kə nīzd) *verb*
Treated rubber with a process of heat and sulfur to make it stronger and more elastic.
▲ vulcanize

weight•less•ness
(wāt´ lis nəs) *noun*
The state of having little or no weight because of the lack of gravity. ▲ **weightless**

wild•life (wīld´ līf´)
noun Wild animals that live in their natural surroundings.

wool•en
(wool´ ən) *adjective*
Made of wool.

a	add	oo	took	ə =
ā	ace	oo	pool	a in *above*
â	care	u	up	e in *sicken*
ä	palm	û	burn	i in *possible*
e	end	yoo	fuse	o in *melon*
ē	equal	oi	oil	u in *circus*
i	it	ou	pout	
ī	ice	ng	ring	
o	odd	th	thin	
ō	open	th	this	
ô	order	zh	vision	

INDEX

Colored page numbers refer to biographical information.

Acknowledgments

Grateful acknowledgment is made to the following sources for permission to reprint from previously published material. The publisher has made diligent efforts to trace the ownership of all copyrighted material in this volume and believes that all necessary permissions have been secured. If any errors or omissions have inadvertently been made, proper corrections will gladly be made in future editions.

Cover and Unit 1 *Chapter by Chapter* Table of Contents: Illustration from YOUNG ARTHUR by Robert D. San Souci. Illustration copyright © 1997 by Jamichael Henterly. Reprinted by arrangement with Random House Children's Books, a division of Random House, Inc. All rights reserved.

Unit 2 *What an Idea!* Table of Contents: Illustration from A PIECE OF STRING IS A WONDERFUL THING by Judy Hindley. Illustration copyright © 1993 Margaret Chamberlain. Reproduced by permission of Candlewick Press, Cambridge, MA.

Unit 5 *Nature Guides* Table of Contents: Photo from SWIMMING WITH SEA LIONS by Ann McGovern. Copyright © 1992 by Ann McGovern. Reprinted by permission of Scholastic Inc.

Unit 6 *It Takes a Leader* Table of Contents: Illustration from TEAMMATES by Peter Golenbock. Illustration copyright © 1990 by Paul Bacon. Reprinted by permission of Harcourt Brace & Company.

Unit 1 *Chapter by Chapter* Unit Opener: Illustration from FAMILY PICTURES by Carmen Lomas Garza. Copyright © 1990 by Carmen Lomas Garza. Reprinted by permission of Children's Book Press. Border by Vicki Wehrman.

Unit 1 *Chapter by Chapter*
"Young Arthur" from YOUNG ARTHUR by Robert D. San Souci. Text copyright © 1997 by Robert D. San Souci. Illustrations copyright © 1997 by Jamichael Henterly. Reprinted by arrangement with Random House Children's Book, a division of Random House, Inc. All rights reserved.

"The Knight's Handbook" from THE KNIGHT'S HANDBOOK: HOW TO BECOME A CHAMPION IN SHINING ARMOR by Christopher Gravett. Copyright © 1997 by Breslich & Foss. Published in the United States by Cobblehill Books, an affiliate of Dutton Children's Books, a division of Penguin Putnam Inc.

"Cherokee Summer" adapted from CHEROKEE SUMMER by Diane Hoyt-Goldsmith, with photographs by Lawrence Migdale. Text copyright © 1993 by Diane Hoyt-Goldsmith. Photographs copyright © 1993 by Lawrence Migdale. All rights reserved. Reprinted by permission of Holiday House, Inc.

"Watermelon" and "Oranges" from FAMILY PICTURES by Carmen Lomas Garza. Copyright © 1990 by Carmen Lomas Garza. Reprinted by permission of Children's Book Press.

"Tales of a Fourth Grade Rat" by Jerry Spinelli. Copyright © 1996 by Scholastic Inc. All rights reserved. Originally published in *Scholastic Literacy Place®*. "Shortstop" from KNOTS IN MY YO-YO STRING by Jerry Spinelli. Copyright © 1998 by Jerry Spinelli. Reprinted by arrangement with Alfred A. Knopf, Inc. All rights reserved.

"Mufaro's Beautiful Daughters" from MUFARO'S BEAUTIFUL DAUGHTERS by John Steptoe. Copyright © 1987 by John Steptoe. Reprinted by permission of Lothrop, Lee & Shepard Books, a division of William Morrow & Company, Inc.

"You and I" from MY SONG IS BEAUTIFUL by Mary Ann Hoberman. Copyright © 1994 by Mary Ann Hoberman. Reprinted by permission of Little, Brown and Company.

Unit 2 *What an Idea!*
"A Piece of String Is a Wonderful Thing" from A PIECE OF STRING IS A WONDERFUL THING by Judy Hindley, illustrated by Margaret Chamberlain. Text copyright © 1993 by Judy Hindley. Illustrations copyright © 1993 by Margaret Chamberlain. Printed in the U.S. by Candlewick Press. Reprinted by permission.

"The Invention of Sneakers" from STEVEN CANEY'S INVENTION BOOK. Copyright © 1985 by Steven Caney. Reprinted by permission of Workman Publishing Company, Inc. All rights reserved.

"The Doughnuts" from HOMER PRICE by Robert McCloskey. Copyright © 1943 and renewed © 1971 by Robert McCloskey. Used by permission of Viking Penguin, a division of Penguin Putnam Inc.

"The Animals Share" from A RING OF TRICKSTERS by Virginia Hamilton, illustrated by Barry Moser. Text copyright © 1997 by Virginia Hamilton. Illustrations copyright © 1997 by Barry Moser. Published by The Blue Sky Press, an imprint of Scholastic Inc. All rights reserved.

"Wings" from WINGS by Jane Yolen, illustrated by Dennis Nolan. Text copyright © 1991 by Jane Yolen. Illustrations copyright © 1991 by Dennis Nolan. Reprinted by permission of Harcourt Brace & Company.

"Dreams" from DREAM KEEPER AND OTHER POEMS by Langston Hughes. Copyright © 1932 by Alfred A. Knopf, Inc. and renewed © 1960 by Langston Hughes. Reprinted by arrangement with Alfred A. Knopf, Inc.

Photography Credits

Illustration Credits

Cover: Jamichael Henterly

Illustrated Author Photos:
pp. 43, 155, 185, 207, 237, 257, 283, 325, 423, 471, 513, 575, 599: David Franck; pp. 63, 85, 107, 141, 357, 383, 403, 453, 495, 551, 619: Gabe DiFiore.

Illustrations:
pp. 284–319: Allen Garns;
pp. 614–617: James Bennett;
pp. 204–205: Paul Jermann;
p. 355: Rob Dunlavey;
pp. 488–493: Steve Jenkins;
pp. 388–399: Tim Spransy.